BUDDHA IS
AS BUDDHA
DOES

Buddha Is as Buddha Does

The Ten Original Practices for Enlightened Living

Lama Surya Das

HarperSanFrancisco
A Division of HarperCollinsPublishers

ISBN: 978-0-06-074729-9

To all the young and awakening Bodhisattvas of this world who unselfishly seek to become more empowered and contribute to a wiser, more peaceful, and compassionate world.

Unless someone like you
cares a whole awful lot,
nothing is going to get better.
It's not.

—DR. SEUSS, "THE LORAX"

THE ESSENCE OF THE
TEN TRANSFORMATIVE PRACTICES

Generosity arises from unselfishness and nonattachment.
Ethics involves virtue, integrity, and self-discipline.
Patience requires resilience, acceptance, and fortitude.
Effort means courage in joyous perseverance.
Meditation implies mindfulness, concentration, reflection, and
    introspection.
Transcendental wisdom includes discernment and self-knowledge.
Skillful means arise from resourcefulness and imagination.
Spiritual aspirations include noble intention and resolve.
Higher accomplishments require leadership, powers, and positive
    influence.
Awakened awareness means pristine realization.
These are the ten arms and legs of the radiant body of the
    Bodhisattva,
whose heart is Bodhicitta, selfless love and compassion.

CONTENTS

Foreword xi

PREFACE Buddha's Gift—The Bodhisattva's
Active Way of Awakening xiii

INTRODUCTION Living the Good Life 1

ONE The Transcendental
Gift of Generosity 21

TWO The Impeccable Virtue of
Ethical Self-Discipline 53

THREE The Transformative Practice
of Patient Forbearance 81

FOUR The Power of Heroic Effort 105

FIVE The Liberating Power of
Mindfulness and Meditation 123

SIX The Panacea of Wisdom 147

SEVEN The Universal Tool
of Skillful Means 165

EIGHT The Profundity and Vastness
of Spiritual Aspirations 185

NINE The Magic of Higher
Accomplishments 205

TEN The Perfection of
Awakened Awareness 237

Spiritual Revolution,
Enlightened Leadership: Prayer of
Accomplishing the Paramita Virtues 263

Acknowledgments 265

About Dzogchen Center 266

FOREWORD

My dear old friend and student Lama Surya Das received teachings from His Holiness the Dalai Lama, the late His Holiness Dudjom Rinpoche, and many other renowned and genuine masters and spent over nine years in strict retreat practice. He has written a number of books on Buddhist philosophy and practices with the aim of introducing Buddhist insight from a modern Western perspective and guiding spiritual practitioners on the path to enlightenment.

Just as his earlier books have served as an eye-opener for both the new and not-so-new Western Buddhist practitioners and helped them understand the true path, I am confident that his latest book, *Buddha Is as Buddha Does,* will benefit those interested in learning and practicing the compassionate way of the Bodhisattva and help them follow the genuine path to enlightenment. I am completely confident that this wise and loving book will go a long way in spreading the teachings of the Buddha in our modern world of conflict and strife, and contribute to developing higher sanity, peace, and wisdom.

—THE TWELFTH GYALWANG DRUKPA
Jigdral Lodo Phende Thaye

BUDDHA'S GIFT

The Bodhisattva's Active Way of Awakening

Train yourself in this way: from higher to higher, from
strength to strength, we will strive, and we will come
to realize unsurpassed freedom and enlightenment.

—THE BUDDHA

The book you hold in your hands offers you a thorough, tried and true map to the richest treasure a human being can find. If you follow its guidelines, you will enter into an extraordinary life of greater joy, energy, clarity, peace, and wisdom than you ever thought possible. At the same time, you will be doing the best you can to make this world into a saner and more wholesome, harmonious, and beautiful place to live, which I personally believe is our highest calling. You will be contributing to a spiritual revolution.

I have no doubt whatsoever that these things will happen; the important thing is to actually begin. We are all participants already; none are exempt. I do not claim credit for drawing this map. It is the gift of the Buddha, a human teacher in the sixth century BCE who was searching for the truth and one day simply woke up to the laws of the universe. What did he see with his awakened vision, his BuddhaVision? He saw that each of us, deep within, is inherently perfect, whole and complete, with the capacity to overcome suffering, transform ourselves into forces for good, and, in so doing, revolutionize and liberate the world. We are perfect as we are, and yet we could use just a little tweaking. This is the Buddha's gift, which we can receive, and which we can give.

According to the Mahayana Buddhist tradition in which I was trained, a person begins this process by taking a vow to be a Bodhisattva. Literally, the Sanskrit term means "an awakening being," but in practice a Bodhisattva aspires to be a helpful spiritual altruist, an activist, and even a service-oriented leader as well as a seeker of wisdom, truth, unconditional love, deathless peace, and ultimate enlightenment. A Bodhisattva lives by a compassionate code that extends far beyond mere self-interest, with its severely limited potential for happiness and fulfillment, to engage more vitally with the welfare of all beings and embody timeless values. A Bodhisattva is on the way to becoming a wise elder, so sorely needed in our benighted world today and tomorrow.

I think "Awakener" is my best one-word translation of *Bodhisattva*. Compassionate as well as sagacious, a Bodhisattva has vowed to work ceaselessly in this life and all possible lifetimes toward the ultimate liberation and spiritual enlightenment of all beings. There is nothing weak or passive about either compassion or wisdom, the two wings of the Bodhisattva. A Bodhisattva is likened in Buddhist scriptures to a spiritual hero, a wish-fulfilling jewel, like one who inexhaustibly provides food for the hungry, water for the thirsty, and protection for the weak and helpless. A Bodhisattva is also called a medicine, an all-illuminating sun, a beacon, a guide, a teacher, a selfless liberator, a benefactor, and a ship captain who helps us cross the ocean of worldliness and reach the other shore of nirvana. The preeminent Indian Buddhist philosopher Nagarjuna offered a Bodhisattva motto when he wrote, "Without regard for reward, provide help to others." The Bodhisattva is a true higher educator and authentic edifier. He or she has fully realized panacean wisdom and unconditional compassion, finding it within the heart and embodying it in life as impeccable action.

The Buddha tells us that he himself became enlightened over many lifetimes of walking the path of awakening as a Bodhisattva, or awakening seeker. He said that if he became enlightened that way, so can we. We see this demonstrated throughout history in the long lineages of confirmed masters—men and women who have followed in the Buddha's footsteps. Lord Buddha himself said, "If one teaching is grasped and known, all of my teachings will be in the palm of your hand. What is this one teaching? It is altruism." A Bodhisattva brings out the best in everyone.

The Bodhisattva ideal is the highest and richest spiritual ideal I know of from my thirty-eight years of spiritual study and meditation practice. It is a universal model that any one of us can emulate by consciously practicing and cultivating its sublime virtues and powers, on the outer, inner, and subtle innermost levels. When we do, we receive blessed benefits, good for now and later, in both this world and other worlds beyond. We find deep meaning, purpose, and loving connection with all that lives.

The Dalai Lama personally taught me that the wish-fulfilling jewel that brings us all we need and seek is the unselfish heart and compassionate mind intent on benefiting others rather than preoccupied with ourselves. This is what Tibetan Buddhists call the indispensable or precious Bodhicitta, the highest intention, the good heart, our best self, our innermost, interconnected Buddha-being. It is the key element in the powerful magic of transformative spirituality. The Dalai Lama's favorite instructional manual on compassion, Shantideva's *The Way of the Bodhisattva,* describes it as the state of being "mounted on the noble steed of awakened heart-mind, riding from joy to joy." The dynamic way of the Bodhisattva swiftly delivers us to the pinnacle of reality, the goal of spiritual life. A Bodhisattva is what we need to be today.

The Bodhisattva cultivates this noble heart and mind in every aspect of his or her existence by following the ten transformative practices— known in Sanskrit as the *paramitas,* generally translated into English as the "perfections" or the "transcendental virtues." These transformative practices are wise principles of impeccable self-mastery that enable us to serve other individuals and be useful in the world to the best of our ability. These splendid qualities appear in many other historical catalogs of virtues: generosity, ethics, patience, heroic effort, mindfulness, wisdom, skillful means, spiritual aspirations, higher accomplishments, and awakened awareness. Without any more information, we can immediately feel that these traits are admirable and worth developing. Over and over again, folktales, news stories, movies, and sermons tell us that these practical yet far-reaching qualities are keys to living a meaningful and truly noble life. We see them echoed in religious, philosophical, and moral codes of conduct throughout human history, including the Ten Commandments of the Jewish and Christian faiths, the seven cardinal virtues of Roman Catholicism, the honor codes of the Boy Scouts and Girl Scouts, and even the guidelines that kindergarten teachers write on their chalkboards. Guitar teacher Julian Gray uses the six strings as a mnemonic device to express his values for correct practice: Enthusiastic Excellence; Attention; Dedication; Generosity; Beauty; Everything Changes. I'm convinced that each of us immediately intuits that these qualities represent the finest, most rewarding, even most overall effective traits a human being can cultivate, and lead directly to enlightened living. At the highest level of their reach and range, the ten paramita virtues can each become panacean; that is, perfecting one cures all ills, just as wisdom is the cure for ignorance and all its attendant complications.

So why aren't we more active in developing and displaying these fine qualities, both outwardly and inwardly?

Why do we find it so difficult to apply the enlightened and enlightening values to our everyday lives on a consistent basis?

Can we actually live in such a way, not just believing in these virtues but actually embodying and practicing them day by day, hour by hour, minute by minute? How can we become the spiritual heroes and active Awakeners that we innately are? How to become a Bodhisattva?

How, specifically, can we make it easier to practice these virtues, especially in the face of competing pressures to earn a living, function in a busy, materialistic society, and cope with endless distractions, temptations, worries, and frustrations? How can we sustain our unselfish spiritual commitment even as we're involved in crises relating to illness, natural disasters, loss, and death?

Throughout the twenty-five hundred years since the Buddha taught the ten transformative practices of his radiant Bodhisattva Code, millions of Buddhists have demonstrated how to put them into action and achieve their liberating results. The same can be said for countless non-Buddhists who have not explicitly taken the Bodhisattva Vow but have obviously proceeded from a similarly wise and altruistic intention to function in a like manner; their commitment to these virtues shows in the quality and effect of what they've accomplished, thought, said, and left behind.

This book is designed not only to give you insights into these exemplary individuals' lives, so that they can serve as your own personal models, but also to deepen your understanding and appreciation of what a Bodhisattva is and what each paramita involves. Here are stories recalling the Five Kinds of Bodhisattvas: cosmological and archetypal; historical founders; lineage masters; contemporary; and anonymous Bodhisattvas, the everyday heroes hidden among us, all of whom aid and guide us in infinite ways, seen and unseen.

This book provides you with tools and techniques that you can use to delve into your own Buddha nature and mine the ore that lies within, so that you can share it with others while awakening the Bodhisattva hidden within. It reveals the Buddha's special enlightened gift—How to be There while getting there, every single step of the way—showing us how to fully inhabit the holy now while embracing all beings throughout the immensity of time and space, for every step of the way is the Great Way of awakening, as the masters say.

Speaking practically, this book will help you motivate yourself to become a Bodhisattva—or, in other words, to live the most enlightened life you can. It will prompt you and assist you in answering common questions about the tasks involved, such as, "Why should I do this?" "What's in it for me?" "Is it genuinely meaningful?" "How can it possibly work?" "How much is it going to require of me?" "How am I going to stick to it?" "What's to keep me from failing?" "How long will it take?"

This book is also crafted to help you listen more closely to your innermost being, what the Buddha called your Buddha nature, the aspect of you that is most intimately interconnected with the entire universe. As you do, you learn that its natural inclination is to manifest the very qualities this guidebook is asking you to exercise more freely in your life. In other words, we realize fully that what we seek is within us: we are already Buddhas by nature. What's more, Buddha nature pervades the entire universe, and we are each challenged to do our part in embodying and expressing it. As Siddhartha says in Herman Hesse's novel of the same name (a book I read and reread in college at the age of seventeen), "This world is not imperfect or slowly evolving along a long path to perfection. No, it is perfect in every moment." This is the ultimate truth, the view from above, the big picture, known in Buddhism as *prajna paramita* (which, as you'll see, relates to wisdom, the sixth transcendental practice).

The minute you start reading these pages you can begin to reorient your life in the bold, exciting, and inspiring Bodhisattva direction of truth and love. It doesn't matter whether you now consider yourself a Buddhist, Christian, Jew, Muslim, Hindu, Jain, pantheist, atheist, agnostic, or devotee of any other spirituality, religion, or philosophy. It doesn't matter if you're antireligious. Although the content of this book appears largely in a Buddhist context, its principles, stories, and suggested activities have universal meaning and application, and could help anyone become a better person and contribute to a better, more beautiful world.

Every description, example, and recommendation here is geared toward enabling you to look more reflectively at how you think, speak, and behave, moment by moment, and to explore more intently your relationships with others. This inner endeavor alone will give you a keener sense of what has genuinely been most valuable, harmful, or problematic in your own experience. Fueled by this wisdom, you can then put more intelligence and enthusiasm into fine-tuning your thoughts, words, and behaviors so that they harmonize more resonantly with the Bodhisattva Code and, as a result, with your own Buddha nature. As you progress along this path, you'll discover that you're creating a marvelous and bountiful new existence for yourself, one that feels more certain, more useful, and, best of all, more alive. You'll also find that the people around you feel this way too, not only about the life they witness you leading but also about their own lives.

Today's world cries out for this kind of impassioned solution on both a personal and a collective level. Who doesn't see the difficult and dangerous state of the world around us, both at home and abroad? In the past few years, Americans have suffered through the 9/11 terrorist attack, a devastating war in Iraq, and, on the domestic front, two viciously divisive presidential elections and an ever-widening gap between the haves and the have-nots. As faith in our leaders steadily erodes, many people feel increasingly hopeless and cynical. Racism, poverty, illiteracy, and fanaticism are ever-greater social problems. AIDS and other potentially epidemic illnesses continue to ravage our population, revealing more and more the inadequacies of our clumsy health care systems. Meanwhile, environmental degradation and global warming threaten us all.

Faced with these dilemmas, popular culture, the media, and the government still pressure us relentlessly to stay self-focused, cocooned, and defensive. They tell us directly and indirectly to fear outsiders, worry about appearances, look good, and accumulate as much wealth and security as we can. With so many of us feeling threatened, insignificant, self-conscious, and acquisitive, it's no wonder that Americans have developed a cult of celebrity. We keep track of the lives of movie stars, elect idols on television, and fantasize about being the victorious, wealthy, self-assured center of envious attention ourselves. We count on winning the lottery, being hired by someone like Donald Trump, or marrying a millionaire to bring us security. We look on reality as a game created by the powers-that-be. Will we win or lose? But isn't this superficial, outer-oriented way of looking at things directly opposed to the way of realizing true happiness, of relating deeply, naturally, and purposefully to the world around us as well as to the inner truth of our own being? Shouldn't we be paying more attention to what our hearts tell us to feel, say, and do, so that we interact more beneficially with others and find our own true place in the world? Why, instead, do we let outside forces dictate to us how we should feel about ourselves and live among others? Don't we know in our heart of hearts that each of us has a special gift to give the world—namely, ourselves? We can be brilliant, truly beautiful, extraordinary; why compromise and settle for mediocrity, or even less? Life is what we *are;* what we do is what we are and become.

I'm certain that we believe this. We all have innately "good hearts" (one of the Dalai Lama's favorite expressions for our Buddha nature). Being human, each of us instinctively seeks to live a life of higher principles, universal values, and cosmic radiance and, in so doing, to help create a loving family and a better world. I call this drive "spiritual tropism": we grow up turning as naturally toward spiritual light as a flower turns toward the sun. Buddhists would say that this inclination is the spontaneous stirring of our inherent Buddha nature. In fact, the Indo-European syllable *bodh,* which is the root of both Sanskrit words *Bodhisattva* and *Buddha* (meaning "enlightened" or "awakened" one), is also the root of the English word *bud,* the beginning of a flower. Extending the metaphor, we can say that it's only when we allow our Buddha nature to unfold in its most natural way that we truly bloom and blossom into life.

We see this spiritual tropism or innate Buddha nature—a natural evolutionary aspiration—most nakedly gleaming in the eyes of young children who have yet to be socially conditioned to distance themselves from others and to compete. If we examine our adult lives carefully enough, we can also catch glimpses and glimmers in them of spiritual tropism. As misguided as many of our own day-to-day thoughts, words, or deeds may be, essentially we all want to become the best person we can be, to see others living the best lives they can, and to leave the best possible world for the next generation. I would like to help you be able to do just that.

Who doesn't want these things? Let me posit that all animals—not only humans and plants—turn toward the light. The Buddha taught that all sentient beings are endowed with luminous Buddha nature—or, in other words, innate spirituality. It's not something that only Buddhists possess. Instead, it is what I call our fundamental Buddha-ness. If we could see it in all the sentient beings around us, we would all look like mirrors reflecting the same, most noble spiritual qualities even here in our shadowy, dreamlike, problematic, yet magical world.

Following the Bodhisattva Code helps us achieve these qualities. It sets in motion a complete turnaround in our lives from being overly needy, self-oriented, and perpetually unsatisfied to being empowered, self-liberated, and buoyantly energized. Because I am so positive that you—and the world around you—will benefit if you bring this helpful code into your life, I'm tempted to shout, "Trust me! Please! Trust me!" But that's not the point. In fact, it totally misses the point. You need to trust *yourself.* Instead of letting the outside world tell you how to live, what to value, and what to fear, you must listen more deeply to your heart of hearts. Then, taking your cues from it, you need to conscientiously examine the truth of these matters; and if it makes sense to you, you could begin making positive, wholehearted differences in how you think, speak, and act—that is, in how you relate both to yourself and to others. This will utterly change your life.

The naked truth of spiritual transformation is that if we don't change our lives ourselves, nothing will change them for us. That's the secret of spiritual self-mastery. No one else can do it for us. Although help is available, we need to take it upon ourselves to find and utilize it.

The Bodhisattva Code is the Buddha's own guide to enlightened living. It provides us with a time-tested map for discovering our own individual path in this enlivening direction. And the current state of the world, despite its many daunting challenges, also presents rare opportunities for taking this all-important journey, both externally and internally. Thanks to tremendous advances in technology over the past half-century, human beings now have the capacity to communicate with each other more directly, swiftly, creatively, and impressively than at any other time in history. Every day more and more individuals utilize these technologies to band together and work more resourcefully and synergistically to solve the world's problems. The possibilities today for positive change on a global scale are enormous. Borders are fading. Interconnectedness and interdependence are being more understood as vital forces at play in our world today. We need each other to live, love, and learn here together. We need each other in order to develop compassion and become enlightened.

Even destructive events, whether on a personal, national, or global level, can trigger promising aftereffects. When hearts are broken open by terror or despair, spirits cry out for healing. From profound suffering can come greater understanding and more bountiful compassion. These powerful energies can then be put to the joyful task of making broken things not just whole again but stronger and healthier than they originally were. A broken heart can lead to more sensitivity to the sufferings of others, and to greater openheartedness, thus transforming wounds into wisdom.

Reinhold Niebuhr, a Protestant theologian, mentioned three of the paramita virtues when he said that we must be strong enough to change the things we can change, patient enough to accept the things we can't, and wise enough to know the difference. You may think you already see fairly clearly how things are in the world and how they should be, but I fervently ask you to look again, more deeply. Positive change most often evolves slowly, like a watershed brought into being by raindrops falling one drop at a time, until the volume of water eventually gathers into a crescendo and forms rivers that flow on to create an ocean. It is the Bodhisattva's challenge and opportunity, as an enlightened leader and heroic spiritual activist, to contribute to the ocean of enlightenment one thought, one word, one deed, one prayer, one smile at a time, day by day, moment by moment.

At a recent conference, an American student asked the elder Tibetan master Khenpo Thrangu Rinpoche how to respond to today's troubling times and live a decent life in a culture like ours, which seems corrupt in so many ways. Thrangu Rinpoche replied, "You must counter the negative energy with as much positive thought and action as you can possibly muster. You must unceasingly sustain Bodhisattva action. It is the Buddha's teaching to make of ourselves an example, a light, a beacon." Speaking more generally of how to meet both the personal and communal challenges of the twenty-first century, including the "fear that our existence is meaningless," His Holiness the Dalai Lama remarked, "Human beings will have to develop a greater sense of universal responsibility. Each of us must learn to work not just for his or her own self, family, or nation, but for the benefit of all mankind."

There is a tremendous spiritual hunger in our world today, and few and far between are those who can meaningfully assuage that sincere yearning. We have a great deal to do. The gap between what we normally feel capable of and what our best selves can actually accomplish is immense, and there is no limit to what we can accomplish *together*. Meanwhile, for lack of vision, imagination, inspiration, and skillful means, our innate natural resources remain for the most part untapped and underutilized. The call for fearless Bodhisattvas and sagacious elders has never been louder; on an individual basis too the marvelous promise of following the Bodhisattva Code of enlightened living has never been sweeter. Many are called; few choose to respond. We cannot afford to wait. That is why I am calling for a spiritual revolution, a veritable groundswell of enlightened leadership and Bodhisattvism dedicated to edifying and awakening the world.

Remember that you too are a Bodhisattva, a peacemaking spiritual warrior and future Buddha. Let's recollect Mahatma Gandhi's clarion message, that we ourselves must become the changes we wish to see in the world. The Dalai Lama says: "It is easier to meditate than to actually do something for others. I feel that merely to meditate on compassion is to take the passive option. Our meditation should form the basis for action, for seizing the opportunity to do something."

May you experience joy and peace, find freedom from greed, anger, cynicism, and illusion, and realize your inner treasure trove of truth and love through the liberating paramita practices of wisdom and compassion, lovingkindness and generosity. May we together activate this delightful freedom in others, and may this book help us along the way.

INTRODUCTION

LIVING THE
GOOD LIFE

The Bodhisattva is like the mightiest of warriors
But his enemies are not common foes of flesh and bone.
His fight is with the inner delusions,
The afflictions of selfishness and ego-grasping....
He is the real hero, calmly facing any hardship
In order to bring peace, happiness, and liberation into the world.

—THE THIRTEENTH
DALAI LAMA (1876–1933)

Exxon Ken is a hero in my life. I haven't seen him or talked with him in twenty-five years, but he continues to inspire me. He was a real backyard Bodhisattva, a diamond in the rough, hidden among the gas pumps and clamor of a small-town mechanics shop.

In 1978 I was living at the newly founded Karma Triyana Dharmachakra Monastery on top of Meade Mountain overlooking Woodstock, New York, and Ken Reynolds owned the local service station down below on Tinker Street, the main drag. Superficially, we seemed like complete opposites. I was a politically liberal, conscientiously smiling monk, raised in the metropolitan New York City area and just back in the United States after years of esoteric studies in Asia. He was a gruff, politically conservative Korean veteran with crew-cut gray hair, and by every appearance, he was a Catskill Mountains good ole boy.

At the time I drove an old, $300 jalopy that didn't start unless I parked it on a hill so I could pop the clutch as it rolled forward. I spent much of an exceptionally snowy Catskill winter either doing that or waiting beside the car for someone to help me push it or jump-start the battery with cables. I couldn't bring myself to approach Ken about getting a new battery or an electric starter because I still owed him money on the four snow tires I'd bought at the beginning of the winter. It wasn't only shame, however, that made me avoid him. I found his whole bearing somehow daunting, and he probably would have intimidated many people with sixties peacenik backgrounds similar to mine. Ken looked as if he belonged to a different species of human being.

One snowy day I pulled up to the Exxon pump and left my car running while I filled the tank with gas. Ken ambled up to me, clutching a big can of his favorite Colt 45 beer, and barked in his usual brusque voice, "Big Man, don't you know it's dangerous to leave the car running while you pump gas? Any teenager should know that!" (I was then twenty-eight years old.) I bashfully admitted why I was letting it run—because I wouldn't be able to start it and drive away if I turned it off. Ken immediately said, "You can't drive around like that! Bring it in tomorrow, early, and I'll fix it. I'll just put it on your account. Pay me when the winter's over. Pay me when you can. Pay me when your ship comes in!" When I later told this story to friends in Woodstock, I discovered that he often did the same thing for others in need, especially welfare recipients and struggling single mothers. Some people told me that he never sent them a bill or brought it up again. I often wonder what happened to him and pray for his good all-American soul.

Exxon Ken is a Bodhisattva. You can find such good-hearted everyday heroes in the most surprising places. More recently, I met one in the form of a bald security guard working the metal detector at an airport, who aided my foreign friends and me with alacrity as well as a smile.

Bodhisattvas are individuals who exhibit an unusually strong and instinctive tendency to relinquish their own apparent gain and self-interest in order to help others, even if it requires a great deal of effort or abandonment of their own personal agenda. Sometimes they act with exceptional generosity. Other times they demonstrate great patience, profound wisdom, or unimpeachable moral character and ethical integrity. Sometimes it can be just a little unexpected kindness, a helpful word, or a smile that expresses the hidden Bodhisattva deep within, coming at precisely the right time and place when one is truly in need of a boost. In every case, they inspire us by the extent to which they apply these qualities for the benefit of others rather than themselves. I believe there are innumerable, ordinary-folk Bodhisattvas like Ken Reynolds among us. Think about those you know who offer genuine help and service wherever they go, and sense the gratitude and appreciation they evoke in your heart. Consider more particularly those humble, unheralded individuals who have made a crucial difference in your own life or the lives of people you know. Maybe one of these ordinary Bodhisattvas helped you, a family member, or a friend learn a significant lesson or showed you how to step up to a higher level of consciousness at some important turning point in your life. Bodhisattvas both ascendant and human are our benefactors, life-changers, allies, guides, and protectors, whether we are aware of it or not.

Although the self-sacrifice of these Bodhisattvas may be illogical from a worldly point of view, it's clearly not pathological—in other words, it doesn't show any signs of coming from sheer madness or any neurotic or psychotic need for approval or self-flagellation. Nor does it stem from codependent, would-be healer behavior or a savior complex, which can lead to burnout, bitterness, and feelings of martyrdom. Instead, these individuals radiate a sense of peace, joy, fulfillment, and naturalness in accomplishing the good things they do. Whatever their external appearance or life situation may be, they seem more deeply in touch with, and empowered by, universal values than their more self-oriented peers are. Doing the right thing is the only reward they need.

Christians sometimes call such people saints or knights, people of honor, and guardian angels. Jews often refer to them as mensches. In every culture, humans consider them heroes, not necessarily in a physically mighty way but certainly in a spiritually effective one. They are the individuals who save us in countless different ways just by being who they are. I'm sure if you take a quiet moment of reflection, you can call to mind special benefactors who have functioned as Bodhisattvas in your life. This recalling of benefactors and their selfless kindnesses is a traditional Buddhist practice to help us open up, soften our hearts, cultivate gratitude, and develop lovingkindness for others. I especially remember my Tibetan Buddhist teachers in this way. They acted as beacons and models in my life and continue to accompany and guide me as an invisible yet almost palpable team of angels and allies, guiding and inspiring me every day.

The title "Bodhisattva," meaning "Awakening being," was applied solely to the Buddha in the earliest years of Buddhism. It was used to describe him during the pre-enlightenment period of his life, when he was known as Siddhartha Guatama (also Sakyamuni, chief of the Sakya clan), who, by most calculations, lived from 563 to 483 BCE and became enlightened in 528 BCE at age thirty-five. Additionally, the title "Bodhisattva" was used to identify him in every one of his previous lifetimes as an animal or human being. During these prior existences, recorded in the beautiful and instructive *Jataka* (or "birth") Tales, he steadily evolved and developed the qualities that eventually led him toward his enlightenment. He later recorded these qualities, the attributes of a Bodhisattva, in the ten transformative practices—the subject of this book.

In a Jataka Tale that I especially like, the Bodhisattva (that is, the future Sakyamuni Buddha) was born long, long ago as a dull, gray parrot. One day a fire broke out in his forest. As he instinctively flew out of the forest to safety, he saw many animals below that were trapped, as well as many plants and trees that were being destroyed, so he resolved to do whatever he could to save the forest. He flew down to the river, scooped up water with his wings, flew over the center of the fire, and shook the drops onto the flames. He did this over and over again, even though his small actions had no noticeable dampening effect on the raging inferno, and even though his feathers were becoming more and more charred by the flames. On a cloud high above, several gods (in Sanskrit, *devas*) were leisurely feasting and watching the parrot. Some were poking fun at his futile efforts, but one of them secretly felt pity for him. This one changed himself into a huge eagle and flew down to urge the parrot to give up his effort and save himself. When the parrot refused, the eagle was moved to tears by the parrot's compassion. These abundant divine tears put out the fire and saved the forest. What's more, some of the tears fell on the parrot's feathers and turned them from gray into a whole rainbow of bright colors.

This Jataka Tale moves me on many levels. I admire the parrot's gumption and fearlessness. I delight in the explanation of how parrots got their colorful feathers. But what I like most about this story is its lesson that we don't need to do great, powerful, spectacular things to make a genuine difference or to become heroes. Nor do we need to be powerful beings or important leaders. We simply need to do the best that we can, even if it seems impossible that we'll wind up doing anything special in the long run. It is purely our motivation and great-hearted Bodhicitta in action that counts, not any attachment to a specific outcome.

Another way of putting it is that we need to focus on what we can do right now rather than wonder about how, specifically, the future is going to unfold. Who knows what wonderful, unexpected things may happen simply because we offer what we can? How easy it is for us to forget that our thoughts, words, and deeds, however insignificant they may seem to us, can affect others in many different, unpredictable, and profound ways. Who knows what help may come from the invisible array of Bodhisattvas and spiritual friends surrounding us?

Stories and anecdotes are universally popular, memorable, and effective means of educating, entertaining, and edifying. There are 547 Jataka Tales in the Pali Canon, the earliest written collection of Buddhist *sutras* (or scriptures), dating from the first century BCE. We can therefore conclude that the Bodhisattva—that is, the Buddha-to-be—went through at least 547 lifetimes before he became Sakyamuni. After the Bodhisattva's breakthrough to realization in this final lifetime, he assumed a new, advanced title, "the Buddha," meaning "the Awakened One." Over the first and second centuries CE, as Buddhism expanded into China and elsewhere and lay practice gathered more strength, a new, more populist vehicle of Buddhism emerged that came to be known as Mahayana Buddhism. According to Mahayana belief, the Buddha chose not to pass into complete and total nirvana after his death—in other words, he put off escaping the endless cycle of birth and rebirth, ever fraught with suffering, even though his enlightenment offered him the means of doing so. Instead, he chose to remain in the cycle in order to continue working toward the enlightenment of all sentient beings. Simply put, he did not consider himself liberated until all human beings were liberated.

For this reason, Mahayana Buddhism—which includes Tibetan, Zen, and Pure Land Buddhists throughout the world—represents a vehicle of universal liberation rather than one of individual salvation. It extends to all its practitioners the opportunity to become a Bodhisattva and to take the Bodhisattva Vow to help to achieve liberation for all. I'll discuss the Bodhisattva Vow later in this chapter. Whether or not you are a Buddhist, you can act in the world as a Bodhisattva by making a similarly selfless commitment in regard to your own life, dedicating your energies now and later to the greatest universal good, and specifically by adopting the ten transformative practices that comprise the Bodhisattva Code.

There are countless human beings whom I would classify as Bodhisattvas in this sense of the term. While the image of the Bodhisattva as an intrepid parrot is still fresh in your mind from the Jataka Tale, let me cite an example of a human Bodhisattva who is working selflessly right now to save her native landscape and the living beings who depend on it: Wangari Muta Maathai, a native of Kenya. After earning a doctorate in biology at the University of Pittsburgh in 1966, Maathai returned to her homeland and was shocked at the damage caused there by deforestation. It was not only ruining the soil but also devastating the lives of local women, who were responsible, by tradition, for collecting firewood and preparing household fires. Having to roam farther and farther to forage for wood, they had less and less time to spend at home tending crops and caring for their children.

Maathai was determined to address this deteriorating situation. She gave up a lucrative and prestigious career to found the Green Belt Movement, an activist organization dedicated to helping women become foresters by planting trees in their own neighborhoods. As she labored tirelessly to expand the scope of the organization, she suffered legal persecution, physical attack, and even imprisonment, thanks to government agents who preferred to sell public lands for private gain rather than let citizens conserve them. Now, after thirty years of struggle, the result has been twenty million new trees in Kenya, empowerment for thousands of formerly impoverished individuals, a frequently adopted model of environmental and economic self-help throughout the world, and, in 2004, a Nobel Peace Prize for Maathai. I sat next to her on an interfaith panel at a church in Harvard Square on September 11, 2002. I was impressed by her dynamism and continue to cherish an image she shared with the rest of us there: "If you're on an unhappy bus and you don't like where it's going, get off it and board a happier bus instead."

I also include in this category of extraordinary human Bodhisattvas a wide variety of well-known figures, historical and contemporary, who have done remarkable things to serve humankind and inspire others to be the best they can be: Moses; Jesus; Mother Teresa; Martin Luther King Jr.; Dag Hammarskjöld, a former secretary-general of the United

Nations; Albert Schweitzer; Jackie Robinson, the first black major league baseball player; Nelson Mandela; Padma Sambhava, founder of Tibetan Buddhism; the Dalai Lama; Dorothy Day, a cofounder of the Catholic Worker movement; Muhammad; Mr. C. T. Shen, a Buddhist philanthropist in New York; Sojourner Truth; Lance Armstrong, the champion cyclist and benefactor to cancer survivors; Aung San Suu Kyi, a campaigner for political freedom in Myanmar; and the firefighters and police officers who risked or gave their lives to rescue people when the World Trade Center buildings and the Pentagon were attacked on September 11, 2001.

My pantheon of human Bodhisattvas also includes unsung heroes like Exxon Ken. He may not have given up as much of his time, energy, and resources to others as, for instance, Mother Teresa, and I'm sure he'd cackle hysterically at the comparison, but he repeatedly went out of his way to act with compassion toward those in need who crossed his path. The relative virtue of an individual Bodhisattva can't usefully be measured in any material way that reflects truth. We can't, for example, say, "Who was the better Bodhisattva: Joan of Arc, the visionary saint, or Joan Van Ark, who runs the local homeless shelter?" This point of view looks at Bodhisattvas from the outside and seeks to judge them merely from that outside point of reference.

In fact, the real transformational miracle, the one that saves all sentient beings, occurs within the individual's life. Different people come to this process from different starting points, but each of us goes through the same kind of growth. And the energy involved—the awakening-life force, the drive to love, grow, understand, connect, and evolve—is the same for every one of us. It unfolds like a lotus, the Asian symbol of spiritual purity, lifting its face up from the muddy waters into the rising sun.

The great American labor leader Eugene V. Debs said, "While there is a soul in prison, I am not free." I define Bodhisattvas as individuals who consistently test their self-oriented limits to relate more fully to others because something deep inside them tells them it's the wisest, most compassionate, and best thing to do. At first, this stretching effort may be difficult for them. They may have to train themselves deliberately to follow through on what they know to be right, breaking unhelpful patterns of thought, speech, and behavior, and reconditioning themselves in more positive directions. Eventually, however, compassion and kindness become second nature. Spiritual warriors develop the habit of going beyond their personal comfort zone and outside of their own small circle of family members and friends to benefit the lives of others in general.

Thinking about Exxon Ken's selfless acts of generosity, we might say to ourselves, "That's very nice of him, but isn't he only doing what everyone should do?" The answer, of course, is, "Yes, but not everyone *does* do it." It's not always so easy, is it? To be a Bodhisattva is not to be superhuman but to be the way human beings should and can be, the way they inherently are—and not just for the greatest good of the species, but for the greatest good of each individual as well. My friend Leonard, who gives up hours of his spare time each week to tutor illiterate adults, is another human Bodhisattva of the Exxon Ken type. So is my friend Lila, who takes it upon herself to clean roadside litter—even dog turds from sidewalks—wherever she goes.

I also classify as Bodhisattvas my many friends and acquaintances who regularly campaign in their own communities and elsewhere on behalf of human rights issues. As Robert Kennedy once said, "Each time a man stands up for an ideal, or acts to improve the lot of others, or strikes out against injustice, he sends forth a tiny ripple of hope ... and, crossing each other from a million different centers of energy and daring, those ripples build a current that can seep down the mightiest walls of oppression and resistance."

I'm sure you have your own personal gallery of Bodhisattvas, including famous individuals who are widely respected for their services to humanity, unsung heroes who have impressed you with their wise and compassionate acts, and revered spiritual figures, gods, goddesses, prophets, or saints. Please think carefully about this matter now and as you read each of the chapters in this book. Start keeping an Awakener notebook to record and write about these vitally important people and spiritual beings in your life. Contemplating and meditating on them can help motivate you to follow their example, turning externally and internally toward that high ground that we all can visit and eventually inhabit.

YOUR OUTER, INNER, AND SECRET BEING

I believe that each of us has three levels of being: outer, inner, and secret. Our outer being consists of our external appearance, presentation, personality, and behavior. Our inner being is made up of all our conscious thoughts, feelings, memories, intentions, daydreams, night dreams, ego—identity and self-image—the story we tell ourselves about who we are. Finally, at the core of our existence is our secret being, our essence or true nature, which Buddhists designate as our inherent Buddha nature, our true nature, our Buddha-ness.

In taking up the practice of being a Bodhisattva, we work with these three forms or dimensions of being, striving to integrate them ever more cooperatively with one another and ever more effectively into our daily lives. For example, in an effort to be more generous (generosity being the first of the ten transformational practices of a Bodhisattva discussed here), we may decide *internally* that it would be a good thing to donate 10 percent of every paycheck to charity. Indeed, beyond even the realm of thought we may know that it's the right thing to do, in which case we've tapped into our *secret* form, our most essential goodness and richness as human beings. In actually going through with the donation project, we are being generous *externally*. However, *internally* we may still hate to give away the money. We may feel that we're somehow shortchanging ourselves or our families, or we may be disappointed that we aren't getting that rosy sense of self-satisfaction about it that we'd been counting on. Nevertheless, as we persevere in our external action and simultaneously work toward a more positive and less grasping and attachment-oriented internal attitude, we find that we draw more and more energy and positive support from our *secret* form, the infinite abundance and contentment within our innate Buddha-ness, which is in fact being increasingly evoked by our ongoing external and internal efforts.

A fully realized way of life, one in which we experience the most satisfying use of our potential and the greatest sense of balance and equanimity, depends on these three levels of existence acting in harmony with one another. The more we persist in indulging our own selfish desires, or craving and striving greedily for worldly gain, or allowing ourselves to succumb egotistically to greed, anger, and delusion, the more we go against the very grain of our innermost spiritual being. How can we help but feel disgruntled with such an off-balance life? Buddhist sutras often compare this kind of existence to an oxcart wheel that wobbles every which way because it's not centered properly on its axle.

We can't help but suffer if we do one thing and think another, all the while assuming that these are two different and separate worlds of functioning: public versus private, other versus self, official versus off-the-record, "this counts" versus "this doesn't count." For example, suppose you have a male acquaintance toward whom you always behave in a very friendly, if somewhat artificial, fashion—smiling, joking, doing all you can to please and charm. In your internal dialogue with yourself, however, you keep reflecting on how often he irritates you, how ridiculous his opinions are, and how much you'd like to avoid him whenever possible. Maybe you pat yourself on the back for being so generous, polite, and patient with him, despite your inner reservations, and yet you can't help but shake the sensation that you're being a hypocrite while also wasting time and energy. You also feel resentment, but is it against him, yourself, or both of you? You can't really tell.

Clearly, if you don't change your overall approach to this relationship, it will never get better, you will never break through your conflict about it, and you'll never feel entirely good about yourself. You need to practice behaving more naturally and sincerely around the other person, and you need to start taking just as much responsibility for *thinking* in a positive manner as you do for *acting* appropriately.

The body-mind-spirit connection is incredibly deep and strong; science and religion both tell us that. As we cultivate the qualities of a Bodhisattva in our deeds and our thoughts, bringing out the Buddha nature that is our secret self, we physically radiate more peace, grace, and compassion. We can literally see this effect when we're in the presence of great humanitarians, like the Dalai Lama and Archbishop Tutu. Something ineffable in the way they look, move, and behave confirms the truth of the path they've taken, reflects the bliss they're experiencing as a result of taking that path, and, most impressive of all, helps others around them share that bliss. They appear extraordinarily open, present, centered, confident, and indomitable.

I'll explore the interplay of our outer, inner, and secret innermost forms throughout the next ten chapters as I discuss how to cultivate each of the ten Bodhisattva paramitas as a transformative practice wisely expressing compassion in action. Meanwhile, please begin right now to note the moments of friction or inner conflict in your life, the times when your actions don't match your thoughts and feelings, or when neither your thoughts nor your feelings quite reflect what your innermost being senses intuitively. Also note the moments of harmony in your life, the times when these three forms of being seem to be in sync. All of this conscious and intentional work on oneself ultimately contributes to great progress on the path of enlightened living.

When we take the Bodhisattva path, we enter into an especially challenging kind of self-training. We commit ourselves to work not just toward self-improvement but toward transcending the whole notion of self and selfishness. This endeavor goes against the grain of every self-help program our culture has conditioned us to seek. Daily we're bombarded with messages that bid us to take a good hard look at our faces, bodies, dwellings, portfolios, job descriptions, leisure-time activities, or relationships with an eye toward making them better for our own personal benefit. Becoming a Bodhisattva means letting go of these desires as we turn our focus instead in the opposite direction and concentrate on what we can do for the genuine benefit of all, out of a felt sense of universal responsibility.

A sublime beauty results from this kind of training. In releasing us from the petty and recurrently painful narrowness of more selfish goals, it allows us to live far more expansively, joyfully, and productively. But if we set out on the path with the objective of attaining this wonderful new life only for ourselves, we're aiming in the wrong direction, hobbling our best selves, and defeating ourselves from the start.

That's just one of the paradoxes associated with the life of a Bodhisattva. More are expressed in the traditional Bodhisattva Vow. As the first step along the Bodhisattva path for formal practitioners of Mahayana Buddhism, the vows help their upholders ensure that their intentions are clear, pure, altruistic, and unmuddied by self-serving motives. They appear in slightly different forms in different Buddhist traditions, but they always contain the same four essential pledges. Here's how I say them each day:

Sentient beings are numberless: I vow to liberate them.
Delusions are inexhaustible: I vow to transcend them.
Dharma teachings are boundless: I vow to master them.
The Buddha's enlightened way is unsurpassable: I vow to embody it.

What does it mean to "liberate" (or, in some versions, "save") all sentient beings? And how can I alone do that, especially if they are numberless? We can't let these questions defeat us from the start. Remember: we're talking about *spiritual intention* here, not a census or strategic planning goal. In a sense, we're vowing to do what hasn't been done yet. We're taking on what the rational mind says is impossible because deep down in our heart we feel that it can happen, even that it must happen, whatever the odds. Because we dare to believe this way, we are helping to liberate that part of us that interconnects with all sentient beings. On a more practical level, we can all agree that what each of us thinks, says, and does has a ripple effect that extends farther out into the world than we can ever know. Thus, one person's transformation helps make the world a better place for everyone. Liberating oneself liberates all, in a mysterious fashion. "To save one soul is to save the world," as the Jewish Talmud says.

If delusions are inexhaustible, how can we transcend (or, in some versions, "put an end to") them? Again, we can't let this apparent paradox stop us from making the effort. Of course delusions seem inexhaustible to us at the beginning, before we've fully developed our Bodhisattva consciousness. Despair over just that fact may be what is compelling us to want to transform our lives. Even though the situation looks hopeless—maybe precisely because it looks hopeless—we must try as vigorously as we can, giving fully of ourselves, not cutting our work to fit certain end-point parameters. There are no parameters involved in the boundless and groundless, wisdom-based ten paramitas, for the eye of all the paramitas is transcendental wisdom itself, which sees through all forms and conceptual limitations.

If Dharma teachings are boundless, how can I master all of them? *Dharma* has two meanings in Buddhism: it refers both to the official body of Buddhist teachings and to every phenomenon in the universe, which has its own unique message or lesson to provide if we're awake to it. Again, why begin this more enlightened learning process if it can never be totally completed? The classic rhetorical answer is the best one here: why not?

If the Buddha's enlightened way is unsurpassable (in other words, "uncontainable" or, in some versions, "unattainable"), how can I embody it? It's like a riddle, what they call in Zen Buddhism a *koan*—a paradoxical teaching question. It's not meant to stop you in your tracks but rather to present you with a key to a whole new mode of perceiving and living. You resolve or break through its mystery in the very process of taking the Bodhisattva path. If the ultimate truth could be said in a more comprehensible way, it wouldn't be the ultimate truth. It would simply be a statement as limited by logic as our worldly lives are boxed up by ego.

The Bodhisattva Vows can seem incredibly daunting, as if they were asking us to do more than we conceivably can. That's one way of recognizing their power. Yes, it is asking us to do more than we're doing right now, more than we can conceive right now, but it holds the outrageous promise of enabling us to do more and conceive more than we ever imagined we could. That's the way the Bodhisattva Vow has functioned in the lives of thousands and thousands of people who have taken it. Once embraced and incorporated into our lives, it manifests its power in ever more magical ways. It's like the fabled philosopher's stone that transforms the dross of ordinary, impermanent, ego-based material existence into the splendid gold of radiant spiritual being.

When I first heard about the Bodhisattva aspiration, I was a college freshman at State University of New York at Buffalo. My roommate David and I went on a weekend retreat with Philip Kapleau Roshi at the Rochester Zen Center, and the whole atmosphere of the vow and all it seemed to entail overwhelmed us. We felt as if we were holding our breath the entire two and a half days. Later I met some Buddhist monks from Thailand at a peace march in Washington, D.C., and asked them about the Bodhisattva Vow. With sweet smiles and definite twinkles in their eyes, they said, "It's probably not for Americans." They appeared quite happy and peaceful themselves. They also were extremely gentle—definitely not something I saw often at school.

Not long afterward, in 1971, I heard much more about the Bodhisattva commitment from my first *lama* (or Tibetan Buddhist teacher), Geshe Thubten Yeshe, at Kopan Monastery overlooking Kathmandu Valley in Nepal. The vow seemed as unattainable to me personally as the high Himalayan snowpeaks glistening on the northern horizon. I thought to my twenty-year-old self, *What an outrageous ambition, to vow to deliver all sentient beings from suffering, no matter how long it might take and how many beings, seen and unseen, there may be!*

I heard a Jataka Tale at the time about the Buddha himself, in one of his earlier lives as Prince Mahasattva. One day the prince was wandering through a forest blighted by drought. Suddenly he came upon an emaciated tiger. Too weak to attack the prince, the tiger curled protectively around her cubs, who were crying with hunger. Moved by compassion, the prince said to himself, *What is this life for, if not to help others?* He disrobed and lay down in front of the tiger. Then he grabbed a sharp stone and tore his flesh until it bled. Smelling the blood, the tiger and her cubs feasted on the body until not a scrap remained. They survived and lived long lives.

Awestruck by the extreme nature of this story, which reflects just how deeply compassion is valued in Asian and Buddhist tradition, I visited Namo Buddha, the very place where this selfless act allegedly occurred. It's situated on a ridge of the mountains east of Kathmandu, and a tree filled with the prayer flags of visiting pilgrims is said to mark the actual spot where Prince Mahasattva offered his life to the tiger and her cubs. I spent a few nights at the small retreat center there and, according to my lama's instructions, contemplated the nature of life, birth, death, suffering, and altruism. Time-bound as I felt, stuck in my own limited sense of identity in this world, and incapable of grasping the possibility of past and future lives, I couldn't honestly imagine unselfishly dedicating myself and each of my lifetimes to the benefit of all. It was difficult for me to believe and to comprehend that the prince's selfless sacrifice had brought him higher and quicker on the path to enlightenment; legend has it that Prince Mahasattva accrued vast merits for his generosity, and was soon reborn closer to the enlightened state.

As I later began teaching English to my lama, it began to dawn on me that he too was a human being not much different from me, not a supernatural avatar descended from heaven. Physically he was much worse off than I was: with a heart weakened by a childhood bout with rheumatic fever, he could die at any time. And yet he gave himself unstintingly to his students, the local villagers, and everyone else who appeared before him. I realized in a way I never had before that it was his Bodhisattva aspiration, far more potent than any egotistical ambition, that lent him stamina, determination, vast vision, and true greatness.

That realization set something in motion deep in my heart. I wanted to bring that aspiration into my own life. Maybe I couldn't envision turning myself into tiger food, but I could at least start doing what I could. One year later, in Darjeeling, India, I undertook the same vow myself in a daylong ceremony with my main teachers, Kalu Rinpoche and Gyalwa Karmapa. I have chanted it every morning and evening since then, and it has gradually taken over my practice and my outlook. It is my purpose for living in this world.

Once I asked Lama Yeshe at Kopan how he could ignore the warnings of his doctors by traveling so much to teach, including taking airplane trips abroad. Without a second of hesitation, and echoing the words of Prince Mahasattva himself, he replied, "What is this life to me if I can't fulfill my vow by teaching and working for others?" I now understand what he meant. Whatever path we take to express the vow, whatever paradoxes life with that vow presents us, once we've come to experience its rightness and power, how can we ever give it up? Why would we?

Bodhicitta (in Sanskrit, "awakened mind") is the very spirit-engine of enlightenment and our prime mover along the Bodhisattva way. If the Bodhisattva is a vessel or vehicle to carry others to nirvana, Bodhicitta is the engine of that great vehicle. Buddhist teachers often describe it as limitless lovingkindness, an active orientation toward seeking the betterment of everyone instead of one's own selfish benefit alone. Practicing Bodhicitta involves bringing our Buddha nature out into the world with our intention (the Bodhisattva Vow) and with each one of our thoughts, words, and deeds (the Bodhisattva path). The Dalai Lama says, "The highest perfection of altruism, the ultimate altruism, is Bodhicitta complemented by wisdom. Bodhicitta—the aspiration to bring about the welfare of all sentient beings and to attain Buddhahood for their sake—is really the distilled essence, the squeezed juice of all the Buddha's teachings." Wisdom and compassion, truth and love in action, are actually inseparable.

The aspiration mentioned by the Dalai Lama is more than just wishful thinking on our part or a philosophical position we take; it's an entire way of life. The root *citta* in *Bodhicitta* means both mind and heart, encompassing the entirety of consciousness. The two entities aren't separated linguistically in many Asian languages. Even in English we think of the heart as the seat of emotions, instincts, and intuitions. So the very word *Bodhicitta* communicates the strong mind-body-spirit connection in walking the path of a Bodhisattva, in pursuing the altruistic career and change-agent lifestyle of a heroic Bodhisattva. We must be wholeheartedly, single-mindedly, body-and-soul committed to it, in order to genuinely accomplish our great aspiration and profound vow to deliver all beings to enlightenment no matter what it takes.

Bodhicitta is our enlightened mode of consciousness. We are not required, however, to become fully realized Buddhas before we can enter into it. In fact, the process occurs the other way around. We can realize for ourselves what constitutes final enlightenment only after we've learned to exercise our enlightened mind and good heart on a continuing basis. We begin this process as soon as we sense its value. We then carry on with it throughout our lifetime and, as Buddhists believe to varying degrees, in every subsequent lifetime thereafter.

The essential feature of Bodhicitta is genuine, heart-quivering compassion toward all. It's based on empathy and a deeply felt sense that we're each interconnected with everyone else in the universe, and that no one person can be free from suffering until everyone is. Feeling and expressing this compassion means going beyond ordinary benevolence toward those who are close to us, share our beliefs, elicit our sympathy, or attract our interest. Instead, a Bodhisattva cultivates lovingkindness toward all beings, all the time, including enemies, and patient gentleness toward all things, even unpleasant and unwanted ones. Thrangu Rinpoche explains:

> The development of lovingkindness for all sentient beings is necessary because we all have one thing in common, the wish to experience peace and happiness and not experience pain and suffering. It is not that 95 percent are longing for happiness and five percent just do not care. One hundred percent of all beings share this common wish of wanting to have happiness and be rid of suffering. Therefore, we have to include every single being in our development of Bodhicitta.

One of my favorite Tibetan terms is *shen-pen,* which means helpfulness, selfless altruism, and consideration for the benefit of others. I have friends who have received this term as a Dharma name from their teachers, an incentive to grow into a true Bodhisattva. Shen-pen is the essence of the Bodhisattva intention and lifestyle. A spiritual secret is that the more we think about helping others, the less egotism and the fewer self-centered attachments we reinforce in ourselves. We thus accomplish the greatest possible transformation of human nature, with all its selfish conditioning and defensiveness, into Buddha nature, our innate goodness and purity. This is the ultimate form of alchemy.

Shantideva, the Peace Master of ancient India, says that all the suffering in the world comes from one culprit, self-clinging and egotistical attachment, and that all the happiness in the world derives from thinking unselfishly of the well-being of others. Helpfulness is the prime product of Bodhicitta, the awakened heart-mind. Even at the simplest level, we can intentionally manifest it—for example, by giving up our seat on a crowded bus to an elderly person or helping an insecure child cross the street. To uncover this enlightened form of consciousness in our own lives, we simply need to rid ourselves gradually of our negative conditioning. Living in a world where there's so much suffering and violence, we tend to become cynical. We're trained to protect ourselves by suspecting the worst from people. We need to open up our hearts more, as fearful as we may have become about doing that, retraining ourselves according to wisdom and compassion.

One of the best examples of this kind of Bodhicitta attitude was expressed by Anne Frank, the German Jewish teenager who, along with her family and four others, hid out from Nazi persecutors for twenty-five months in an Amsterdam attic before being deported to a concentration camp, where she died in March 1945. Shortly before she was betrayed and captured, she wrote in her diary: "It's a wonder I haven't abandoned all my ideals, they seem so absurd and impractical. Yet I cling to them because I still believe, in spite of everything, that people are truly good at heart." How could such radiant, splendid words of wisdom spring forth from such a young and inexperienced woman if the clear light of Buddhaness were not inherent within her?

Anne Frank's words have resonated with millions of people who have read her diary or seen plays or movies based on her life, and they impress us still today. We instinctively recognize their fundamental truth and value. In tribute to their worth, an international committee bestows Spirit of Anne Frank Awards each year on people who have taken bold steps to fight discrimination and teach tolerance. It's one way of acknowledging that the campaign for world peace and harmony must start with individuals. Visiting the house in Amsterdam where her family was hidden, I could feel the living inspiration of her indomitable and true heart.

We are all essentially good at heart. We would also be good in thought, word, and deed if only we could give full expression to that heart. Cultivating the paramitas, or transformational practices of a Bodhisattva, that are described in this book is largely a matter of unlearning bad habits while raising our spiritual sights. When we stop agonizing over our private share of worldly happiness and unhappiness and falling under the spell of our personal ego-story, we free ourselves not only to benefit the world as a whole but also to live our own life more fully and spontaneously.

Pema Chodron, the American Buddhist nun and director of Gampo Abbey in Nova Scotia, wrote in her 1991 book *The Wisdom of No Escape* about the tremendous effect that this self-liberating activity can have:

> In the early seventies, a friend kept telling me, "Anything you can learn about working with your sense of discouragement or your sense of fear or your sense of bewilderment or your sense of feeling inferior or your sense of resentment—anything you can do to work with those things— do it, please, because it will be such an inspiration to other people...." Remind yourself that it's up to you whether you actually experience gratitude and the preciousness of your life, the fleetingness and the rareness of it, or whether you become more resentful and harsh and embittered and feel more and more cheated. It's up to you how the law of karma all works out.

THE TEN PARAMITAS: HOW A BODHISATTVA LIVES

The ten paramitas—the transformational practices that constitute the Bodhisattva Code—are far-reaching, well-rounded principles for living the truly good life, one of truth and integrity. Often the word *paramitas* is translated into English as "perfections," but this doesn't mean that we need to enact them perfectly in the sense of getting a perfect score on a math test, nor should we give in to the internal tyranny of perfectionism as we strive to cultivate and further develop them. These panacean virtues don't come with precise measurement criteria, although they definitely do become evident as they emerge. The perfection aspect refers to the fact that all ten paramitas, each perfectly complete in and of itself, together combine perfectly to create the total way of being a Bodhisattva, and that when we walk this way, we release our innate perfection. According to my friend Donald Altman, a former Buddhist monk and author of the recent book *Living Kindness,* there's a more mystical dimension to the perfection of the paramitas. "It means that each individual principle illuminates and possesses all of the ten principles," he explains. "This makes each principle entirely whole and inseparable from the others. Imagine a single, flawless diamond containing ten brilliant facets, or virtues. Whenever you express any one of them, you are really expressing and practicing them all."

For example, suppose that we manifest the first paramita, generosity, by grocery shopping for someone who is sick. Intrinsic in this act, as in all generous acts, are aspects of each of the other paramitas: ethics (or, in simple language, doing the right thing), patience (tolerating the inconvenience and time involved), effort (working diligently on the sick person's behalf), skillful means (by doing it correctly and efficiently), and so on.

In practice, each paramita functions not only to nurture joyful and beneficial qualities in the way we function but also to remedy painful and destructive ones. The two activities go hand in hand. To continue the example of grocery shopping for a sick person, let's say that this act of generosity requires that you give up an hour or two of watching television, working on a report, cleaning out your garage, or taking a nap. Whatever activity you relinquish, you are ceasing to cling to your own narrow agenda and instead giving something of yourself by voluntarily helping out someone who is in need. By opening your heart and your schedule to help another person, you are going beyond the limits of your self-orientation to lead a larger life with a greater scope in the world, accumulating meritorious good karma through doing so.

The first six paramitas (starting with generosity and building up to wisdom) are laid out in the Pali Canon, which is said to record the actual words of the Buddha. Later, in Mahayana sutras, these six were expanded to ten, partly to flesh out the path more clearly. I find it helpful to think of the first six paramitas as the key Bodhisattva characteristics and the additional four as advanced and enlightened applications of those characteristics. The classic Indian Buddhist text on the paramitas and Bodhicitta remains Shantideva's thousand-year-old *The Way of the Bodhisattva* (*Bodhisattvacarya-avatara*). I still remember clearly the day in 1973 when my beloved young Nyingma teacher, Tulku Pema Wangyal, introduced me to it for the first time, in the library of his father, Kangyur Rinpoche's, monastery in Darjeeling. I immediately received much richness from it, and it continues to illuminate my life.

I begin each of the following ten chapters with a prayerful affirmation related to the paramita discussed in that chapter. Please use each prayerful affirmation as a focus for your thoughts and meditations, especially at moments when you feel challenged to exercise the particular transcendental virtue it extols. For example, you may one day find yourself feeling road rage when someone cuts you off in traffic. That would be a good time to invoke the prayerful affirmation that goes with the third paramita, patience and forbearance, often extolled as the antidote to anger. Or perhaps one night you experience some dullness or even depression, in which case it would help to invoke the prayerful affirmation that introduces the fourth paramita, joyous effort. I recommend posting each affirmation, as you're first working with it, on your computer monitor, bulletin board, or dashboard as a constant reminder of it, so that you can eventually internalize it through repetition and practice.

Right now, as you take up this glorious, spiritual adventure, this incorporation of the Bodhisattva Code into your life, I extend to you this prayer:

> *With one eye on this world and one on the next,*
> *And a third focused on the timeless dimension,*
> *Throughout this life and all possible lifetimes*
> *Until enlightenment be achieved,*
> *May I inexhaustibly endeavor in the Bodhisattva way*
> *And follow the path of unconditional compassion*
> *And selfless altruism,*
> *So that all beings everywhere may be delivered*
> *And freed from the ravages of suffering and confusion*
> *And reach the other shore, great peace, deathless nirvana.*

ONE

THE TRANSCENDENTAL
GIFT OF GENEROSITY

May I perfect the sublime virtue of generosity,
which liberates and releases craving, grasping,
and attachment,
and brings joyous contentment.

Dana, the ancient Sanskrit word for the first paramita, or transformative
practice, is most often translated into English as "generosity," but the full
meaning of dana is much richer and more far-reaching, as we will see in
this chapter. It refers not only to giving away our time, money, resources,
or labor to help others, but also to having a liberality of spirit that doesn't
erect barriers between self and others. True generosity is giving everything you have to every moment, and is the way of nonattachment.

In many respects, dana is similar to the Christian concept of *caritas*
(Latin for "charity"). Being charitable in this sense means selflessly bestowing compassion and benefits on others without expecting any sort of
return. Instead, the charitable person comes to experience the act itself
as its own natural reward precisely because it's the best thing to do for
everyone involved. An act of charity is, in essence, the purest way to apply
the Golden Rule: "Do unto others as you would have them do unto you."

Being generous according to the Buddhist concept of dana calls for the same kind of dynamic shift in consciousness. It means breaking through the self-oriented attitude that we're making a sacrifice or that we're martyring ourselves when we put the needs of others ahead of our own self-interest. We learn to welcome occasions for generosity as golden opportunities to express our noble Bodhicitta and, in doing so, realize the wealth and abundance of our innate goodness. In giving, we too receive. Through being generous, we erase the troublesome, dualistic distinction between giver and receiver. Buddha said, "Generosity brings happiness at every stage: in framing the intention, in the act of giving, and in rejoicing afterward."

It can be difficult for any human being, concerned about survival needs and subject to countless preoccupations and desires, to rise above self-centeredness toward this kind of generosity. Living in an especially competitive, materialistic, narcissistic, me-first culture, we Americans are even more inclined to devalue and even fear generosity. Although we all respect philanthropy and support charities up to a point, each person is expected to pull his or her own weight. Unlike in more traditional Old World cultures, here beggars are regarded as bums. Rich people are exalted as heroes, often without regard for how they may have come by their fortune. Feeling isolated from each other, we are led to fear poverty as the greatest disaster and wealth as the highest mark of success.

The Vietnamese Zen teacher Thich Nhat Hanh was once teaching students about the six realms of existence in the Buddhist worldview. Just above the infernal demon realm is the realm of creatures called hungry ghosts, who are forever plagued by having huge stomachs (or addictive appetites) and extremely constricted throats, so that they can never satisfy their appetite. One student asked, "What is life like in the realm of the hungry ghosts?" Thich Nhat Hanh replied, "America." The hungry ghost symbolizes the starving spirit plagued by incessant and insatiable desire. The six realms of existence represent psychological states as well as places where beings are said to actually be reborn. For example, the angelic state of the devas, or deities, is a pleasurable realm of sensual satiation and complacent happiness, suggestive of those people who seem to have everything go their own way and enjoy lives of satisfaction, comfort, and ease without a care in the world, at least for the time being.

With this conditioning in our background, we may find it hard to accept or appreciate why generosity is so important to our spiritual growth.

The Buddha, on the other hand, deliberately put generosity first on the list of paramitas. This contrast in attitude reminds me of a story told by my old friend Sharon Salzberg, a founder of the pioneering Insight Meditation Society, in her book *Lovingkindness.* A traditional forest monk from Thailand came to this country to observe Buddhism in America firsthand. After a few months, he confided to Sharon something that perplexed him. "In Asia," he said, "the classic sequence of the teachings and practice is first generosity, then morality, and then meditation or insight. But here in the United States, the sequence seems to be meditation first, then morality, and after some time, as a kind of appendix, there is some teaching about generosity. What's going on here?"

What *is* going on here? One response I'd make to this question is that even when we Americans do strive to break away from the materialistic, self-aggrandizing focus of our society, we still bring with us our cultural training as individualists. Many of us come to Buddhism in the first place as a means of self-improvement, and our initial focus tends to be on things we can do all by ourselves, and seemingly all for ourselves, such as meditate. It's true that meditation is a vitally important practice in Buddhism. As the fifth paramita, meditative mindfulness also permeates each of the other paramitas, so that effectively practicing generosity can't be separated from effectively practicing meditation. But the question remains: why did the Buddha give fundamental value to generosity by making it the *first* paramita or panacean practice in the sterling Bodhisattva Code?

For one thing, despite the fact that we may have some initial stinginess to overcome or override, it's relatively easy to be generous. We can begin right now, where we are, to be more compassionate and giving to others in our thoughts, words, and deeds. As we continue this process, we learn fairly quickly and vividly how good it feels and how valuable it is. This makes generosity an excellent, viable, readily accessible starting point for practicing Buddhism in the day-to-day world at any age.

An even more significant aspect of generosity, however, is that it acts as a direct remedy in our life for the primary cause of suffering and dissatisfaction: desire, craving, resistance, attachment. By giving up our own private agenda and possessions to help others, we help free ourselves from our misguided dependence on transitory things to define who we are and provide us with happiness and fulfillment. By manifesting a generosity of spirit, we help realize the true wealth and value that stem from our deepest identity. Giving more of ourselves reinforces our best selves.

Wild monkeys run around everywhere in India, like squirrels and pigeons in New York City, so catching a monkey is a common subject of interest there. They say if you put out a large, heavy, narrow-necked glass jar with some nuts inside, a monkey will reach in, grasp the nuts, and get caught. Why? Because the monkey is unwilling to relinquish its grip, release the nuts, and thereby free its hand from the jar. The monkey probably doesn't even experience the problem as unwillingness. To the monkey, the wish for the nuts is so overwhelming that it feels absolutely incapable of letting go.

This is how we are with our ruts, our unsatisfying, habitual, self-perpetuating patterns of living. We need to pull ourselves out of our ruts by reorienting our point of view. Shantideva, the eighth-century Indian Buddhist master whose teachings had a profound impact on Tibetan Buddhism, also refers to the six realms of existence when he writes about our need to replace greed with generosity: "'If I give this, what will I have left to enjoy?' Such selfish thinking is the way of demons. 'If I enjoy this, who else can I give it to or share it with?' Such selfless thinking is a quality of the gods." Through the cultivation of generosity—an openhanded, openhearted giving of ourselves—we realize the virtue and freedom of nonattachment. We relax our grip, and instead of losing control, we feel new power, energy flow, and mobility.

KNOWING HOW TO BE GENEROUS

> The sage accumulates nothing,
> but the more he does for others
> the greater his existence;
> the more he gives to others,
> the greater his abundance.
>
> —LAO TZU, *TAO TE CHING*
> (TRANSLATED BY RED PINE)

According to the Buddhist master Tsong Khapa of fifteenth-century Tibet, giving is a wish-granting jewel that fulfills the hopes of all sentient beings. It cuts the knot of miserliness and greed, builds indomitable courage, and develops meritorious good karma, wealth, and good reputation in the best way possible. He cautions, however, that generous acts are best guided always by the "clear eyes of prajna wisdom" (prajna being the sixth transformative practice). If not, they are often ineffective, misguided, or diluted by selfish motivation, and can even cause further problems.

To teach this truth, I often use a simple example involving a young Tibetan monk who was visiting our center in the Catskills in the seventies. It was his first trip outside of India, where he grew up as part of a refugee community. One summer morning I came outside to find him in the parking lot, spraying cars with a water hose. They'd become very dusty during the night, and it was clearly his intention to do a good deed and surprise everyone. I took a closer look and broke out laughing. I said to him, "If you really want to do a good job, you have to close all the windows before you start spraying!" Several of the cars were already soaked inside, much to their owners' dismay. Fortunately, my car was not there at the time!

Tibetan Buddhist teachings say that ideally a donor is endowed with the seven jewel-like Bodhisattva qualities: faith, integrity, nonattachment, learning, discrimination, modesty, and conscience. This endowment helps make possible a prototypical Bodhisattva's pure power of selfless generosity. Aside from preventing misfires of generosity, it keeps the genuine Bodhisattva free from condescension and pride. In addition, it does away with any chance of humiliating the recipient, feeling regret about the gift, or being personally attached to what the recipient does with it. Practically speaking, however, most of us need to give what we can, as we can, and not wait until we have all these perfectly pure and exalted qualities.

Tibetan Buddhist teachings also describe three kinds of generosity. The first or most basic kind is the giving away of material things, including food, clothes, medicine, money. Higher than that kind of generosity are gifts of the spirit: for example, giving someone encouragement, inspiration, reassurance, love, protection, fearlessness, or hope. We can be emotionally generous rather than stingy as well. The highest form of generosity is to bestow the sublime Dharma, the gift that keeps on giving, the timeless truths that lead one to ultimate wisdom, compassion, and joyful enlightenment. This most exalted gift helps recipients to help themselves. There is an old Chinese saying that applies here: "If you give a man a fish, he has lunch and maybe dinner today. But if you teach him how to fish, he has meals for himself, his family, and his village forever."

To share the Dharma does not necessarily mean to preach to people. Preaching can easily get out of control and turn into shoving dogma down people's throats, mixed in with all kinds of dualistic illusions, impure motivations, and unconscious drives and desires. Tradition tells us that there are four ways a Bodhisattva-like teacher helps convey Dharma wisdom to others so that they can mature and develop spiritually. The first is through the generous sharing of ourselves, in order to establish a trusting relationship with others and be both attractive and accessible. The second is through interesting and meaningful discussions with others regarding what is of true benefit to them, as opposed to self-serving chatter, idle gossip, or the dissemination of distorted and hurtful views. The third is through encouraging others to implement and internalize what they have learned and understood. The fourth is through walking the talk, practicing what we would otherwise preach and, in the process, serving as an example, a beneficent role model. These four ways to help teach others are at the heart of the application of each and every one of the ten paramitas as well as all of them taken as a whole—the Bodhisattva Code, the munificent Awakener's dynamic way of life.

Buddhism uses lists like the ones I've just mentioned as skillful means (or *upaya,* the seventh paramita) to assist a practitioner's memory and motivate him or her to meaningful action. Sometimes, however, these lists can seem daunting. Do we really have to start following, right away, each step in each list if we're going to be truly generous? Not exactly. These lists lay out the blueprint and help set up our aspirations. Meanwhile, the Buddha himself suggested that we start with small acts of giving and work our way up. Once he was approached by a businessman who complained that he was simply incapable of giving, even to his own children, despite his exceeding wealth. The Buddha said, "First try giving them milk sweets, and then, later, increase your largesse."

"I can't even do that!" the businessman replied.

The Buddha countered, "Surely, sir, you can begin by moving some coins from one pocket to another or from one hand to the other. This would loosen up your stuckness and help set in motion the gracefully flowing tide of give-and-take. Eventually this tide will overflow your stinginess."

The businessman followed the Buddha's advice. It eventually helped him to become generous and to realize all the advantages that come with that blessed state of being.

OUTER, INNER, AND SECRET GENEROSITY

The Buddha taught that the greatest act of all is the act of giving. He advocated what he termed "kingly giving"—let's call it "royal giving"—which means giving the best of what we have, graciously and unstintingly, without reservations, hesitation, or regret. Does this mean that we should start giving away our most valuable things, the possessions to which we're most attached, to anyone who wants them? Is our gift worthless if we feel in any way uneasy about making it? How much is it fair to keep for ourselves?

These are inevitable and important questions to consider. The fact that the Buddha is clear about the need to be wholeheartedly generous in order to evolve spiritually does not change the fact that generosity is a complex subject. True generosity does not involve mindlessly handing over everything to anyone who asks. For example, the parent who gives his spoiled child every toy the child wants may be showing more laziness than generosity and ends up spoiling the child. The spouse who tolerates or even enables a partner's addiction in the name of love may be more codependent than generous, thus doing harm while trying to be helpful. The worker who allows an exploitative corporation to take advantage of his or her willingness to work overtime for free or without appropriate benefits is exhibiting more fear than generosity. One must find what Buddha often called the Middle Way, one of balance and appropriateness.

Buddhism always encourages being responsible for our own welfare as well as looking out for the good of others. It also emphasizes the need to combine compassion with wisdom in everything we do, so that we know the best thing to do in the specific time, place, and circumstances in which we find ourselves. It's helpful to keep in mind the Buddha's famous dictum on the value of the Middle Way: "Practice and cultivate freedom from extremes in all things." He once compared this practice to tuning a lute: the strings shouldn't be too tight or too loose, but tuned just flexibly enough to play the instrument well.

Learning to exercise true generosity is a growth process. Given the Buddha's mandate, we must continually look at our own needs and the needs of others in light of the present situation, which is often changing. Our constant aspiration is to expand our capability of giving generously while at the same time reducing our craving and clinging. This means we always need to test our limits, and willingly tolerate and accept a certain amount of difficulty, discomfort, and ambiguity in our noble quest. We are not required, however, to go to extremes that don't represent how we truly feel. We all start from different places. Some people are genuinely challenged by the prospect of giving money to a panhandler or donating a couple of hours a month to helping out at a homeless shelter. Others are fully prepared to devote their entire life to fighting poverty, racism, and injustice of all kinds, perhaps even enduring great hardships to live in a place their charitable mission requires. We need to start from where we are. For each of us, the path lies right beneath our feet, and as Lao Tzu famously said, a journey of a thousand miles begins with a single step. So make this step, and the next step, count.

In training ourselves to exercise more refined and deeper generosity, it's very helpful to think about the subject in terms of each of our three levels of being: the outer, or physical, behavioral level; the inner, or mental, attitudinal and emotional level; and the secret, or spiritual, subtle innermost level. On the outer, or physical, level, generosity involves actually giving things to other people or sharing things with them. In addition to material things like money, food, shelter, clothing, tools, recipes, breath mints, and bandages, outer generosity includes the words that we say or write to other people. Among these words are the statements of support, gratitude, forgiveness, encouragement, acceptance, or good humor that enrich other people's lives as well as our own. It's easy to forget our need to be generous in words as well as deeds, particularly when it comes to appreciation, gratitude, and forgiveness. Finally, there is the outer dimension of sharing our time and energy with others, whether it's a matter of lending them an ear or literally helping them fix their car, set up their computer, or rebuild their house.

On the inner level, we experience our thoughts and feelings about our outer acts of generosity. These internal attitudes should harmonize with the acts involved. Otherwise, we are not engaged wholeheartedly in royal giving. The most important thing to clarify in our mind is the intention behind our act of generosity. Why are we taking this action? Is it a means of impressing the other person, bolstering our influence over him or her, or enhancing our own self-esteem? If so, we are still attached to and reinforcing our egocentric self rather than giving of self, and so we are not yet being really and truly unconditionally generous.

The Buddha pointed out that there are many possible motivations behind giving, including ambivalence or mixed motives. We can give out of fear ("Will I be disliked or suffer other bad consequences if I don't give?"). We can give mechanically in accordance with tradition or peer pressure ("I have to get Aunt Martha something for Christmas!" "I have to buy five tickets for the office raffle!"). We can give with the expectation of getting something in return ("If I help Jenna with her taxes, she'll feel more obligated to take care of my dog while I'm away"). We can give in order to secure our reputation ("I'll donate to this museum because they'll put my name on a plaque on the wall"). We can give out of guilt ("I guess I owe this person a favor"). We can give simply to get rid of stuff ("I'll give Tony this lamp because I can't use it anyway"). We can even give in hope of a better rebirth ("If I do this, I'll get good karma, have higher rebirth, and require fewer lifetimes until reaching perfect enlightenment"). Or we can give for the sheer joy it creates in the world for everyone involved, without much concern for what we might receive in return.

We must also consider the thoughts and feelings we have that do not necessarily relate to our specific deeds or statements but that we keep to ourselves. Whether or not we realize it, these thoughts and attitudes can affect the shape and influence of our lives just as powerfully as the thoughts and states of consciousness we put into overt action. I'm referring to the attitudes that we carry toward people, both individuals and groups. For example, what grievances, jealousies, and petty feuds do we harbor? Looking at each of the people or groups that upset us—who may not agree with us—can we find some means of moving away from our negative feelings toward more positive ones, such as compassion, forgiveness, or even gratitude? Examining our negative, unhelpful attitudes about ourselves, our lives, and the world in which we live, can we take the same proactive approach, turning wounds into wisdom and recognizing difficulties and hardships as one of the greatest precipitants to genuine growth and transformation?

Whenever we consider our inner thoughts about anything, it's crucial to bear in mind that we *can* change them. Being visited by negative or selfish thoughts doesn't make us bad people. It just means we're conditioned human beings. Nor do we have to be forever at the mercy of these thoughts merely because they occurred to us. We can cultivate positive thoughts to replace them, thus skillfully and intentionally reconditioning and eventually deconditioning our energy and ourselves. When the Buddha said, "We are what we think," he was asking us to take responsibility for our inner life. That's the crux of why meditation and awareness cultivation are such vital practices in Buddhism. They enhance our ability to manage more skillfully our own thoughts and feelings, including our thoughts about generosity—a truth that, again, illustrates how all the paramitas are interrelated and mutually supportive.

To engage in royal giving, we need to decide internally that we're going to make our gift out of love and compassion to the best of our ability. The issue here is being conscious of what is occurring in our consciousness, monitoring it, and making sure that we're clear with ourselves. Yes, we may have mixed motives at first, but we're going to let go of the selfish or heartless ones and not shape our outer actions to cater to them or disguise them. This self-observation practice helps us be more generous and authentic emotionally, rather than repressed, constrained, overly controlled.

It's all too easy to let ourselves get slack in this regard when it comes to specific actions, even with the best intentions. In 1976 I was translating for Lama Norlha, a Buddhist monk from Tibet who was visiting New England for the first time. We journeyed by bus and train through a heavy snowstorm to Boston and stayed with some of Kalu Rinpoche's students at their modest home, which they hoped to make into a Dharma center. The students were all vegetarian, Birkenstock-wearing, antimaterialistic, nonviolent, good 1960s folk. When it came time to prepare dinner for the visitors, I overheard one of the students say, "Here's a perfect chance to get rid of those faux hot dogs that have been in the freezer for so long." That kind of giving was not what the Buddha meant by royal giving. It may seem like a small thing, but our lives are made up mostly of small things.

A supreme example of royal giving was offered one hundred years ago in Tibet by the Dzogchen master Patrul Rinpoche (1808–1887), also known as the Enlightened Vagabond. One day he laid his body across the small path through a narrow mountain pass to thwart warring clans of horsemen from carrying on a longtime feud by raiding each other's valleys. The enlightened yogi reclined on one side of his body for a while, praying in the direction of one clan's valley, then he reclined on his other side for a while, praying in the direction of the other clan's valley. As he continued to do this back and forth, the warriors coming from either valley, as a gesture of respect for the great enlightened yogi, had to get off their horses and walk carefully around him. This slowing down of their bellicose activities spurred their consciences to reflect. Eventually, the two clans called off their conflict. When he was later asked how he managed to bring the feud to an end, he famously said, "Compassion is contagious. May all be infected by it!"

Another example of royal giving involves Lama Norlha, the recipient of the faux hot dogs I mentioned. Once his retreat center in Wappingers Falls, New York, had an auction to raise money for its building fund. When the auction started, Rick, the auctioneer, banged his gavel and said, "All right, we'll start with this basket of fabulous silk flowers." Lama Norlha immediately bid $5,000, and Rick said, "Sold!" You could hear the lama's nun attendant say to the lama, "No, no! This is for real! Those flowers aren't worth more than $100!" But Lama Norlha said, "I am not joking! Write out a check." Flashbulbs went off all around him. Someone said aloud, "Don't be attached to what you get!" Everyone laughed, the ice was broken, and the charity auction proceeded successfully, with much more money bid on each object than the planners had anticipated. Sometimes you just have to get the giving going by starting somewhere.

We must always be conscious of our thoughts and feelings, monitoring them, and making sure we're clear and in integrity with ourselves. Only then do we enable ourselves to give compassionately, wisely, and unhesitatingly, using skillful means and making sure our hearts and minds correspond to our actions every time we engage in generosity. When we do this, we create wonderful, life-giving karma in the world for both others and ourselves. As the Buddha said:

> *Generosity brings happiness*
> *at every stage of its expression.*
> *We experience joy in forming*
> *the intention to be generous.*
> *We experience joy in the actual act*

of giving something.
And we experience joy in remembering
the fact that we have given.

Inner generosity also means cultivating nonattachment, acceptance, and contentment, so that we are more open to whatever the needs of others might be. Meditation and conscientious self-inquiry can greatly help us in this effort. Critics of meditation often say, "Isn't meditation selfish? Doesn't it mean cutting yourself off from the rest of the world? Isn't it unproductive?" Nothing could be further from the truth. By meditating, we're learning to disengage ourselves from habitual clinging and disperse the defilements and obscurations that hinder our capacity to serve others, such as illusory feelings of scarcity and fears of deprivation. We gradually learn to be more conscious and make better choices. We develop simplicity instead of complexity, open-mindedness instead of narrow-mindedness, flexibility rather than rigidity. We free ourselves to be more available to others and to give more generously of ourselves.

Finally, there is generosity as it relates to our secret or innermost spiritual level of being, the incandescent immensity of innate Bodhicitta, which Buddhists call our "suchness," our Buddha nature. This is our connection with the infinitely abundant truth and inexhaustible source, the Dharma or universal law. When we realize its limitless possibilities, we know how little we need from the outside world or anyone in it and feel content, supported, fulfilled. With this delightful knowledge, we give freely of ourselves at all times, without preconceptions or specific goals in mind. When we surrender to what *is* and learn to let go and let be, we exist as agents of pure generosity, like a clear channel for the flow of the cosmic energy of enlightenment.

Our secret level of being is the inherent domain of complete nonattachment, where we live with wide-open mind, heart, and hands. The more we cultivate generosity in our outer and inner lives, as clumsy as our efforts may sometimes be, the more we resonate with the secret and subtle level of our being, releasing its amazing, inexhaustible energy into our lives and into the world. When we realize the truth of the Buddhist adage that deep spiritual contentment is the ultimate form of wealth, we liberate ourselves to practice generosity to its fullest extent. We re-enter the marketplace with bliss-bestowing hands and a large bag of gifts on our backs, ready to dispense them.

WHAT IS YOUR EXPERIENCE WITH GENEROSITY?

Right now, take a few moments to review your past in terms of the generosity you've received and bestowed. Ask yourself the following questions and note the first images that come to mind. Strive to make this a routine practice each time you feel blessed by someone's generosity or challenged to be more generous yourself.

- When have I especially appreciated another person's act of generosity toward me? How did it feel? Why did I appreciate it so much? How did I respond? Try to feel some gratitude for these kind benefactors.

- When have I been especially generous to others? How did I feel? Why? What charitable cause or causes could I support better now?

- What individuals and groups of people do I find it hard to think compassionately and open-mindedly about? Considering each individual and group separately, why do I experience this difficulty? How might I work toward overcoming it?

- Thinking of individuals in my life now, what gift would I like from them? Why?

- Thinking of individuals in my life now, what gift would they most appreciate from me? Why? What would I most like to share with them?

- Am I usually on the giving or the receiving side of relationships? Have I realized that true generosity includes both giving and receiving, just like breathing in and breathing out?

WHAT GOES AROUND COMES AROUND

The result of generosity is always richness. The result of miserliness is always poverty. This principle is constant.

—SAKYA PANDITA
(THIRTEENTH CENTURY, TIBET)

Whenever I address the issue of generosity, I'm reminded of the old saying "What goes around comes around." This adage corresponds perfectly with the Buddhist doctrine of karma. Literally, the law of karma states that every cause has an effect. It's not unlike the scientific law of thermodynamics, which states that for every action there is a reaction, and the energy involved in that exchange is constant: it can be neither created nor destroyed. On a practical level, this means that each of our thoughts, words, and actions sets in motion a related chain of events that reverberates in the universe as a whole as well as in our own individual lives. If we fail to be generous, kind, and giving, we not only diminish the potential existence of these qualities in the world around us but also create a life for ourselves that is in many ways impoverished.

According to my lamas, the Buddha taught that our wealth and station in life, and even our state of mind, are all our own karmic responsibility and are intimately interrelated with our responsibility for our own temporary happiness as well as ultimate enlightenment. In other words, we alone predominantly determine the cause-and-effect process that runs through our lives, our quest for liberation, and our Bodhisattvic commitment to help save others. When we give good things to others, whether it's much-needed money or more hope and enthusiasm for life, we come to be endowed with similarly positive things ourselves. When we don't give good things to others, or when we give them bad things, we initiate a negative karmic result for ourselves; what we sow we shall reap, as the Good Book says.

If we had been fortunate enough to study with a learned Tibetan lama of old, we would have devoted much of our time to a text called *The Jewel Ornament of Liberation,* composed by a Tibetan scholar named Gampopa, who lived in the eleventh and twelfth centuries, became yogi master Milarepa's principal disciple, and founded the famed Kagyu lineage of practice. This classic treatise explains to students why they should practice all the paramitas, including generosity, and how to practice them most successfully and ascend through all the stages of a Bodhisattva's development until reaching complete Buddhahood and enlightenment. Kalu Rinpoche used to tell me and the other disciples at his monastery in Darjeeling, India, that this *Jewel Ornament* was the only book we ever needed to read. In the section on generosity, Gampopa says, "When we are not liberal, we are unable to work for the benefit of others so that we do not attain enlightenment. As it is said, 'He who has never given a gift remains without wealth [and] is unable to attract other beings, to say nothing of his inability to attain enlightenment.'"

Mahatma Gandhi, himself an exemplar of generosity for giving his life to the cause of social justice and freedom in India, had a similar understanding of the cosmically reciprocal effect of generosity. When a reporter asked him, "Why do you give so much to others?" he replied, "I don't give to anyone. I do it all for myself." By "myself," he was not referring to the egotistic or social persona that might expect a specific this-for-that reward. He was referring to the inner self, which is not attached to any concept of reward but is the pure spirit of generosity that must give to live. He was echoing the old adage that virtue is its own reward, and doing the right thing is the best thing to do, personally as well as more generally.

In 1988 I participated in a wonderful generosity fest that radiated this kind of spirit. My friend Lama Norlha took a large group of American students to visit Kalu Rinpoche, the senior Kagyu meditation master, in Bodh Gaya, India, the site of the Buddha's enlightenment under the Bodhi Tree. The object of the journey was to pray for the aged Kalu Rinpoche's longevity as well as to feed the many homeless beggars who congregated there. His students and ordained *sangha* (spiritual community) members contributed a great deal of money so that many people could travel and the offerings to the homeless would be substantial.

In Bodh Gaya, Lama Norlha announced to the beggars, "Come to the tree tomorrow and you'll be fed." His words were like the song of the Pied Piper to them. At least five hundred street people showed up the next day. Lama Norlha and his helpers were able to put a piece of bread covered with cooked lentils in each person's hand. Then he told them to come the following day with a bowl. Lama Norlha's group, doing all the cooking themselves, continued to feed poor people for forty-nine days, while the elder Kalu Rinpoche watched, smiled, and blessed the entire affair from his seat near the top of the stone steps in front of the enlightenment shrine; and when Ani Palmo tried to hold an umbrella over his head, the frail old master insisted on holding it up himself.

During that forty-nine-day period, the number of people in the crowd grew to over two thousand per day. Sleeping only two hours each night, Lama Norlha got up early in the morning and labored in the kitchen, ensuring that the food was well spiced and delicious. Then the rest of the day he supervised the crowd so that everything proceeded in an orderly way, without chaos or clamor. On the last day, he gave one of the nuns a huge bag of Indian money to distribute to the beggars. Others also did this, including myself. I found one poor man asleep in the Dalai Lama's monastery there and stuck coins under his blanket. I walked by kids and gave them money, praying with each donation that it would help lead that human being along the path to enlightenment. Slowly but surely, all the money was given away, while abundant good karma was set in motion.

Once we open our wisdom eyes, we see that the entire universe functions according to this basic karmic principle of generosity: what goes around comes around. In this sense, the word *generosity* is an ideal translation of *dana,* because *generosity* shares the same root as *generation:* the causing to be, the procreative force. Ralph Waldo Emerson, in his seminal essay "Nature," declares that earth itself is dependent upon "the endless circulation of divine charity": "The wind sows the seed, the sun evaporates the sea, the wind blows the vapor to the field . . . the rain feeds the plant, the plant feeds the animal." When we're sensitive to the full impact of generosity as a driving force in the cosmos, we become more grateful for our existence. We respect life itself as a gift instead of taking it for granted as an entitlement. And we extend the same spirit to all sentient beings in our life—the people, plants, and animals who share our world.

The Bodhisattva Code's call to be generous, which is its very first instruction, asks us to stretch our arms, hearts, and minds, holding nothing back. I hear this call in certain lines from a poem by Edna St. Vincent Millay. I don't think that Millay had any Buddhist inclinations, and the poem is undoubtedly a romantic love poem written to another person, but the lines describe to me what generous intentions of the purest sort are like:

> Love in the open hand, nothing but that,
> Ungemmed, unhidden, wishing not to hurt,
> As one should bring you cowslips in a hat
> Swung from the hand, or apples in her skirt,
> I bring you, calling out as children do:
> "Look what I have!—And these are all for you."

The last line of the poem, "Look what I have!—And these are all for you," spells out one of the most interesting karmic aspects of transcendent generosity. When we open up so fully to give of ourselves, we receive instantaneously a great blessing: our own full awareness of how much we have to give, how marvelously endowed we are. "Look what I have," the poet cries. "And these are all for you." The words are reminiscent of the Buddha's great joyful call of invitation, "Come and see!" The act of giving shows us that we have gifts to give. And in fact, those gifts are inexhaustible because they are ever-renewing.

Speaking personally, I have been the beneficiary of a great and powerful legacy of timeless wisdom and enlightenment, passed along to me by my Tibetan gurus, who asked little or nothing in return. Now it is my heart's desire to pass this legacy along to you and, in so doing, thank them for their unrepayable generosity by paying it forward. I wish for my students and readers what every authentic teacher wishes—that they may each surpass their teacher.

WHAT ABOUT BOB? THE NITTY-GRITTY OF DAILY GENEROSITY

If you want others to be happy, practice compassion.
If you want to be happy, practice compassion.

—THE DALAI LAMA

Now that we've spent a few exhilarating moments considering the cosmic, karmic dimension of generosity, it's time to get a bit more down to earth. How do we go about actually navigating and negotiating the complexities of generosity that so often present themselves in real-world situations? Every day we face countless direct and indirect appeals for help from our family members and friends, from letters mailed to us by worthy causes, and from images of suffering and devastation we see on television. We can't address all of them with 100 percent of our resources. How do we choose? Where do we draw lines in determining how much to give? What if we feel inadequate to meet someone's need? What if we're not sure we're addressing someone's need in the right way?

Let's imagine a man named Bob, sitting in his office thinking about his plans for the weekend. His phone rings; it's his mother. Normally he enjoys talking with her, but her tone today quickly lets him know that she is about to ask something of him, something that he isn't too sure he wants to do.

"Bob," his mother says, "I know your sister Cheryl already owes you money, but she's having bad financial problems again. She wanted me to ask you for help—she's too nervous to ask you herself."

"How much this time?" Bob is exasperated, and his voice shows it.

"A thousand dollars," his mother replies. "She has only six more months of grad school, and as soon as she gets a job, she'll be able to pay you back."

"Listen, Mom," Bob says, "I don't want to upset you, but I know my sister. As soon as she finishes grad school, she'll want to go to law school or medical school or dental school. She's thirty-six years old, and she has more degrees than a thermometer!"

"If your father were still alive, I wouldn't be asking you, honey. And if Cheryl wasn't still upset about that awful divorce and rotten ex-husband, neither would she."

Bob can hear the tears in his mother's voice, and he begins to feel guilty. After all, as he is often reminded, he introduced his sister to the rotten ex-husband, who'd been his best friend at the time. He thinks for a moment about Jason, his current best friend. Jason has always been a generous, hardworking man and is now struggling desperately to pay medical bills that his insurance won't cover. Bob has been secretly planning to loan Jason close to a thousand dollars. If he gives the money to his sister, he can't do that.

"Bob?" says his mother in that same teary voice. His guilt gets the better of him.

"Okay, okay, I'll do it. But ask Cheryl if she can watch the twins over the weekend. She keeps talking about how much she loves Jill and Amy and how she wants to spend more time with them. This will be her big chance."

Bob hears his mother hesitate and feels sorry that she is stuck in the middle. "It's okay, never mind," he tells his mother. "I'll ask her."

"You don't have to ask her, honey," his mother says. "The girls can stay with me. We'll have a good time."

Bob wants to shout, "You and I both know Cheryl never wants to stay with the kids. She's too damn selfish. All she knows how to do is take, take, take, and I'm sick and tired of hearing how upset she is. She's always upset! Tell her to grow up and get over it!" But he bites his tongue because he doesn't want to make his mother cry. By the time he gets off the phone, his head is beginning to pound, and he feels a disturbing combination of anger, resentment, and guilt. He knows that Cheryl has had a hard time, and he wants to be kind to her, but he also worries that her demands and requests will never stop.

It's sure a long way from Edna St. Vincent Millay's open arms to Bob's pounding head, isn't it? Many real-life situations are just too complicated for us to take a simplistic, overly idealistic attitude toward generosity. Much as we aspire to respond to every genuine appeal with open arms, we simply may not be able to do so. We need to confront our own limitations as well as other barriers that are outside of our control, and then do the best we can. Sorting out which particular needs to address, and how far to go in addressing them, becomes, out of necessity, a balancing act.

In these situations, it can be helpful to recall again the Buddhist doctrine of the Middle Way: consider the full picture, avoid extremes, and give each of our responsibilities an appropriate (or, in Buddhist terms, "right") share of our attention. As we handle challenges to our generosity in this manner, however, we should also work toward stretching our capacities so that each time we give a little more than we originally thought we could and take the opportunity to rejoice in the goodness and virtue of doing so. I personally try to remember to be grateful that I am in a position to be able to help.

There are several things I hope Bob considers now that he's hung up the phone. Although everyone needs to make his or her own decisions about what to do in a given situation, there are also some things that I wish he'd taken the time to consider *before* reacting one way or the other to his mother's request, based on my own experience with family and friends.

First, Bob is clearly conflicted about giving his sister money, not because he's stingy and tight, but because he doesn't want to encourage what he's convinced is his sister's ultimately self-destructive habit of relying on handouts. I would advise Bob to consider what psychologists call "tough love" here: giving a lesser amount of money to cover immediate emergencies and then saying no to giving any more. It's a practice that establishes healthy boundaries that benefit all parties in the long run.

Otherwise, Bob is acting as an enabler, one who colludes with a wrongdoer out of misguided love, as though he were giving sugar to a diabetic or booze to an alcoholic. Chögyam Trunga Rinpoche referred to this kind of would-be generous thinking and behavior as "idiot compassion." In its place, he advised "ruthless compassion": saying no in those situations when saying yes means assisting someone in remaining foolish, dependent, abusive, or even criminal. By not giving his sister all that she's requesting, Bob may have to disappoint his mother temporarily, but it's a risk he may need to take out of genuine love for both of them. After all, his mother should not have to be making the call in the first place.

In addition, I hope that after Bob hangs up the phone he makes a sincere effort to question and investigate all the inner attitudes and reactions he experienced during the conversation. Maybe then he'll be moved to start working constructively to understand and integrate them more harmoniously so as to reduce his stress level during future calls of this type from his mother or sister—or, for that matter, during appeals of a similar nature from anyone else.

I hope, for example, that Bob learns not to attach specific expectations to his generosity, such as assuming that his sister should be willing to spend more time with his kids if he gives her the money. Although it's easy for me to sympathize with this assumption, and although it may sometimes be appropriate (if not exactly generous) to hammer out a quid-pro-quo exchange, the situation with his sister is clearly too emotionally loaded to bear the weight of his counterdemand. It would be much better for him to make a separate, more openhearted attempt at influencing his sister to *want* to spend time with his kids.

I also hope that Bob learns to forgive himself for having introduced his sister to her "rotten" ex-husband. It surely wasn't Bob's intention to make her miserable when he did this, and his own guilt is yet another factor complicating their relationship. If he's going to give $1,000 to someone, I'm inclined to agree that he should consider giving it to his sister rather than to his best friend Jason—family comes first. But any intelligent act of conscious generosity toward her should be motivated by love, not guilt.

I could go on and on expressing hopes about Bob or giving him advice. Couldn't we all? It's so much easier to critique another person's dilemma than to accurately perceive and tackle our own. What I'm attempting to illustrate here is that one strategy simply doesn't work for all occasions. Each generous deed needs to fit its context, and wisdom needs to guide each giving hand. Remember that young Tibetan monk who tried to do something good by washing the cars and only wound up soaking their interiors!

As we train ourselves to open up and expand our capacity for wise and compassionate generosity, we constantly need to investigate, analyze, reflect, intuit, experiment, and contemplate as we go along. Whenever we enter into a complex situation that calls on us to be generous, we would do well to explore the full range of our intentions, motivations, hopes, fears, anxieties, expectations, talents, back story, and abilities in the light of what we truly feel best serves the needs of others. Each time we do this, we deepen our intuitive understanding of what's right or wrong, too much or too little, helpful or harmful, for the particular situation at hand.

THE SPECTRUM OF GENEROSITY

Without exception,
All suffering comes from wanting happiness for yourself.
Perfect Buddhas are born from wishing to benefit others.

—NGULCHU THOGME
(FOURTEENTH CENTURY, TIBET)

Learning to become an ever more generous Bodhisattva requires more than thinking carefully about ourselves, the specific people in our lives, and the particular situations we face with these people. We must also remain mindful of the full spectrum of generosity that human beings are capable of experiencing. When we do this, we not only draw steady inspiration from examples of great generosity but also avoid overlooking the countless small opportunities to be generous that present themselves every day.

The first time I remember hearing about Buddhism was in 1963, when I was barely in my teens. That's when a Vietnamese monk named Thich Quang Duc doused himself with gasoline, sat in a cross-legged meditation posture in the middle of a busy intersection in Saigon, South Vietnam (now Ho Chi Minh City, Vietnam), and set himself ablaze as a protest against the persecution of Buddhists in that country. A photograph of the burning monk was immediately reproduced around the world, shocking all who saw it and dealing a heavy blow to the credibility of the South Vietnamese government.

This terrible image is definitely seared into my memory. At the time I saw it in an American newspaper, I wasn't sure how to evaluate an act of such magnitude. I remember asking myself, *What is it about Buddhism that would motivate or even allow a monk to do this?* I couldn't really answer these questions at the time. Neither could my schoolteachers. Years later, however, one of my Dharma teachers drew a parallel between Thich Quang Duc and Jesus, saying that they both literally gave their lives for the sake of the rest of humanity.

Quang Duc's final act—which in succeeding months and years inspired a handful of other Buddhist monks and nuns also to immolate themselves—represents a practice of supreme generosity that has its roots in the Lotus Sutra, one of the most significant scriptures of Mahayana Buddhism. Because these Vietnamese monks and nuns had realized their ultimate, unborn, deathless nature and were no longer attached to an idea of the physical body as the self, they were free to use their bodies to deliver a powerful wake-up message to others. You could say they transformed their bodies into torches to illuminate the terrible suffering of the Vietnamese people. Only those Bodhisattvas who have truly liberated themselves by seeing deep into the profound prajna truth of the universe can undertake this ultimate gesture of generosity with complete clarity and wisdom and without doubt or negative karmic repercussions. Contemporary master Thich Nhat Hanh, who knew Quang Duc personally, remarked on Quang Duc's act, "It was not made out of despair, but out of the wish to help, out of his great love for humankind." It has taken me years to understand this statement, but it has been worth the journey.

At one end of the spectrum of generosity we have the inspirational examples of Quang Duc, Prince Mahasattva (of Namo Buddha), and Jesus, who gave totally of themselves, surrendering their own lives to save sentient beings. We also have the Buddha himself, who not only devoted his entire life to teaching the way to enlightenment but also renounced nirvana in order to do it. In other words, he voluntarily chose to re-enter *samsara* (the world of suffering) as a Bodhisattva, giving up his own liberation until all sentient beings were free.

Another individual at this end of the spectrum is the late Mother Teresa. When she was only eighteen years old in Albania, she was so inspired by accounts of the charitable mission of Roman Catholic Jesuits in Calcutta, India, that she joined an Irish order of nuns. She left that order two decades later to live and work more directly in the slums of the city, helping some of the poorest people in the world meet their basic food and health care needs. Soon afterward she founded her own order, the Missionaries of Charity, which went on to establish centers in other parts of India and in many other countries as well.

Through her faith and goodness of heart, Mother Teresa became one of the greatest charitable forces in the modern world. And how did she accomplish this transformation? She gave herself, body and soul, to her Lord—and through him, as she understood it, to the weakest, lowest, and most miserable of his creatures. She served God by serving humanity day after day after day; that is transcendental giving. She was only one individual, and not very tall at all, but by going beyond selfish concerns and preoccupations, she ultimately benefited millions of people, both the direct recipients of her charity and those of us who continue to be inspired by her example. Her selfless lifework donation of her single diminutive female form reminds me of the New Testament miracle of the small portion of loaves and fish that Jesus turned into food for a multitude—a meal that many still find nourishing in the deepest, most spiritual sense of the word.

Mother Teresa never advised others to follow her lead exactly and devote their entire life to the poor. She well understood that she was only responding to what her own heart and mind had told her to do. In her writings, she counsels us to do the same: start where we are, and do what we genuinely feel we can, repeatedly testing our limits as we go. A story she shares in her 1985 book, *My Life for the Poor,* tells of a very rich Hindu woman who wanted to work alongside her. As they talked together, the woman told her, among other things, how much she loved beautiful saris. The one she was wearing cost eight hundred rupees, in contrast to Mother Teresa's eight-rupee sari, and she confessed to buying a new one every month. Mother Teresa writes:

I prayed a little bit to our Lady to give her the right answer how she would share in the work. And I said, "I'd better begin with the sari. You know, next time, when you go to buy a sari, instead of buying a sari of eight hundred rupees, you buy a sari of five hundred rupees and with the remaining three hundred you buy saris for the poor people." And so the poor thing has come down to paying one hundred for a sari. I have told her: "Please do not go below one hundred!"

Isn't this a good demonstration of the commonsense wisdom and even necessity of following the Middle Way?

Throughout the spectrum of generosity are many wonderful and moving examples of people consistently working to help others in the course of their everyday lives. One hidden Bodhisattva who comes to mind is Mr. C. T. Shen, a now-retired Chinese American businessman who owned the American Steamship Company. Always an ardent supporter of spiritually related projects and good works, he founded the Institute for the Advanced Study of World Religions in New York. He also gave significant assistance to those of us who established Gyalwa Karmapa's monastery in Woodstock during the 1970s. He never claimed any credit or privileges for his financial aid and wise counsel, not even a plaque or the honorary dedication of a room, wing, or library. Shen just liked to make solitary meditation retreats at the Karmapa's hilltop monastery.

Joy Peterson, my loving mother-in-law, is another very giving anonymous Bodhisattva. After devoting herself to raising four children with her late husband in Louisville, Kentucky, she now has her own unofficial, one-person charity organization. Two days a week she makes hospicelike visits to several shut-ins. As if that weren't enough good work to earn her a place in my Bodhisattva pantheon, every morning at six AM, when she takes her walk, she takes curbside-delivered newspapers right to the front doorsteps of all the houses along her long suburban street. It has become such a regular service that her neighbors—including people she's never actually met—let her know if they're going to be away from home, so that she doesn't worry about them. This very week she is also providing meals for her aged brother-in-law and his wife, who has just returned home from surgery. Aptly named, Joy is nearly eighty years young. One day she offhandedly remarked to me that the more she gives, the less she needs.

The head of my Dzogchen Foundation and centers—who, characteristically, prefers to remain anonymous—is also someone I consider to be a discreet Bodhisattva. A retired hospital administrator, P. puts in fifty to sixty hours of volunteer work per week as our executive director and managing editor, year in and year out. He says that the only payback he wants is to know that I feel he is furthering my teaching efforts and our mission to bring the Buddhist Dharma and, more specifically, the fruits of the Dzogchen tradition of practice to the Western world, helping ensure that our planet is a safer and saner place to live.

One of my students recently told me a story about two unlikely looking Bodhisattvas who came to her rescue while she was traveling from Minnesota to Boston for one of my winter Dzogchen retreats. Soon after she boarded the early morning train for the thirty-hour ride, she discovered that she'd left her wallet behind, which meant that she suddenly had no money or credit cards with her. During a layover at Union Station in Chicago, she went to the Amtrak office in hopes that she could get a personal check cashed there. No way! The office was filled with agitated travelers, all of whom were disgruntled for various reasons. One middle-aged man next to her, dressed in bright red sweats, was trying vociferously and unsuccessfully to get to a model train convention on time. At last acknowledging defeat, he turned to my student and shouted, his face as red as his sweats, "Lady, if I can't get to Birmingham, at least you can have your supper!" Snarling and growling all the while, he nevertheless gladly swapped her a signed $25 traveler's check for her personal check in the same amount.

Unfortunately, my student and her Bodhisattva number one didn't realize that a traveler's check isn't good unless it's signed in the presence of the person cashing it. My student found out when she stood in front of the cashier at the Union Station Pub with a tray full of vegetables and mashed potatoes. At that moment, Bodhisattva number two showed up: a tired-looking blond woman who was tending bar and sniffling from an apparent cold. "You go ahead and take that check," the bartender yelled to the cashier. "If there's any trouble, I'll cover it."

When I heard this amusing story during the subsequent retreat, I thought to myself, *Hidden among us are the best of Bodhisattvas, disguised as unhappy wage slaves and lost travelers. How marvelous!*

A smile is the shortest distance between two people, between I and Thou. At the far end of the generosity spectrum from giving an entire life to save all sentient beings may be simply smiling at another person. One of the Five Pillars (main supports) of Islam is *Zakat,* or charity. As a demonstration of Zakat, Muslims traditionally make periodic offerings of money to help those in need. For Muslims who can't afford this kind of donation, giving a smile is deemed sufficient.

GENEROSITY MEANS NOT KEEPING COUNT

I've just discussed generosity in terms of a spectrum. I use this image to convey that acts of true generosity may be different from each other in degree, but they all share the same liberating Bodhisattva spirit of self-giving for the sake of others. I don't use this image to imply that we should set up some rigid standard of evaluation by which we determine the relative worth of each generous deed. This kind of reckoning too easily leads us to see ourselves as superior or inferior to other people. At the very least, it can inhibit, paralyze, or complicate our genuine inner urge to help, to give, to be good. Mother Teresa said, "We cannot all do great things, but we can do small things with great love."

Instead of making dualistic judgments, we need to take a wiser, more compassionate approach to the differences in degree we notice between one generous act and another. When we're tempted to feel that we're more generous than others, we need to remind ourselves that we may well be in no position to make that kind of determination, for how hard it is to correctly judge and evaluate intention and motivation. When we are especially impressed by someone else's generosity, we need to allow that impression to inspire us rather than disturb us. Celebrating their virtuous act helps contribute to furthering our own virtue, just as jealousy erodes it.

My friend Celia told me about an experience that taught these lessons to her. She lives in a third-floor walk-up apartment in Manhattan's East Village. Today the East Village is a chic neighborhood dotted with upscale boutiques and trendy restaurants. Until recently, however, it was largely inhabited by poor immigrants who came to this country from Ukraine. Celia's apartment is in an old tenement that still has one elderly Ukrainian resident who has lived there for fifty years, her upstairs neighbor, Nadya.

Following a heavy snowstorm last winter, Celia was leaving her apartment in a big hurry because she was late for an important dinner date. As she locked her apartment door behind her, she spotted Nadya clumping her way up the stairs dragging a shopping cart and two large plastic bags filled almost to the bursting point. Nadya would take one bag a few steps up, drop it, sigh, go back and get the other bag, and then, finally, the cart. Knowing that Nadya had poor eyesight, Celia couldn't resist hoping for a few seconds that Nadya wouldn't see her in the hallway; Celia felt very pressured to be on time for dinner, and she didn't feel like stopping to help her neighbor. Nevertheless, she couldn't bring herself simply to abandon Nadya.

"Nadya," she finally cried. "It's Celia. Please, let me help you."

It took Celia at least ten minutes to get the cart and two bags up to Nadya's door. As Celia labored, she couldn't help congratulating herself for being so generous. She wondered what Nadya had in her cart and bags and envisioned cans and cartons of food. She knew that Nadya lived on an extremely limited income. In fact, she'd once seen Nadya standing in line at a local homeless shelter where they distributed free cheese once a month. Celia wondered to herself, *Why does Nadya have so much food with her now? She should plan her trips better.* Then, feeling even more proud of herself, she thought, *Maybe I should talk with her about this. It might help.*

"Nadya," Celia began, "is this all food you're going to eat right away?"

"Oh, this is not food for me," Nadya said. "It's for the birds. They can't find much to eat when there's so much snow on the ground. They suffer terribly. What can I do? I try to help. I take this food up to the roof for them."

Nadya began unpacking. Sure enough, the cart and the bags were all filled with ten- and twenty-pound containers of birdseed.

Celia confided to me, "At first I felt deflated. Here I was feeling so saintlike, both wise and helpful, in comparison to this poor, dim-sighted elderly woman who didn't plan well. Actually, Nadya had been aware of something that hadn't even occurred to me: the plight of the birds in the bad weather. And she was depriving herself of food to take care of them! I truly felt ashamed of myself for worrying so much about my own little dinner date. But then, as I thought about it, I felt extremely grateful that I'd discovered what she was up to. It made me feel better about the world I lived in and more determined to help not just human beings but other critters as well."

Many people have a hard time accepting generosity. For example, I know one person, I'll call him Ted, who is extremely uncomfortable about getting presents or even letting someone do him a favor. Ted himself, however, is often generous to others. He says he just doesn't want to be "beholding" to anyone. His word choice here indicates that he sees generosity as a tally-sheet issue: if someone is good to him, that act imposes a debt on him, according to his worldview. He seems to hold this opinion even though he doesn't believe his own generosity puts others in debt to him.

I'm not sure why Ted feels this way. Maybe he has an inferiority complex or feelings of unworthiness. Perhaps his parents or other authority figures taught him to think as he does. Whatever the case, his attitude deprives others of the pleasure of giving because he hijacks that role for himself. In addition, he misses out on the wonderful, life-affirming feeling of gratitude one gets through accepting the generosity of others and the mutual give-and-take of unrestricted generous sharing.

Many people I know consistently approach acts of generosity in an accountant-like manner: "He gave me a $25 gift—I can't give him one that costs $35," or, "I called the last time—it's her turn. She *owes* me a call! I'm not calling again!" Living as we do in a balance-sheet culture, we may all have such thoughts from time to time. The point is not to let this kind of thinking dominate our attitude toward generosity. We need to give without attachment or expectation and with our whole heart and mind, not merely dispense justice according to our own calculating terms.

We also have to remember that dana paramita, the panacean practice of generosity, is as much about receiving things in the right spirit as it is about giving things in the right spirit. Buddhists are asked to be mindful at all times that the universe supports them—giving them ground to stand on, air to breathe, and wonders to appreciate every moment, and that all are interwoven and interdependent.

Through cultivating gratitude for all the ways in which we are blessed, we come naturally to wish and work for the good of all sentient beings. "The Dervish in the Ditch," a teaching tale from the Islamic tradition, helps us appreciate the shift of consciousness involved here. Once a dervish (or Sufi teacher) was walking down the road with one of his disciples. Suddenly a man with a scowl on his face came barreling down the road. Rather than walk around the dervish, the scowling man simply shoved the dervish aside, causing the dervish to fall in a ditch. His disciple helped him out. When the dervish was back on his feet, he cried out after the scowling man, now far ahead of him, "May all good things happen to you, so that you are fully content."

The disciple was shocked. "Why do you wish this man well," he said, "when he was so nasty to you?"

The dervish replied, "If he is fully content, he won't be so mean anymore to others. Don't you want that to happen?"

TONGLEN: A MEDITATION FOR BECOMING MORE GENEROUS

> The problem with the world is that we draw our family circle too small.
>
> —MOTHER TERESA

The practice of *tonglen* (literally, "giving-receiving"), brought to Tibet by Master Atisha in the eleventh century, is an ideal one for opening up, facing fear and difficulty, recognizing the dreamlike nature of things, and expanding our capacity to be generous. It helps us let go of our isolated self-clinging and transform our egocentric perspective, step-by-step, into a universal one, filled with unconditional love and oneness. Specifically, tonglen bids us to confront (or take in) all the suffering that exists in the world and then, to counteract that suffering, give away (or send out) our own joy and happiness. We do this with our whole heart, to the rhythm of our breath. Breathing in, we imagine siphoning up the world's suffering into our own being, where it's dissipated. Breathing out, we envision discharging our own positive energy as a replacement for that suffering.

Tonglen is not a practice to be taken lightly, as if it were an empty litany. One of the most powerful practices I know, it demands a great deal of fearlessness, concentration, insight, and honesty. I admit that I was originally quite intimidated by it. *What am I risking,* I'd wonder, *by volunteering to suck up every bit of trouble, illness, and negativity that's out there?* I was conscious of how little we really know about the interconnections of mind, body, spirit, and energy, and I'd think, *What if I'm somehow asking to get a horrible disease? What if I'm polluting myself with all this negative energy coming in?*

Engaging in tonglen was definitely a leap of faith for me, but one that proved immensely rewarding. For each ounce of courage I put into it, I gained a pound of fearlessness as a result. The more sincerely I made my resolutions as I inhaled and exhaled, the more completely I felt integrated with the flow of the universe. I was giving up my identity as a lone human being who was desperately attached to his own "skin-bag" (as the Zen master Dogen calls it) and entering into a much larger, more meaningful, connected, and abundant mode of being.

Here's how I recommend practicing tonglen (sending and taking):

1. *Breathe and visualize in harmony.* Each time you engage in tonglen, first assume a comfortable posture that facilitates meditation. Relax and focus your mind, centering yourself in the present moment. Then, just for a few seconds, flash on absolute Bodhicitta as you understand it—the natural state of uncontrived awareness, empty yet lucid. Rest in this unborn, uncreated, present awareness, the innate Buddha-mind. Your mind is filled with nothing but pure warmth, peace, acceptance, as if it were a bright, empty sky. Enjoy the perfection of this incandescent Bodhicitta flash and your own infinite, radiant, and empty mind. Breathe, relax, focus, and take it easy.

    Then start following your breath; observe your breath. As you breathe in freely through your nose, visualize that you are vacuuming up dark smog that represents pure suffering and delusion. Hold your breath for just a brief moment, letting the smog dissolve completely in the perfect groundless and boundless emptiness of your vast, open mind. Then, as you breathe out freely through your mouth, visualize that you are sending forth sunlight and fresh spring breezes that represent all the pure joy, love, and truth you have inside you.

2. *Be generous to yourself.* Imagine yourself as having two parts. One part consists of all your suffering. The other part consists of all your joy and love. As you breathe in, visualizing smog, silently resolve, pray, and affirm, "May all the suffering in one part of me be absorbed into the empty and essential nature of my joyful, wise, and loving part." As you exhale, visualizing sunlight and spring breezes, silently resolve, pray, and affirm, "May the suffering part of me have all the joy and love in the other part of me."

3. *In widening concentric circles, expand your generosity beyond yourself to all sentient beings.* After you've practiced tonglen on

yourself for a while, and you start to feel the healing energy of that work, shift your focus one step further beyond yourself to your loved ones—your family members and friends. As you inhale, visualizing smog being sucked through your nostrils, silently resolve, pray, and affirm, "May all the suffering of my family members and friends be absorbed into the empty nature of my innate Buddha-mind." As you exhale, visualizing sunlight and spring breezes, silently resolve, pray, and affirm, "May my family members and friends have all my joy, peace, wisdom, and love." You may feel a special need to focus tonglen practice on one or more individual family members or friends—for example, someone who is ill—as well as the group as a whole. Do separate rounds of breathing for each recipient—individual or group—enfolding and suffusing them with radiant light rays.

When you've reached a point where you feel you've completed the exchange with your family members and friends, move on successively to other individuals or groups, including your neighbors and acquaintances; your enemies; all the people involved in the job you do; all the people who live in your state; all the people who live in your nation. Ultimately, you can work up to practicing tonglen for all sentient beings, human and otherwise.

4. *Gradually relax all the guided imagery.* Let it dissolve back into the empty, luminously clear, skylike nature of innate Buddha-mind, where it all began and arose from. Rest in the uncontrived presence of pristine awareness itself, in the inseparable union of oneness and noneness, at home and at ease in that, savoring the sacred afterglow.

May your blessed acts of charity and self-giving make the world a better place for all of us!

TWO

THE IMPECCABLE VIRTUE OF ETHICAL SELF-DISCIPLINE

May I develop and accomplish
the pure virtue of ethical self-discipline,
which dries up the boiling river of greed,
hatred, and delusion
and is a kindness to the whole world.

"Sentient beings are numberless; I vow to liberate them." What an awesome, outrageous vow this is! As the opening statement of the Bodhisattva Vow, it's the first step we need to take on the path to becoming a Bodhisattva ourselves. But how can we make this vow sincerely—how can we even *dare* to make it at all—without really knowing the steps and challenges involved?

The answer is that our heart tells us it's the right thing to do. We know that transforming ourselves helps transform the whole world. Deep in the part of us that is most intimately interrelated with everything else in the universe, we realize that our own true happiness and fulfillment are inseparable from the true happiness and fulfillment of all other living creatures. We resonate with the notion that we won't really be free unless the world around us is also free, and we genuinely believe we must incorporate that purpose into our life, whatever it may entail.

In this respect, taking the Bodhisattva Vow resembles taking a romantic or marriage vow, such as, "I will love and care for you forever, and I will never do anything to harm you." When we're deeply in love with someone, we say these words with our whole body and mind, although we have little, if any, practical understanding of what, specifically, keeping this vow will involve in our day-to-day lives ahead. We should not mistake schooling for true education, but formal education at least does something to prepare us for life in our society, getting along with others, speaking a language, solving a math problem, driving a car, mastering a software program, or acquiring a marketable job skill. However, it does virtually nothing to help us bring to life the vows we make to sustain a significant relationship. It's no wonder we so often fail to do so and, as a result, harbor vague but indelible feelings of shame, guilt, failure, and bitterness.

The same painful scenario often occurs with vows we make to bring ourselves spiritually to life. Unless we have a practical structure to support that vow—particular guidelines to apply and specific practices so that we can translate the vow into our everyday thinking, speaking, and acting—we can easily wind up forgetting or forsaking it, even against our best intentions and fervent wishes.

When it comes to realizing the Bodhisattva's wish, we have the ten paramitas, or transformative practices, to assist us. They are the Buddha's own principles of enlightened living—a guidebook, an operating manual—and they help us to become enlightened as well as to live in an enlightened manner every step along the way. I call this "being there while getting there." We must learn how to be focused, dedicated, and disciplined to maintain this kind of life. We cannot afford to lose sight of the forest for the many individual trees that can distract our vision. We cannot risk losing sight of the general welfare of all and the highest good for everyone in favor of our own limited, self-centered concerns. Thus, the Dalai Lama always says, "My religion is kindness." He repeatedly affirms his intention to remain in this world and be reborn again and again until all beings are liberated.

I am Jewish on my parents' side, but Buddhist by choice and training. Like Buddhism, Judaism emphasizes this-world ethics and the importance of belonging to a beloved community; the shared value of *tzedakah:* the giving of oneself and one's resources generously; and the commitment to social justice. We are meant to take part in the healing (*tikkun,* or restoration) of our world. Sometimes this means taking a stand or speaking up, even when it is not easy to do so. Rabbi Hillel of ancient Judea beautifully expresses a Bodhisattva's Golden Rule of universal responsibility:

> *If I am not for myself, who will be for me?*
> *If I am only for myself, what am I?*
> *If not now, when?*

My friend Janet Surrey adds, "If not together, how?" To me this is a guide to leading a good life. It reminds us that we must learn how to be a good friend to ourselves and, at the same time, a good friend to others, always keeping their feelings and needs in mind, side by side with our own.

Generosity is the first or prime paramita because it involves opening up our hearts so that we can palpably *feel* the value of relating to others more expansively. Acts of generosity summon our most subtle, innermost being, our Buddha nature, to manifest itself dynamically in the potent form of Bodhicitta, or active lovingkindness. Once we've tapped that essential part of our being and set it in motion, we've begun the awakening process, which transports us toward enlightenment through enlightened living.

In our quest to be a Bodhisattva, the next dimension is to move the process forward very deliberately and conscientiously. Here's where the second paramita, ethics—or, in Sanskrit, *sila*—comes into play. We need guidelines to plan, chart, assess, and inspire our progress as Bodhisattvas, and we find them within the realm of moral ethics. This realm includes the virtues associated with living more wisely, compassionately, and harmoniously among others on an everyday basis. Among these moral virtues are self-discipline, integrity, decorum, faithfulness, temperance, tact, justice, honesty, reverence, and modesty. Bringing these qualities into our practical lives gives us integrity and good character, precisely because we're synchronizing our three levels of being—outer, inner, and secret—on a moment-by-moment, day-by-day, year-by-year basis. When we're doing this, we're living the good life and helping to usher in a better world. We cannot wait for the Buddha of the future to come; it is up to us as sangha members to find nirvana right here amidst samsara.

Above all, any discussion of moral and ethical values today must include tending not only to lapses in our own personal virtue but also to social, political, and economic evils on a global level, such as racism, sexism, chauvinism, imperialism, poverty, crime, injustice, genocide, health care inequalities, and environmental degradation. We do this by striving ceaselessly to manifest the power of ethical and moral goodness in everything we think, say, and do. There is a Tibetan saying, "The upright, like a precious jewel, never change at all." In a world of constant change, I find this statement quite comforting. Lama Shabkar, a nineteenth-century guru in the Dzogchen lineage of Buddhism, in which I was trained, sang: "Until you have removed the ulcer of deceitfulness, persevere in self-discipline. Moral discipline is like a stairway to liberation: guard it as you would your own eyes—all right?"

The Sanskrit word *sila* means "that which cools or calms." In this context, cooling or calming refers to taming the virulent, seething passions that can easily overwhelm us, sometimes damaging ourselves as well as others. Specifically, the practice of ethics serves as an antidote to our tendencies to be careless, meretricious, irresponsible, cruel, false, exploitative, and unfair. Moral living exemplifies compassion in action.

Buddhist teachers often describe sila as like a shade tree that guards us and our immediate environment from the rays of the scorching desert sun. Sila protects us from being burned by our negative karma and habitual ego-conditioning. It helps us to develop the wisdom that knows right from wrong, helpful from harmful, wholesome from unwholesome—which is the essence of Buddhist morality. Under the influence of sila, we coolly, calmly, and masterfully create our own new and intentionally directed positive momentum toward enlightenment and Bodhisattvism, which we experience simultaneously. This is what I mean by "being there while getting there," every single step of the way.

Individuals with a strong sense of sila, or ethics, are true to standards that reflect and elicit not only the best in themselves but also the best among human beings in general. They make promises to themselves and others to uphold these standards, but once these promises become second nature to them, they don't restrict their lives, as others might expect they would. Instead, these promises lend clarity and power to their lives, allowing them more freedom and opportunity to live positively, grow spiritually, and help others naturally along the way. They are no longer focused on, and upset by, the wrongdoings of others, but rather are intent on improving themselves so that others might benefit. As Patrul Rinpoche says in *Heart Advice on the Two Ethics* (spiritual ethics and worldly ethics), translated by my Cambridge, Massachusetts, neighbor and friend Tulku Thondup Rinpoche, "If you desire to enjoy happiness in this life and the next, don't keep talking about others' qualities, but watch yourself and examine your own path. This is the entire means of achieving both spiritual and worldly accomplishments." As the Buddha himself said:

> *Seeing myself in others and others in myself,*
> *Whom would I harm, whom could I exploit?*

The moral self-discipline of sila involves training through familiarization and repetition, which is what we Buddhists call practice. If a bear can learn to ride a bicycle, as I have seen at a circus, just imagine what a human being can accomplish! All the various kinds of vows and precepts in Buddhism are training guides or spiritual exercises to be used in taming and refining our own rough, intransigent tendencies toward greed, anger, meanness, cruelty, and jealousy. They are not whips or scourges to be applied to others, but like mirrors to better see and know ourselves.

In Buddhism, all of ethics relates to two key principles: avoid doing harm and seek to do good. The ideal exemplar of these principles is the historical Buddha himself—a human being of immaculate integrity who was heart centered and guided by inner principles rather than outer events, conditions, and circumstances. When Rahula, the Buddha's son, was ten years old, the Buddha came to visit him. Rahula said to his father, "My mother told me to ask you for my inheritance. Someday I will be king of this land, and I'll need great riches."

The Buddha answered, "Son, you ask me for an inheritance that does not last and without fail leads to suffering. I cannot and would not give you this kind of inheritance. Instead, I will impart to you a legacy that is everlasting and will always make you rich. When you wish to do anything with your body, speech, or mind, first ask yourself whether it will result in harm for yourself or anyone else. If the answer is yes, then such a thing is not right, and you should not do it. If you can't keep yourself from doing it, then admit what you've done, so that it will be easier to avoid doing it the next time. But if you wish to do anything with your body, speech, or mind that is not harmful and that you know to be good, do it. These right deeds lead to joy and peace. Train yourself diligently, day and night, to do right things." We have all heard that virtue is its own reward; this is why. Nagarjuna, one of ancient India's most prominent Buddhist teachers, said: "Moral ethics is the basis of all excellent qualities." The virtuous man or woman is the very heart of every society. This is universal law—truth itself. Character is at the root of action.

In the scope of world history in general, perhaps the most famous model of ethical standards is Confucius, the great educator and political figure who was active in China during many of the same years that the Buddha was teaching in India. Like the Buddha, Confucius believed that following ethical standards should be not simply a matter of spiritual observance—that is, performing specific acts of piety and behaving in a certain manner during sacred times and at sacred places—but a complete way of life.

Confucius's ethical system was based on the same core truths espoused by the Buddha. In his masterwork, *Analects,* Confucius identifies the fundamental virtue as "Ren," which means benevolence, humanity, love, and kindness. He also states, "The great person understands Yi [morality, duty to one's neighbor, altruism, and politeness]. The small man understands only Li [profit and personal advantage]."

One of the most famous stories illustrating Confucius's devotion to living ethically concerns a time when he was seriously ill. His disciple Tzu-lu asked permission to offer a prayer. Confucius asked, "Was such a thing ever done before?"

Tzu-lu replied, "Yes, it was. It was done to honor the gods above and the gods below."

"In that case," Confucius said, "I have long been offering my prayers." This statement is interpreted to mean that Confucius had been praying all his life just by avoiding harm and aiming toward good in everything he did. No formal prayer on his behalf was necessary to pay tribute to the gods throughout the universe. He'd already taken care of that.

Often people who live very ethical lives wind up speaking truth to the powers-that-be in an especially compelling manner. Mahatma Gandhi did so when he launched his nonviolent disobedience movement, called *satya-graha* (literally, truth-force), against the evils of British imperialism in the mid-twentieth century. The whole point of his movement was not so

much to cause trouble for the British as to engage other individuals—and ultimately the British as well—in exercising their own best, most honorable, and ethical selves. He was confident that the combined effect of these activities would cause positive change without bloodshed, and his confidence was rewarded when India peacefully won its independence. As he said many times, "The spirit of democracy cannot be imposed from without. It has to come from within." We each can and must liberate ourselves.

Some five hundred years earlier, Sir Thomas More, lord chancellor of England, spoke truth to the powers-that-be when he refused to go against his principles by approving the convenience-driven divorce and remarriage of the Roman Catholic king, Henry VIII. It was a courageous stand that brought More a death sentence but has since inspired generations of people struggling to lead more ethical lives. In 1935 the Roman Catholic Church canonized Thomas More as a saint.

Today we have Aung San Suu Kyi as a shining example of a moral Bodhisattva who is campaigning with honor and personal sacrifice against unethical powers-that-be. The daughter of General Aung San, who helped found the modern state of Burma, Suu Kyi (a Buddhist scholar and activist) was democratically elected as the leader of Burma in 1990, after which she was immediately placed under house arrest by the ruling military junta (who have since changed Burma's name to Myanmar). She remained housebound for six years, and her movements are still restricted by military guards. Nevertheless, she has relentlessly led a nonviolent, grassroots effort to end the many human rights violations of the junta and to restore democracy in her country.

The junta has offered to let Aung San Suu Kyi leave Myanmar altogether, but she has refused, knowing that the junta would not permit her to return and that her cause might fail in her absence. She wouldn't even let herself go to her beloved husband's side when he was dying of cancer in a London hospital. When she was announced as the winner of the 1991 Nobel Peace Prize, she wouldn't travel to Oslo for the awards ceremony but declared in her acceptance speech, "To live the fully responsible life, one must have the courage to bear responsibility for the needs of others ... one must want to bear this responsibility. Concepts such as truth, justice, and compassion cannot be dismissed as trite when these are often the only bulwarks which stand against ruthless power."

Like millions of other people around the world, I have long found an impeccable role model of an ethical human being and a person of moral conscience in the Dalai Lama. A devout monk and lover of science as well as meditation, yoga, and philosophy, he has traveled the world tirelessly as a statesman, ambassador, and human rights activist in favor of peace, international cooperation, and each person's universal responsibility. Since childhood, he has maintained 253 monastic vows covering every aspect of his hardworking daily existence; simultaneously, he has cultivated on an inner, mystical level the utmost, let-it-all-hang-out authenticity and internal freedom of mind. Yet, despite all this esoteric training, he relates immediately and genuinely to everyone he encounters, spontaneously manifesting simple good humor and a very modern, practical sense of being "right here, right now." In Tibetan Buddhism, he is what we call a Three Vows Master, one who exhibits a commitment to his vows on all three levels of his being: outer, inner, and secret. As I've said before, we can see it in his face and in each of his acts, even the smallest gestures. This is the joy of sila paramita.

Think of people you know and respect who lead very ethical lives and treat everyone they meet with thoughtfulness and compassion. Don't they seem to shine with a light from within? The late John F. Kennedy Jr., who met the Dalai Lama on several occasions, said that whenever they parted, "it was like the man carrying the lamp left the room." Don't such Bodhisattvas seem filled with the joy of life? Don't they effortlessly uplift all with whom they come into contact? That is their job description: to uplift, to edify. Bodhisattvas are wisdom warriors.

Very few of us have taken 253 monastic moral vows to follow the Buddhist monks' way, as the Dalai Lama has. Even fewer of us have found ourselves in direct physical opposition to unethical, ruthless heads of state. However, thanks to the vibrant examples of those who have done these things, we can bring their indomitable spirit to the vows we do take and the resulting conflicts we inevitably face, using these exemplary modern Bodhisattvas as inspiring role models.

From a Buddhist perspective, the most important vows to consider are the Bodhisattva Vows, which we've already examined, and ethical vows to follow each of five basic, purifying training precepts that arise from the Buddha's overall counsel to "avoid doing harm and seek to do good. Purify the heart and mind." These Five Precepts are: do not kill,

do not steal, do not deceive, do not engage in sexual misconduct, and do not indulge in intoxicants, which cause heedlessness. I'll discuss each of them more specifically later in this chapter.

On the surface, these moral precepts, with their "do nots," remind us of the Ten Commandments. However, they are most definitely precepts rather than divine commandments in the strict sense of the term. Precepts are not fixed and absolute rules imposed on us from the outside that we must obey without question. Instead, they are preliminary guidelines that accord with our own innermost spiritual being, whether we call it our Buddha nature, our soul, or our better self. We must then take it upon ourselves to examine their potential advantages and benefits in order to apply these guidelines thoughtfully, skillfully, and compassionately to the realities of our lives. As Hildegard von Bingen, one of my favorite medieval Christian mystics, once sang: "I, the fiery light of divine wisdom ... I am the yearning for good."

As we undertake this grand enterprise, we will often experience doubt and confusion regarding just whether or how an individual precept fits a particular situation. At any given point along our way toward incorporating the ethical precepts more fully into our lives, we may decide, after stretching ourselves as much as we can, that we can only go so far at that moment. In that case, we need to be patient and compassionate toward ourselves, just as we would be toward others who are doing as much as they can to be virtuous. We must befriend ourselves and make our mind into an ally rather than a tyrant. We must listen and cooperate with this moderate inner friend, rather than merely bowing down and helplessly giving in to some inner taskmaster of extreme perfectionism.

The precepts define themselves in the context of our lives. We should aspire to express them naturally and automatically, so that there is no separation between them and our day-to-day existence. Until we can do this, however, there may be many instances of legitimate doubt, fear, uncertainty, indecision, unwillingness, and other difficulties that we need to work through, for ethical morality is a complex area of life without many easy, black-and-white, preconceived answers. Our conscience must be our guide.

Consider the many gray areas of ethical life where ethics may not be so very clear, questions abound and viewpoints vary. People often ask me what I think—or worse, what they should do—about questions relating to abortion, euthanasia, capital punishment, living wills, and so forth. How are we to decide what is the wisest, most compassionate, and most appropriate decision to make when we're dealing with such complex issues? This is precisely where the sixth transformative practice, wisdom paramita, comes in. It informs our ethics, our morals, our entire practice of sila. As Samuel Johnson, the eighteenth-century British philosopher, once said, "Integrity without knowledge is weak and useless, and knowledge without integrity is dangerous and dreadful."

Ethical intelligence, like all the paramita virtues, is a multilevel individual and social intelligence, which you can always tap into at different depths and levels. All of the paramitas have their egocentric, outer behavioral aspect, including bodily intelligence; their inner ethnocentric or attitudinal aspect and emotional wisdom; and their world-centric or most vast and inclusive, subtle spiritual aspect or wisdom. To make effective judgments and wise decisions we usually need to include this integral style of thought and analysis, rather than settling for easy, canned answers.

Buddhists would say that we have to do the best we can according to the universal truths available to us through our ever deeper understanding coupled with the intuitive wisdom of our innermost Buddha nature. When I'm faced with dire decisions, I like to ask myself, "What would the Buddha do? How does this situation relate to enlightenment? Can I regard this through my open Wisdom Eye, which intuits unity while simultaneously seeing the many disparate elements involved? What would unconditional love do and call forth in this situation?"

THE THREE KINDS OF SILA

An aspirant who unfolds the fragrance of virtue, unravels the luminosity of spiritual wisdom, experiences the profundity of universal life, and ascends the heights of superconsciousness, with no need to indulge in pride and its numerous expressions.

—JOYA MA, AMERICAN HINDU TEACHER

The Buddhist sutras poetically inform us that sila is a perfume not unlike sandalwood, whose fragrance is said to reach up to the realm of the gods. Sila is considered the highest form of virtue and the cause for a divine rebirth. It is widely understood that it is not the robe but the inner spiritual discipline that makes the holy man or woman divine. One Buddhist sutra (scripture) says:

> *Train in meritorious acts that bring long-lasting bliss.*
> *Develop a life in tune, and a mind of goodwill.*
> *These three things cause the wise*
> *to inhabit a blissful world.*

Sila encompasses moral discipline, virtue, integrity, kindness, character development, and healthy ethics. Tradition teaches that there are three basic kinds of sila: the moral discipline of restraint from nonvirtue, as reflected in multiple precepts that bid us to avoid doing harm to ourselves and others in either the short term or the long term; the virtue of accumulating positive qualities and merits, good karma and good fortune, through good deeds and generous offerings, as described in numerous vows and rituals; and the discipline of selfless service and benefit to other beings, of all forms, without regard for oneself.

The first kind of sila is mainly external and behavioral. The second kind is somewhat behavioral but more internal, relating to our attitude and spiritual aspirations. The third, and highest, kind of sila is that of the true Bodhisattva: boundless altruism that issues from radiant Bodhicitta and connects most closely to dana paramita (thus showing again how the paramitas support each other).

The third kind of sila is not explained in detail in Buddhist writings, primarily because it is based on one's own realization of the profound, innate, groundless ground of prajna wisdom. The ultimate level of virtue—the innermost and mystical-transcendental level of sila—is being in touch with our innate purity and untrammeled, luminous spirit or pure, unadulterated Buddha nature, which is uncorrupted by whatever mistakes we may have made or foibles and regrets we may have. It implies connecting totally with the primordial purity and uncreated radiance at the heart of everything and everyone. This innate purity and radiance is the Bodhisattva way and the means combined in one, which makes possible rehabilitation, forgiveness, and hope, no matter how far we may have fallen or gone astray.

THE FIVE PRECEPTS:
VOWING TO BRING OUT YOUR BEST

Now let's consider each of Buddhism's five basic training precepts individually in the light of what it states and what it leaves unstated for us to realize.

1. Do Not Kill

The precept "do not kill" comes first, and from a Mahayana perspective, it seems an especially crucial guideline, given the Bodhisattva's mission to save all sentient beings. Actually, each of the precepts can be seen from both a prohibitive and an affirmative perspective, so an alternative expression of this one might be "Support, cherish, and protect life."

This double-sided directive—"do not kill; support life"—can also be interpreted many different ways, according to our three levels of being. On an outer, or physical, level, it clearly directs us not to murder another human being—a violent act often motivated by greed, anger, passion, or delusion run amok. Many people, especially Buddhists, extend this guideline to include not killing animals maliciously or for sport. Some even invoke it as a reason not to kill animals that may seem harmful, like mosquitoes, or not to kill animals for food or support slaughter by eating meat. There are even Indian puritans who refrain entirely from using leather, fur, silk, ivory, and all other animal-related products, for similar reasons.

Here we start getting into areas where our personal conscience must intervene to make a final decision: the Buddha himself didn't offer much specific advice beyond "do not kill." For example, some people resolve the question of whether or not to eat meat by deciding they will avoid excessive eating of meat, give conscious thanks for each meal they eat (including ones with meat), and do everything reasonably possible to avoid eating meat that comes from large, animal-abusing producer-processors, such as industrial chicken farms. Many Zen schools as well as a few other Buddhist sects claim that plants are sentient beings too, so avoiding meat doesn't solve the problem for them. Instead, they also choose a middle way, like the one I just described. The same strategy goes for Buddhists who live in areas where vegetables can't easily be grown, such as in large sections of the Himalayas. Even a vegetarian or fruitarian must be aware of the harm to insects and worms caused by farming, whether or not pesticides are used. There is simply no way to opt entirely out of Rudyard Kipling's famous "nature red in tooth and claw." The question is, *How* aggressive and violent are we?

On an outer level, this precept also argues against fighting in wars. King Ashoka (304–232 BCE), the greatest emperor of ancient India, was originally a fierce warrior and conqueror who was also guilty of fratricide, but he was almost instantly converted by the peaceful, silent presence of a wandering holy man who turned out to be a Buddhist monk. Ashoka became the first known ruler in history to renounce the glory of conquest through violence in favor of the pacifist ways taught by the Buddha. He applied these ways to politics and government through his renowned Ashokan Code, a fourteen-point edict of compassionate and nonviolent conduct for both society and individuals; it remains carved on pillars and statues around the subcontinent today, over two millennia later. Among the fourteen points is the following: "You are true to your own beliefs if you accord kindly treatment to adherents of other faiths. You harm your own religion by harassing followers of other creeds." In his kingdom, which came to be called the Kingdom of Kindness, King Ashoka made imperative the practices of honesty, compassion, mercy, and nonviolence. His threefold lion emblem persists even now as the official symbol of India, and is prominent on its rupee notes.

The same precept against taking life exists as a religious prohibition in the Nation of Islam; in 1967 it guided the American heavyweight champion and Black Muslim Muhammad Ali to refuse to be drafted into the U.S. Army to serve in Vietnam. His official statement at the time was, "I have searched my conscience and I find I cannot be true to my belief in my religion by accepting such a call." More characteristically, he chanted the following poetic verse to a crowd of reporters:

> *Keep asking me, no matter how long*
> *On the war in Vietnam, I sing this song*
> *I ain't got no quarrel with them Viet Cong.*

I consider Ali a Bodhisattva for taking this stand, which made a strong public statement in favor of peaceful coexistence. It cost him his heavyweight title, as he knew it would, and subjected him to several years of court battles to avoid a prison sentence for draft evasion. Finally, in 1971, the U.S. Supreme Court reversed his conviction. Interestingly, three years later, Ali regained the heavyweight title by defeating George Foreman.

Ali has always radiated a clear sense of values, great pride in his humanity, and active compassion for people of all nations, as evidenced in the myriad good works accomplished by his World Foundation. I met Ali once in the late 1970s at a restaurant on Fifth Avenue in New York City and was struck by his charismatic glow and the immensity of his energetic presence. To me he looked like one of the giant Nagas, who, in Buddhist cosmology, are part divine and part animal. He revealed the same kind of intense passion mixed with grace that the Nagas (like water dragons) are said to display. I'm sure this quality related not only to his physical gifts but also to his ethical integrity.

On the outer level of our being, the precept "do not kill; support life" also bids us to create safe conditions for others—for example, to drive our car responsibly for the well-being of our passengers, to make sure our home environment is free from hazards or toxins that might endanger both family and visitors, and to offer healing words and assistance to others in need so that they might live healthier and more fulfilling lives.

But what does this precept tell us to do in regard to aborting a child, supporting capital punishment, or ending the life of a very old pet or a desperate person who's terminally ill and totally dependent on life-support machinery? Again, we must resolve certain ethical dilemmas for ourselves, with deep consideration for all the circumstances and individuals involved. This difficult work takes place on our inner level. As we struggle to reconcile our thoughts and feelings, we become ever more receptive to what our secret level of inner being holds dear and true. We must trust that we will make the right decision, not only for ourselves but also for all beings. The clearer our hearts and minds are, the truer and more congruent with reality our decisions and actions will be.

Meanwhile, on the same inner level of our thoughts, feelings, and conscience, we also need to avoid even the most casual thoughts associated with killing others or with their deaths, such as, "I could just kill him!" or, "Things would be so much easier if she would just die." In fact, we need to guard against any thoughts or feelings that entertain the notion of harm or misfortune occurring to someone else. This kind of inner-level activity does not support life. For the same reason, we must not entertain morbid thoughts relating to ourselves, such as, *I wish I were dead!* or, *What reason do I have to live?* Because our outer and inner selves are intimately and, in many ways, imperceptibly connected in terms of cause and effect, we need to be just as responsible for our thoughts, intentions, and feelings as we are for our physical acts.

2. Do Not Steal

When we think about stealing, we tend to conjure up stark images of masked robbers swiping some precious object that doesn't belong to them. The precept "do not steal" certainly covers such acts, but it also applies to more subtle manifestations of greed, covetousness, exploitation, and misappropriation.

This precept calls us not only to be respectful of things that belong to others, but also to avoid desiring a lot of things for ourselves. Otherwise, we may wind up stealing without being clearly aware of it: for instance, by laying personal claim to otherwise unowned trees and bushes in the forest, by hogging all the attention at a gathering, by accepting an unfairly large salary relative to our peers, or by utilizing more than our fair share of our neighborhood's and even our planet's resources. This kind of stealing is proscribed in the traditional nonmaterialistic Buddhist injunction against "taking what is not given." It is up to us to be more aware of our actions and intentions as well as their possible repercussions and to decide where, when, and how to draw the line between our legitimate needs and our greed.

In many respects, following this precept involves the same mind-set and activities as practicing the first paramita, generosity. If we learn to live more simply, less selfishly, and with greater awareness of the welfare and rights of others, we inevitably avoid stealing and more subtly appropriating for ourselves what is not freely and clearly given. Otherwise, we run the risk of justifying all kinds of essentially stealthy acts, thinking only that we've been clever at getting away with a good deal or getting off scot-free. That kind of thinking overlooks—or worse, disregards—the law of karma.

Let's consider a hypothetical example of ethical decision making and its attendant issues. Shana, an antique dealer, has a neighbor who has offered to sell her some old metal garden chairs for $10 each. She has seen the chairs and realizes their true worth. If they are just cleaned up, she's confident she can take them to a large show on the East Coast and get anywhere from $500 to $800 for each chair.

Shana is delighted about making such a big profit, but deep down she wonders if it's right for her to take advantage of her unwitting neighbor's overly low sale price. To feel better about the deal, Shana reminds herself that she spent years gaining the expertise that enables her to know how much antiques are worth. She also tells herself that she will most likely have to devote a few days to cleaning the chairs properly. Then she will need to store them until the first day of the show, when she will have to get up at 4:00 AM to put the chairs in her van and drive three hours to the show, unload them there, and sell them. Still, she wonders, does she deserve to keep that much profit for herself without giving some of it to her neighbor?

Shana at least wonders about the ethics of her situation, which is certainly an appropriate response whenever we sense in our inner being that we've engineered a "steal." In real-world terms, Shana is clearly within her personal and professional rights to get away with whatever she can, as long as it's legal. However, her instincts are telling her that she should be less stealthy and more generous to her neighbor, and it is important for her to honor these instincts in some manner. Doing so will make both her and her neighbor feel better, which is a double good. I might recommend that she explain to her neighbor what she thinks the chairs are worth before she buys them. Then I'd say that Shana is even freer to do whatever she wants with the chairs and to let the chips fall where they may.

I offer this example and discussion to illustrate how complicated the "do not steal; give freely" precept can be in real-world scenarios. After all, Shana does need to gain some kind of profit in order to make a living, which brings us back to finding the balance between need and greed. Her conscience is clearly engaged by the large discrepancy between her neighbor's asking price and what she considers to be the value of the chairs; this fact alone means that something needs to be done if she's going to have lasting peace of mind. On a very mundane level, how would Shana feel if her neighbor found out about this discrepancy? How would her neighbor feel?

This last point reminds me of a wonderful story that Tulku Thubten Rinpoche tells about an unnamed Kadampa master he knew. One day this master was having lunch at someone's place before going on a retreat.

After lunch, everyone else went outside, leaving the master alone in the house to prepare for the retreat. He suddenly remembered that he had no tea to take with him on retreat. He found a huge bag of tea in the kitchen, and stuck his hand into the bag to scoop some out for himself. Suddenly, he realized he was stealing. He remained in that same position, with his hand in the bag, and called everyone else back inside the house. "Look at me!" he said when his hosts were all gathered around him. "I'm stealing your tea!" The uncompromising monk was making sure that he learned a lesson he'd never forget: not to take the precept "do not steal" too casually and not to fool himself or others about when he was violating it. He said that after that lesson it was unlikely he'd forget his moral vows again.

3. Do Not Deceive

Mahatma Gandhi tells us, "Be truthful, gentle, and fearless." The precept "do not deceive" refers to not lying in thought, speech, or action. When we deliberately give someone false information—whether we're trying to hide something wrong we did, put ourselves in a better light, or simply fool the other person—we are violating this precept. The same is true when we don't actually say anything but knowingly allow someone to believe a lie, or when we flatter people to their face and then cut them down behind their back, or even when we engage in denial, talking ourselves into one way of looking at a situation that we know in our hearts is not the truth. The Buddha's Lovingkindness Sutra says, "This is what should be done by one who is skilled in goodness and who knows the paths of peace: Let them be able and upright, straightforward and gentle in speech, humble and not conceited, content and easily satisfied.... Let none deceive another."

Honesty is an awesome quality. How can we claim to be seekers of truth and reality if we can't at least be honest, straightforward, and authentic in day-to-day life, both externally, with others, and internally, with ourselves? No one wants to be a hypocrite or values that negative quality in others, yet there is an enormous amount of hypocrisy and hidden corruption and injustice in the world. How is that possible except as the result of dishonesty, denial, and lack of clear-sightedness, all conspiring to produce an epidemic of self- and collective blindness?

In my opinion, nondeception is the most difficult precept to maintain with any precision. For example, even if we manage not to tell flagrant

lies to others—and thus avoid being sent to the precepts penalty box—
what about the minor fouls that seem to come automatically and, so we
think, innocuously? These include the little white lies ("No, that dress
doesn't make you look fat!"), the slight exaggerations ("I'm late 'cause I
was stalled in traffic over an hour!"), the convenient forgettings ("I don't
recall seeing him there"), the sugarcoatings ("Don't worry—his bark is
worse than his bite"), the self-defensive evasions ("Well, boss, I'm not
sure how I feel about it—how do you feel?"), the self-serving stories we
tell ourselves ("I know I said I'd quit smoking, but today was so stressful, I deserve a cigarette"), and our jokey rationalizations ("Calories don't
count, do they, if I snack quickly while standing at the refrigerator?").

In addition, there are other little ways in which we deceive others and
ourselves that seem not just socially acceptable but even encouraged. In
this category we can put dyeing our hair, cosmetic surgery, padding our
résumé, claiming tax deductions for personal expenses, even maintaining
a fancier home than we can comfortably afford merely to maintain appearances and keep up with the Joneses.

Granted, we shouldn't deceive either others or ourselves about "serious" matters, but what's wrong with simply bending the truth a bit to
make life a little bit easier? Truth seems so malleable, especially in these
postmodern days of relativism and deconstructionism. Whose truth is
true anyway when there seem to be so many possible versions in our plu-
ralistic world? What's the harm in my particular, even if slightly skewed,
version of the truth? The answer is as simple as it is hard to digest or apply:
the more we go about bending the truth or creating our own perspective
on the truth, the easier it becomes to do so, and the more likely we are to
do it again. As a result, we become less and less authentic, lose touch with
our genuine selves, and contribute more and more illusion and confusion
to the world around us. We must never forget the karmic cause and effect
of our thoughts, words, and deeds. Even the simplest deception can set in
motion a chain of dishonesty that sooner or later adds to human suffering
by destabilizing the ground of trust most of us need to walk on. Just look
at the effect that parental lying has on children and that public scandals
have on our current relationship with political leaders. Bear in mind that
the affirmative expression of this precept—be truthful—challenges us not
only to avoid deceit but to embody truth and project it into the universe,
which means we need to know truth and realize it for ourselves.

Having said that, I need to add that many situations call for our conscience—our inner-self link to our secret, higher self—to negotiate between the absolute demands of this precept and the relative world of samsara. Our conscience functions as an internal tuning device or gyroscope that keeps us oriented toward what is genuinely right in a particular situation. Suppose, for instance, that a friend who cares a great deal about writing poetry asks you to read one of her poems and tell her what you think about it. You recognize the courage underlying her request: she's never shown her work to anyone else, and you're well aware that she's quite shy and hypersensitive to criticism, even if it's constructive and well intentioned. So you read the poem, but you don't like it. In fact, you thoroughly dislike it. You think the entire work is trite, clumsy, sophomoric, and overwrought. What do you say to her?

It is probably wrong to say to your friend, "Your poem is wonderful!" This statement clearly violates the precept against lying. Nevertheless, if you believe that the unadulterated truth (which is only your opinion, after all) will do more harm than good to her, will hurt and undermine her, and may even cause her to give up her only creative outlet, you might let yourself say something ambiguously appreciative and marginally positive, even if it misleads her into thinking you like her poem more than you do. You might say, for example, "It meant so much to me to read your poem! You clearly poured your heart into it. There are a few changes I could suggest that you might want to consider. Would you like to hear what they are? If not, I can respect that you'd want to keep it just as it is. I hope you'll keep writing."

Your specific approach to this problem, however, has to hinge on what you know about this person, on the particular nature of the relationship the two of you have, and on all the other circumstances surrounding the event. Only then can you exercise what Buddhists call *upaya*, or skillful means (the seventh transformative practice), in interpreting this precept wisely and compassionately to fit the case at hand. As a teacher, I constantly have to apply this strategy. After all, my goal is not to produce the perfect teaching, ritual, or meditation experience but rather to encourage and empower individual students to keep practicing, learning, and enhancing their competencies so that they can achieve their own genuine excellence and surpass even that of their teachers.

There's no escaping the fact that this kind of truth mixed with tact requires courage, timing, attention, and skill, but the long-range effects are well worth the trouble. I'm reminded of the time when I was in college and my first real girlfriend told me she loved someone else, an old friend who lived some distance away. Naturally, I was hurt, but thanks to her care in telling me, I was also very moved. Through my pain and disappointment, I even felt loved and well considered, although not quite in the way I selfishly desired. Her honesty explained many things that had perplexed me about what had been going on between us. It helped me realize that I wasn't really crazy or insufficient as a lover after all. It also saved our warm and long-lasting relationship as close friends— something she definitely wanted but was clearly putting at risk by being so forthcoming.

More than anything else, we need to be honest with ourselves; then we can't help but deal honestly with others.

4. Do Not Engage in Sexual Misconduct

The precept "do not engage in sexual misconduct" is not a prohibition against sex itself. Although many monastic orders in Buddhism require monks and nuns to be chaste and celibate as a means of avoiding distraction and interpersonal conflicts, there are no specific rules in Buddhist sutras for the laity that prohibit, for example, premarital sex, masturbation, or homosexuality—or divorce, for that matter—as there are in the scriptures of other religions. Instead, engaging in sexual relations is considered an honorable and joyful experience for body, mind, and spirit, as long as the sexual partners avoid doing harm to each other or to people outside the relationship. For this reason, the affirmative version of this precept might be "respect yourself, your partner, and others in all forms of healthy sexual expression."

So, once again, part of the burden lies on us to realize—either through listening to our secret, innermost being or through actual experience, or both—what is harmful and what is not. Clearly, prostitution represents sexual misconduct, not because it's illegal (in many areas of the world, and even some in the United States, it's not, by the way), but because it's based on an inequality between the two partners, and opens up all kinds of opportunities for exploitation and abuse. The sex trade often represents a loathsome objectification of a person as a mere commodity and a dangerous bartering of flesh verging on slavery. One party is definitely the boss; the other is the relatively powerless employee or even chattel. This mercantile use of sex demeans its essential beauty and power.

The same problem occurs whenever we use sex manipulatively to get what we want in spite of the other person, or whenever we willfully suppress, abuse, or inflict pain on our sexual partner against his or her will. We can also agree that being unfaithful to someone who we know would be hurt by our infidelity—or who has good reason to be upset about our infidelity—is also sexual misconduct, whether we're married to this person (in which case it's officially adultery) or not. In addition, it's clear to most of us that sex with minors and sexual addiction represent abuses of our inherently healthy sexuality. One can also be unfaithful and cheat emotionally, with other partners, even without the intimate sexual connection.

Other forms of misconduct are less obvious and therefore might seem easier to justify, despite the fact that they can cause a great deal of suffering and confusion. Engaging in sexual teasing and wearing provocative clothing in social, school, or workplace situations may seem innocuous acts. After all, aren't we simply displaying our cool in exactly the way that movies, television shows, and ads tell us is sexy? Isn't it commonly understood as acceptable, even attractive, behavior? Sadly, in all too many cases the answer is yes. We're taught from a shockingly early age to project media images of sexual hipness to one and all rather than to allow our authentic sexuality to reveal itself in a more natural and timely manner to appropriate individuals. This kind of careless exhibition can be fun and even exciting from time to time, but it can easily wind up giving us warped ideas about sex; our conduct can also mislead, disturb, embarrass, tempt, exploit, provoke, or even harass others.

Our inner world is a rich realm where many sexual fantasies can take place. It may be difficult to intervene in these fantasies with wisdom, skillful means, and compassion, rather than just abandon ourselves to them with lust. Our libido certainly urges us in the latter direction. Yet here is precisely where we need to do much of the work of liberating ourselves from attachments. Sexual energy can be channeled and redirected, as well as sublimated into a propellant for deeper development. Sexual fantasies can be extremely powerful in shaping the ways we think, speak, and act, especially in our relationships with others. We need to wean ourselves from entertaining fantasies that involve manipulating, abusing, dehumanizing, or otherwise mistreating other people, and use our yearning and longing for heart-connection to lead us closer to wholeness and oneness, rather than just to the next sensual fix.

Simultaneously, we need to guard against letting our thoughts and feelings about sex get ensnared by fear, ignorance, prejudice, or self-righteousness. A Zen teaching tale addresses this kind of insidious trap. Once two monks were walking through the woods when they came to a shallow river. On the other side, a beautiful woman in wedding clothes was clearly anxious to cross the river, but she was afraid it would ruin her clothes. Moved by the troubled look on her face, the older monk said to the younger, "I will volunteer to carry her across."

The younger monk was shocked. "But we've taken a vow never even to touch a woman! It can stir up all sorts of dangerous desires. What about that?"

The older monk replied, "What about compassion? Look—she's crying!" The older monk immediately waded to the other side of the river and then carried the woman back across without letting her clothes get wet. She thanked him profusely and walked on.

As the two monks continued on their journey, the younger one remained silent and scowling for hours. Finally, he could contain his anger no longer. "You shouldn't have carried that woman on your back!" he said to the older monk. "You know the rule!"

The older monk said, "I set down that woman hours ago. It seems that you're still carrying her."

5. Do Not Indulge in Intoxicants

On the surface, the precept "do not indulge in intoxicants" would seem to be the easiest one of the five to practice: just don't drink alcohol! With a little thought and reflection, however, we realize that there are many more potential intoxicants available to us than alcohol alone. In addition to drugs like marijuana, cocaine, crystal meth, acid, heroin, and a host of other legal and illegal uppers, downers, and psychedelics, we have at our disposal a host of technological fixes that can numb, overstimulate, or otherwise bend our minds. For example, how many of us deliberately and addictively let ourselves zone out for hours in front of a television or computer screen? Besides taking control of our consciousness, how much do these machines and their programs artificially alter the way we see reality? Isn't this also a form of intoxication?

Mindfulness is at the core of living an awake, aware, and responsible life. From a Buddhist perspective, a clear mind is a critical component of effective meditation, conscious living, and, eventually, enlightenment. If we seek to be mindful and aware, and especially if we strive to attain enlightenment, how can we cloud our mind with intoxicants that cause heedlessness?

Frankly, we can do it quite easily. Living in a consumer culture, we're encouraged to indulge ourselves. Advertisers encourage it; politicians even tell us it's our fundamental right, our hard-earned way of life. They don't necessarily mean we should smoke crack, but they do mean we should be free to get as much fun out of life as we can. As a result, we can justify pretty much any indulgence we want to allow ourselves, including even a mind-blowing intoxicant, especially if it's the only way we can seem to experience the euphoria we see other people enjoying in the media, or the only way we can escape a misbegotten sense of having missed out on what our culture calls "our due."

Often my students ask me, "Does the precept against indulging in intoxicants mean I can never have a beer or glass of wine?" I tell them that they have to make these kinds of decisions for themselves. The heart of the difficulty in mastering this precept is knowing where to draw the line. Some people are not exactly indulging or intoxicating themselves by having one or even two glasses of wine in the course of an evening. For others, it is an indulgence because two drinks are too many, or they aren't always able to limit themselves and they do often wind up clearly intoxicated, in which case they're all the more capable of harming themselves and others. For an alcoholic, even one sip is far too many.

My students also ask me, "What about caffeine and nicotine—do we need to abstain from these drugs as well? And what about sugar?" Although the degree of danger involved is certainly much less than it is in the case of the harder drugs I've already mentioned, the same rationale applies to the mind-buzzers caffeine and nicotine: some people aren't significantly affected by them, and others are. Some people can control their intake, and others have problems doing so. Each person needs to be honest and forthright in determining which kind of constitution he or she has and what to do about consuming such products. In fact, we can even stretch this precept—and this advice—to include any type of addictive behavior that can blur mental clarity, including television watching, Web surfing, eating, sleeping, gambling, shopping, and making phone calls. For some, the best solution may be to follow the middle way. For others, the only realistic answer may be complete abstinence.

We have only briefly examined each of the five basic precepts of Buddhism. As I mentioned earlier, there are other, longer lists that apply to laypeople as well as monastics. And yet, in confining our attention to just these five precepts, think of how many complex and interconnecting issues are raised. Does that mean we should stop here? Why not simply confine our moral and ethical practice to these five precepts? Aren't they enough to worry about?

In Buddhist terms, following precepts alone, whether it's five or five hundred, does not bring about enlightenment; nor does living according to any system of ethical morality all by itself. Granted, either approach has many virtues and positive outflows, but if you aspire toward enlightenment, as every Bodhisattva must, you need to embrace sila paramita in its totality, which is suffused by each of the other paramitas, most especially prajna wisdom. In other words, sila is a direct portal into realizing all the other dimensions of the Bodhisattva way and, ultimately, enlightenment.

I believe this is one reason why the venerable senior monk and abbot Kalu Rinpoche once explained to his students that if we took Buddhist training vows and even became fully ordained monks or nuns, our lives would be more simplified and focused, so that our meditation would be better as we simultaneously grew in moral virtue and deepened our inner development. He said, for example, that the more we straightened out our mind and life by ceasing to lie, the less we would be wondering what we said to whom about what. Thus, it would be much easier for us to concentrate on mindfulness, leading to insight and realization, and we would attain enlightenment in this very lifetime.

I have found this to be absolutely true. The more truthful I am with myself and others, the more my conscience is clear and tranquil. Thus, I can more thoroughly and unequivocally inhabit the present moment and accept everything that happens without fear, knowing that what goes around comes around (the law of karma). Ethical morality and self-discipline represent the good ground, or stable basis. Mindful awareness is the skillful and efficacious growth-path, or way. Wisdom and compassion constitute the fruit, or result. This is the essence of Buddhism as taught in the three liberating trainings (*sila, samadhi,* and *prajna*) that are encoded in the Buddha's Noble Eightfold Path to enlightenment.

ETHICS IN ACTION:
JOURNALING AND THE THREE GATES

In the beginning, love; in the end, love; in the middle, we
have to cultivate virtues.

—SWAMI CHIDVALISANANDA

Examining each of the five precepts individually—or, for that matter, any list of ethical do's and don'ts—we can see how daunting it is to practice thinking, acting, and speaking in a wise and appropriate manner. We have to pay close attention to our own lives as well as the world around us to identify the specific challenges and determine what we can realistically do to meet them. We also have to accept that the process will be messy and, at times, even painful. We're bound to confront things we'd rather not face, to feel obliged to do things we'd rather not do, and to experience many setbacks, discouragements, and mistakes along the way. Meanwhile, as we develop more character and integrity, we realize a growth in consciousness, spirit, reverence for all forms of life, and communion with others that is wondrously revitalizing and unobtainable in any other way. This is where self-knowledge, wisdom, and discernment come into play. The better we know and understand ourselves, the better we understand and relate to others. Buddha taught that ignorance is the root of all evils.

To engineer this shift in attentiveness, I highly recommend keeping a journal of your daily thoughts, feelings, words, and behaviors as they relate to the ethical considerations involved in the five precepts. This endeavor can be so absorbing, revealing, and rewarding that you may want to focus solely on it for a month rather than immersing yourself in the other activities suggested in this book. You could also focus on one precept at a time, such as "do not kill," for a day, a week, or a month and see how that goes.

In the mid-1970s, my Tibetan guru suggested that I practice one paramita at a time to see how it was and what in particular would come up for me; he also recommended that I record in a journal several times a day all my difficulties, successes, temptations, doubts, insights and discoveries, hesitations, desires, transgressions, and other issues. In my practice as well as in my journal, I was advised to consider all three levels of my being—outer, inner, and secret. How did my day-to-day experiences associated with this paramita resonate on each level?

When I concentrated on the ethics paramita for a month, I diligently pondered whether my daily words, deeds, intentions, thoughts, and feelings were helpful or harmful, skillful or unskillful, virtuous or not. I was astounded by what I learned about myself. I realized that in each and every moment, my mindstream and feeling world was a mixed bag of all kinds of pollutants and obscurations, fears and prejudices, habitual responses and knee-jerk reactions, selective memory, personal storytelling, sharp desires and semiconscious confused longings. Although I'd been dimly aware of some of this stuff before, it all became much more obvious and more identifiable to me. As a result, it became much easier for me to do something about it. I found out that I was much more capable than I'd imagined of redirecting my life on all three levels of being to become healthier, more productive, and more Bodhisattvic. This completely boosted my spiritual energy and interest.

I find in my journal from that time the following words of Shantideva:

> Whenever I wish to move or speak,
> First I shall examine my state of mind
> And then act firmly in a suitable manner.
> Whenever my mind becomes attached or angry,
> I shall not react in kind;
> I shall remain unmoved, like a tree.

Along with these words I found my own note to myself: "Don't numb out and suppress feelings, but remember this verse whenever you feel angry or upset, and instantly try to examine the feelings and states of mind rather than blindly reacting to outer people and circumstances. Then you will be master rather than victim of conditions and circumstances."

Just as I was urged to consider all three levels of my being in both my practice and my journal, I encourage you to do the same. Remember that outer sila is virtuous behavior, nonviolence, helpfulness, honesty, and integrity. Internal sila, which has more to do with character, involves being straightforward, unselfish, tolerant, humble, unbiased, authentic, and true to your highest self and deepest principles, regardless of what others might say or think. Secret sila means intuiting your innate purity of heart, your perfect and complete Buddha nature, the basic goodness at the core of your luminous being.

In addition to keeping and using a journal, I suggest incorporating the Four Gates practice into your daily life. Whenever you're troubled by a particularly bothersome train of thought or feeling, or when you're tempted to say or do something that you're not sure about, put yourself through these four questions, or "gates," which will help make you a real team player:

1. Is it truthful?
2. Is it helpful?
3. Is it kind?
4. What is my motivation and genuine intention here?

If you can say yes to each question—if you can pass through each gate—then go ahead. If not, stop and go no further. You do have the ability to control whether you stop or go, even in the deepest recesses of your mind. Please don't think you are powerless to do whatever is good for yourself as well as whatever is good for others. Remember: the two acts are one and the same.

THREE

THE TRANSFORMATIVE PRACTICE OF PATIENT FORBEARANCE

May I perfect the noble virtue of patience,
which can face naked reality,
forgive, accept adversity, and turn it into an ally.

We live in an era that's in love with all things new, swift, convenient, and hassle-free. As we run each day to keep up with the ever-accelerating pace of life, we rely more and more on fast food, quick service, instant messaging, high-speed Internet access, same-day delivery, and snap judgments. If we're told we have to wait for something, we're immediately bummed out. If the correct answer to a question doesn't pop up in our minds right away, we get upset. If anyone or anything gets in our way, we're automatically angry. If a commercial appears on the TV screen while we're watching a movie, we impatiently switch channels.

Even when we do realize how much we suffer from the rush of things, we often turn toward some sort of speedy, short-term solution. Searching for peace of mind, we try to buy time by multitasking our chores, streamlining our schedules, and bringing products into our lives that rev up the way we cook, clean, exercise, learn, meet people, travel, or make a living. Ironically, the result is often an increase in our craving for painless speed and a decrease in our ability to tolerate the inevitable challenges of life and to handle situations that call for calm reflection, restraint, and long-term bigger-picture thinking—in other words, situations that slow us down or require more nuanced consideration.

My first lesson in patience came from my baseball team manager in fourth grade, Mr. Ittic, who taught me to be more patient and not to swing at every pitch. "But, Coach," exclaimed my nine-year-old, lefty-slugger self, "I'm here to hit the ball!" Mr. Ittic patiently explained, "Wait them out till you get what you want to hit, and then hit the ball." Following his advice, I became a Little League All-Star with a lifetime average of .400.

The true solution to our personal and cultural "speed trap" lies in practicing the third paramita, patience (in Sanskrit, *kshanti*). It sounds like such an old-fashioned virtue, doesn't it? Don't we tend to think of truly patient people as saints? These impressions in themselves are strong symptoms that we're living too fast for our own good. We've lost touch with what patience really means, and how vital it is to everyone's well-being. Patience means steadfastness, peacefulness, tolerance, and stoicism in the face of harm and anger. Patience isn't some otherworldly ideal, but a here-and-now necessity, especially as we confront escalating global problems involving terror, anger, intolerance, and inequality.

The best teaching tale I know on this issue is a classic Tibetan Buddhist story about Patrul Rinpoche, the beloved vagabond lama who spent his life wandering throughout Tibet and dispensing his wisdom. Patrul was deeply committed to keeping people focused on the practical essence of spirituality rather than on its formal observance. He never hesitated to deflate pomposity or pretense. One time he heard about a renowned hermit who had lived for a long time in seclusion. He decided to visit this hermit. When he arrived unannounced at the hermit's cave, he peered inside with a big grin on his heavily lined face.

"Who are you?" asked the hermit. "Where have you come from, and where are you going?"

Patrul replied, "I come from behind my back and am going in the direction I'm facing."

The hermit frowned, wanting a more precise answer. "Where were you born?" he asked.

"In this world," Patrul answered.

The hermit was even more annoyed. "What is your name?" he demanded.

"Yogi Beyond Action," said Patrul. "And now let me ask you something: why do you live in such a remote place?"

The hermit answered with pride, "I have been here for twenty years, meditating on the transcendental perfection of patience."

"That's a good one!" The mischievous Patrul laughed out loud. Then, leaning forward as if to confide something, he whispered, "Perfect patience? A couple of old frauds like us could never manage anything like that!"

The hermit, flushed with anger, rose from his seat and shouted, "Who do you think you are, disturbing my retreat like this? What made you come here? Why couldn't you leave a humble person like me to meditate in peace?"

"And now, my dear friend," said Patrul calmly, "where is your perfect patience?"

In many ways I sympathize with the frustrated hermit in this story. Sometimes I feel exactly like him. Yesterday, for instance, I was working at my writing desk. As I was struggling to resolve my thoughts and sort out some notes, I was repeatedly startled by interruptions that made it difficult, if not impossible, to concentrate. Some of them came from the outside world. A phone rang. A huge truck rumbled by. A beautiful red cardinal landed on the windowsill. The doorbell rang, and it was the FedEx man. Other distractions were internal. I suddenly remembered an appointment the next day. I started feeling thirsty. An image left over from a dream the night before kept coming back to pester me. Finally, upset with my lack of progress, I put off working until later. *What the heck,* I said to myself, *I'm a free man. I'm outa here!*

Both of these stories illustrate the difficulty we face when we try to practice perfect patience in an imperfect environment. It almost seems as though this roiling world is conspiring to test our patience at every turn. In fact, it is. With this in mind, we would be wise to look on our imperfect environment as a teacher rather than an antagonist. It constantly shows us that we need to be patient on an ongoing basis, not just every now and then, if we're going to realize true inner peace, happiness, and fulfillment. As Marpa the Translator, Milarepa's guru, said,

"The greatest, most supreme paramita is patience. Patient forbearance is the hardest paramita for me."

Probably each of us is already very patient in some ways but amazingly impatient in others. For example, I have a friend who prides herself on being incredibly gracious and tolerant with demanding customers at the dress shop where she works. She admits, however, that when she gets home, she's not nearly as patient with her own husband and children when they get on her nerves. Meanwhile, she notes that her husband is extremely patient with their children but has great difficulty waiting in line. Because of this problem, he even refuses to go to the supermarket. She wonders why it's so hard for people to be patient in one context but not in another. Do we each have patience visas that, like cell phones, work only in certain places?

Don't we all share this question? The secret to moving beyond this limit and expanding our capacity for patience is first to demystify what patience means in our minds. Being patient is not simply putting up with something or someone that's boring, annoying, or downright infuriating. Nor is it strictly a matter of learning to control our restlessness, irritation, disagreement, or rage. These forms of emotional self-management are certainly part of it, but the full practice of patience is much broader in scope. Instead of being a way to react only when we encounter an unwanted situation, patience is a way to act at all times, so that negative situations occur less frequently and less destructively. Rather than being simply a passive way out of a bad situation, it's a proactive way of being an agent for harmony and mutual understanding in the world.

The Dalai Lama recently told us a story about an old lama who escaped not long ago from Tibet and eventually made his way to Dharamsala, India, to meet His Holiness. After the old lama spoke about his long decade and a half of incarceration and torture for being a religious cleric in a Communist state, the Dalai Lama cried. Then he asked, "What was your greatest fear during this time?"

The old lama replied, "My greatest fear was that I would lose my Bodhicitta and Bodhisattva Vow through losing my patience and compassion for my captors." This he feared above everything else, and that fear gave him strength and perseverance. The Dalai Lama concluded, "He is truly a Bodhisattva."

The sixth chapter of Shantideva's masterwork, *Bodhisattvacarya-avatara* (*The Way of the Bodhisattva*), is devoted to patience, and it begins very bluntly with these two bold statements: "There is no evil so great as anger. There is no religious practice so powerful and arduous as patience." Why is anger the primary evil? Because anger represents the most terrible and destructive manifestation of self-driven desire, and leads to hatred, cruelty, and violence. We're never more separate from others—and therefore never more selfish, greedy, and deluded—than when we're afraid of and angry with them. And we're never more estranged from the true core of our being, our peaceful Buddha nature, than when we're angry with ourselves.

Why is patience considered the most powerful and difficult spiritual practice? Because patience is the antidote to anger. Just as the first paramita, generosity, opens up our hearts to practice all the other transcendental virtues, so patience sets the right rhythm and tone for that action. When we're patient, we don't dance to the jerky, ever-changing beat of worldly circumstances. Instead, we think, speak, and act in a measured way, as if to a steady internal heartbeat—a tempo that comes from our deepest, most secret being. When we achieve this degree of patience, how can we get carried away by anger, much less rattled by petty irritations? We may feel anger, and know it, certainly; then we can consciously choose how exactly to relate and respond to it.

Buddhism is often characterized as a religion of peace, serenity, and patience. The Sanskrit word for peace is *shanti,* which is closely related to *kshanti* (patience). Practitioners challenge themselves to work patiently through countless lifetimes toward achieving the bliss and nirvanic peace of enlightenment. In most paintings and statues of the Buddha, patient calmness radiates from his benign, half-smiling face. Meditative mindfulness itself, the central practice of Buddhism, strikes many as nothing but the practice of patience in its purest form. As we'll see in chapter 5, when we examine meditation as a paramita, it involves much more than simple patience, but patient acceptance is definitely a major aspect of it.

Of course, patience as a paramita is, by definition, intimately interrelated with all the other paramitas. When we're patient with someone, we're clearly giving him or her the benefit of our open-minded generosity, the first paramita. Patience is also essential in disciplining ourselves to live according to the second paramita, ethics; doesn't it take tolerance to practice lovingkindness and, for example, to accept the fact that even your critics, competitors, and adversaries have their story too? As a key component in courage, patient endurance and perseverance are likewise indispensable qualities in exercising the fourth paramita, heroic effort. In fact, as we review every one of the other paramitas, we realize anew each time the power, beauty, and panacean value of cultivating patience in our lives and expressing it in the world around us.

How does unconditional patience lead directly to lovingkindness, compassion, forgiveness, equanimity, and acceptance of reality as it is rather than as we'd like it to be? I am reminded of a story told by Richard D. Parsons, CEO of Time Warner (originally, like me, from Brooklyn).

> People tend to learn more from mistakes than from anything else. My parents gave the New York City school system permission to spank me. But there was never any question in my mind that I was loved, no matter how outrageous I got. I was seven when I burned my house down. I was playing with matches. We had to live in my grandmother's house for three or four months. I remember my father ran in to save my younger brother and sister. She got burned a bit and had to go to the hospital, but she was okay. It was so egregious, but what is a parent to do? They said, "Everybody is alive." They said, "Don't do that again."

PATIENCE IN OUR OUTER BEING

Buddhism teaches three kinds of patience. In our endeavor to understand more clearly what patience means, it helps to look at the different but connected and mutually supportive ways in which it unfolds in our outer, inner, and secret levels of being. Let's begin with the outer level—how we interact with the outside world in our thoughts, words, and deeds. In Buddhism, the practice of patience has three aspects that are especially important for a Bodhisattva to consider on this frontline level where we "hang in there," not allowing ourselves to be overwhelmed with impatience, anger, or self-righteousness. These three aspects of patience are gentle forbearance, endurance of hardship, and acceptance of naked truth.

Gentle forbearance, the first aspect, comes into play in that instant when we feel ourselves becoming impatient. It then lasts as long as it takes to calm ourselves down, so that we can function more effectively. We may be on the verge of screaming at a child who is throwing a tantrum. Perhaps we're just about to make a cutting remark to a colleague who is giving us trouble. Maybe we're seething with violent energy directed toward someone who has horribly offended us. Whatever the trigger, we need to recognize it as a danger signal, warning us that if we simply let our frustration, anger, or outrage run its course, we may wind up hurting not only the actual target of our animosity but also ourselves and a host of other people we may not even know about. We must learn to recognize and feel the difficult emotions if we are to have any real hope of intelligently dealing with them.

It's at the very moment of the upsurge of, for example, anger that we need to remind ourselves to do no harm. During the initial stages of practicing forbearance, we may have to force ourselves consciously to take a deep breath, count to ten, or smile through our teeth. Eventually, however, we see more deeply into the helpful effects of this practice on others and on ourselves as it creates within us a lasting peace of mind and serenity that leads to greater insight and more skillful management of various matters. These positive results far outweigh the possible instant gratification that may come from merely venting our anger when it first arises. When we learn to appreciate this truth, the habit of forbearance eventually turns into our natural, unassisted response. We're no longer at the mercy of automatic prickliness and uncontrolled reactivity when things don't go our way. We no longer require total agreement from the outside world in order to experience harmony and even inner tranquillity. Leonardo da Vinci said, "Patience serves as a protection against wrongs as clothes do against cold. For if you put on more clothes as the cold increases, it will have no power to hurt you. So in like manner you must grow in patience when you meet with great wrongs, and they will be powerless to vex you."

I seem to have become very patient in my old age, if I may say so myself. I attribute it to a couple of things. First, I've learned that the bigger picture trumps the momentary accomplishments and tribulations and even the epiphanies, many of which turn out to be just scenery along the way. It doesn't matter so much what happens at any given moment. Far more important is overall sincerity and ongoing, long-term spiritual development. I have simply learned to do my best and not to be overly invested in outcomes; to trust, to surrender, to let go and let be.

Once the Buddha was staying in Kosambi, a town in northern India, to teach. A wicked man living there hated the Buddha, so he spread lies about him that turned many other residents against the celebrated wise man. The Buddha's disciples were finding it increasingly hard to get food when they went begging, and they often suffered taunts and blows from disaffected strangers who saw them approaching. Finally, the disciple Ananda said to the Buddha, "We'd better leave this city. There are other places that are more likely to be hospitable."

The Buddha said, "What if we go to another city, and it's just as difficult for us? What shall we do in that case?"

"If that happens, we'll move on to another city."

"No, Ananda," replied the Buddha. "It is better for us to stay here and forbear than to respond in a negative or impatient way. Eventually, the bad treatment will stop; then we can proceed to another city. This world is filled with gain and loss, falsehood and honesty, reward and punishment, praise and criticism, pleasure and pain. The enlightened person is not ruled by such external things."

When I think of gentle forbearance, I think of the life of Peace Master Shantideva himself, who wrote so eloquently about these qualities. For years he quietly tolerated all the barbed criticism, slander, and gossip aimed at him by the monks of Nalanda Monastery, where he lived. They didn't understand why he spent so much time in his cell instead of with them in active community life. They nicknamed him "Bushuku," meaning wastrel or vagabond (literally, "old rice bag"). Meanwhile, Shantideva, despite his awareness of being personally attacked, always treated his fellow monks kindly and never wavered in his efforts to become enlightened and compose the glorious *Way of the Bodhisattva,* which he left as a departing gift—much to their amazement.

Taking a more contemporary perspective, I also think of Jackie Robinson, the first black player in American baseball's major leagues. Growing up during the 1930s and early 1940s, he patiently withheld his anger during the many times he was verbally assaulted with racial slurs, physically abused, or denied admittance to restaurants or hotels. While he was in the U.S. Army during World War II, he was barred from playing on its baseball team and told to play on the black team—which didn't exist. When he launched a formal protest against a reprimand he'd received for sitting next to a white woman on a military bus, Jackie was court-martialed. He was acquitted only after officials discovered that the woman in question was in fact a light-skinned black woman. Still he refused to let his temper get the better of him, and in so doing, he helped ensure that people would eventually respect not just him but his cause as well.

After Robinson was chosen by Branch Rickey to play for the Brooklyn Dodgers, breaking the racial barrier, he continued to be subjected to abuse, which he chose to bear patiently. At one game, Philadelphia Phillies players sitting in the dugout aimed their bats at him like rifles. At many games, people in the stands yelled racial epithets. He also put up with far more than the average number of fastballs coming at his head and spiked shoes "accidentally" injuring his flesh. He even received death threats, both mailed and hand delivered. Jackie even retaliated.

Jackie Robinson, along with his legendary teammates Duke Snyder and Pee Wee Reese, played in the first major league baseball game I ever attended, when I was five years old. I was taken to that game at Brooklyn's Ebbets Field by my Grandpa Rothouse, my partner in listening to the Dodgers on the radio. When the Dodgers finally won the World Series in 1956, it was as if the entire borough of Brooklyn was on its way to heaven. Robinson was a big part of the Dodgers' success in those days, as a Rookie of the Year, an All-Star, and an MVP, but it was his role as a pioneer in opening American sports to black people that earned him the highest regard. He certainly helped me, a Brooklyn boy descended from Eastern European Jewish immigrants, to appreciate that victims of prejudice, hatred, and injustice have many different kinds of faces. For this reason, he's one of my personal Bodhisattvas.

The second aspect of patience, endurance of hardship (which includes voluntarily bearing the difficulties of spiritual life), is an extension of the first aspect, gentle forbearance. As John Quincy Adams said, "One moment of patience may ward off great disaster. One moment of impatience may ruin a whole life." Beyond experiencing occasional irritations and injuries, we are each called upon to endure certain long-term situations in our lives, whether it's dealing with ongoing poverty, a chronic illness, a difficult family member, the much-delayed gratification of a cherished goal, or something else entirely. The First Noble Truth (taught by the enlightened Buddha in his famous original Four Noble Truths), "life is difficult and full of suffering," means that unenlightened life itself is a condition of constant impermanence and repeated dissatisfaction, so you could say that simply to live is to endure.

Nevertheless, to endure hardship *with patience* is not to be simply submissive to the hardship but to work with it constructively, fearlessly approaching it with wisdom and compassion rather than retreating into our shells so that we can numb ourselves to it as much as possible. In many respects, the passive denial of hardship is just as destructive as constantly raging against it or seeking to escape it altogether by abandoning our responsibilities to ourselves or others. When we simply hunker down like an ostrich with its head in the sand and wait for hardship to go away without doing whatever we can to turn it around, it's as if we're already dead. Above all, enduring hardship means going through it, not waiting it out. We can learn to find the light even amidst the darkness. Thus Shantideva teaches us, "The enemy is our greatest teacher. Through difficulties pride is dissolved, karma is purified, inner strength is furthered, and equanimity attained." Hardships and obstacles become our friend.

A classic Hindu tale, "The Tiger's Whisker," conveys exactly what I mean. Once a man came back home from war with an illness no doctor could cure. His wife tried everything to make him healthy or at least comfortable, but nothing worked. He refused his favorite foods. He wouldn't speak to her. He wouldn't even let her touch him. Finally, she visited a holy man who had a reputation for concocting magic healing medicines. After listening to the woman describe her husband's symptoms, the holy man sadly shook his head. "I'm afraid there's nothing I can do," he said. "The only thing that could possibly help would be the whisker from a tiger's jowl, and I have no such thing."

The woman left in despair, but as she kept on thinking about what the holy man had said, an idea occurred to her. After asking everyone she knew, she found out that a wild tiger lived in a cave in the forest. She bought some meat and walked to that cave. Getting as close as she dared, she put the meat on the ground and then ran off, but not so far that she couldn't still see the meat. Sure enough, the tiger appeared, devoured the meat, and, satisfied, curled up and took a nap. Every day for the next six months she brought meat to the cave at exactly the same time, only each day, struggling against her fear, she set the meat a little closer to the cave, and she herself moved a little closer to the meat. Finally, at the end of that time, she was sitting right next to the meat while the tiger ate it. Then the tiger, accustomed to the woman, curled up and took a nap beside her. Very carefully, the woman leaned over and snipped off a whisker from the tiger's jowl.

With great excitement, the woman immediately ran to visit the holy man and said to him, "Look! I have a tiger's whisker! You said it would help cure my husband!" She gave him the treasured whisker, and he quickly threw it into the fire.

"What have you done!" the woman cried in horror and disbelief.

"My dear woman," said the hermit, "a wife who has tamed a tiger has no need for magic medicine to tame her husband." Similarly, anyone who can take on the Bodhisattva's universal mission of awakening and enlightening all beings need not fear mere everyday difficulties and disappointments.

This woman brings to my mind Julia Butterfly Hill, a lovely contemporary Bodhisattva who patiently put herself through an incredible ordeal in order to help save the environment. On December 10, 1997, Hill, age twenty-three, climbed high into a thousand-year-old redwood tree in the Headwaters Forest of Northern California. There she set up house on a little platform barely big enough for her to lie down. Her aspiration was to prevent a logging crew from cutting down the forest because it would be impossible to do that without killing her.

For two years, Hill lived up in that tree without ever coming down. Aided by activists who sent up food, water, and other supplies, she persevered through some of the biggest storms of the decade, not to mention a great deal of cold, deprivation, fear, and harassment from loggers. Meanwhile, her campaign attracted the attention of celebrities, journalists, and politicians, many of whom either visited her or talked with her on her mobile phone. Among these people were harsh critics, avid supporters, and those who assumed she was simply a freak. She discovered that one of her biggest challenges was learning how to interact skillfully with each kind of individual in order to further her efforts to save the tree.

Eventually, on December 18, 1999, Julia climbed down the tree she had affectionately named "Luna." She had finally managed to strike a deal with Pacific Lumber/Maxxam Corporation to spare not only Luna but also every tree in a three-acre buffer zone around Luna. Since then, she has created the Circle of Life Foundation, which, in her words, is meant to "inspire,

support, and network individuals, organizations, and communities so together we can create environmental and social solutions that are rooted
deeply in love and respect for the interconnectedness of life."

Probably the hardest spiritual practice I ever endured was completing the *Vajrayana ngöndro,* or fundamental practices, which I undertook
for the first time in Darjeeling in the early 1970s, with the support of
Kalu Rinpoche and which took several years to complete. These practices
involved learning and doing over 100,000 full-body prostrations while
reciting the refuge and Bodhisattva prayers while contemplating their attendant visualizations; chanting over 100,000 purification mantras; and
performing over 100,000 mandala offerings as well as several hundred
thousand *guru yoga* mantras, prayers, and practices. I had to stop and start
this endeavor again and again as I was compelled to move from Darjeeling
to Bodh Gaya in India and then to Nepal and then back again to Darjeeling because of inclement weather, passport complications, visa exten-
sions, and my own fluctuating youthful inspiration. And all of this effort
occurred while I was living a basically solitary, mendicant life in hovels,
Tibetan refugee camps, cheap hotels, caves, ashrams, and monasteries.
Needless to say, this lifestyle taxed my patience and energy to the utmost,
but it also proved to me that the more you put into a spiritual practice, the
more you get out of it. Patience furthers.

The third aspect of patience, acceptance of truth, involves the ability
to endure "not-knowing" and objectively to face naked reality, whether or
not it fits our expectations, our desires, or even our sense of justice. This
naked reality is what we call *sunyata* (or emptiness) in Buddhism, signifying the emptiness or hollowness of all our conceptual imputations su-
perimposed upon reality. This can sometimes be difficult to face. It does
us no good, for example, to look upon our human enemies as demons or
forces of evil rather than as human beings. In fact, it's not even helpful to
look on them as enemies. Instead, we need to look beyond the personal
to the universal, asking, "What *is* the complete situation here? How does
it look from each person's point of view? Given the reality at hand, and
all the people involved, and the world around us all, what work needs to
be done to bring a peace that everyone can share?"

St. Augustine of Hippo said, "Patience is the companion of wisdom."
Acceptance of the truth or bare, unadorned reality doesn't mean allow-

ing injustice to go unchallenged or doing nothing to overcome adversity. It means taking care at all times, even as we work toward change, to see things clearly and with acceptance rather than through the squinty-eyed stance of self-righteousness, malice, resentment, fury, fear, prejudice, or even wishful thinking. When we open up our eyes, minds, and hearts to being as fair and impartial as possible, we put ourselves in the best possible position to do objectively the right thing. Once the sculptor Auguste Rodin was asked how he came up with the ideas for his works. He replied, "Sometimes I have a subject in mind, sometimes I don't. In either case, my best ideas come from quieting my mind and letting the stone speak to me about all its characteristics and possibilities. It may take a long time to do this, but that is fine. Patience is also a form of action."

Often this opening up to the bigger picture beyond our own perspective means giving up whatever is strictly personal, such as winning an argument or forcing someone to apologize, in favor of striving toward what's best for everyone or everything involved in the long run. Certainly it means abandoning statements like "I can't forgive," "I refuse to listen," or, quoting Pontius Pilate, the official who wouldn't intervene to spare the Christ, "I wash my hands of the whole situation." When we say things like this, we're really not saying much at all. The only thing that a listener hears is our anger, hatred, or limitations and avoidance. It's like that joke about the self-defeating do-gooder who says, "If there's one thing I can't tolerate, it's intolerance! I hate that!"

The ancient Tibetan tale "The Mani Man" gives an illuminating, if extreme, example of accepting the truth with patience rather than rushing to impose upon it a particular judgment, interpretation, or attachment. The word *mani* refers to a prayer (or mani) wheel that the hero of the story constantly turns in his hand. It's a traditional practice that still exists among Tibetan Buddhists. Inside the wheel are slips of paper covered with prayers; by stirring them around, the practitioner is, as it were, "reciting" them for the edification of all.

The practitioner-hero of this tale is an old man who lives with his son and one horse on a tiny plot of land. One morning the mani man wakes up and his horse is gone. His neighbors wail with grief on his behalf, but he keeps turning his wheel and saying, "We must give thanks for everything. Who can tell what is good or bad?"

The next week the horse comes back with two wild mustangs tagging along behind him. "What luck!" his neighbors cry, eager to help the old man celebrate.

He replies, "I am grateful, but who knows what the world will bring? We must simply wait and see."

Two days later, while training one of the wild mustangs, the old man's son falls and breaks a leg. The old man's neighbors rush over crying to console him, but the old man, still turning his prayer wheel, says, "The mere fact of my son's life continues to be a blessing to me, and I am grateful. What has happened cannot be called good or bad."

The following day a military recruiter appears to take the old man's son off to war. Because the old man's son is bedridden, he can't go, so the recruiter has to leave without him. The old man's neighbors, many of whom have sons in the army facing death, congratulate the old man on not having to send his son to fight. The old man keeps spinning his wheel and says, "Nothing is known for certain. We shall see."

This tale no doubt has longer versions: it's the classic Tibetan version of the good old shaggy-dog story. In any version, however, it illustrates a never-ending truth about life. We must accept the givens of a particular situation without projecting upon them too quickly or too clumsily our own passion-driven, reactive list of highly subjective likes and dislikes, goods and bads, rights and wrongs, victories and defeats.

In modern times, the Dalai Lama has offered an incredible example of this kind of patience and acceptance. Despite losing his homeland to Communist China in a brutal military takeover in the fifties, he does not advocate violent recrimination against, or hatred of, the Chinese people. He told a reporter in 1998, "As a Buddhist monk, when I pray for all sentient beings, that means a greater part of my prayer includes China, because it has the largest population." He even cites the Chinese oppressors of Tibet as being among his greatest teachers, because they have compelled him to cultivate patience, compassion, humility, and wisdom all the more diligently.

Although his attitude toward the Chinese is benevolent, the Dalai Lama is not simply lying down and doing nothing in response to what happened to him and his homeland. Quite the contrary; he's devoting all his energy toward causing a revolution. In fact, he argues for a much stronger, more dynamic revolution than we ordinarily associate with the term. In his *Ethics for a New Millennium,* he writes:

The great movements of the last hundred years and more—democracy, liberalism, socialism—have all failed to deliver the universal benefits they were supposed to provide, despite many wonderful ideas. A revolution is called for, certainly. But not a political, an economic, or even a technical revolution. We have had enough experience of these during the past century to know that a purely external approach will not suffice. What I propose is a spiritual revolution.

PATIENCE IN OUR INNER AND SECRET BEINGS

As we've just seen, patience on the outer level of our being requires practicing gentle forbearance, endurance of hardship, and acceptance of reality in our interactions with the outside world. To help ensure that these qualities develop and manifest themselves naturally, we need to cultivate a sense of balance, equanimity, and inclusiveness on the inner level of our being, the domain of our private thoughts and emotions as well as what we call our conscience. I remember my Tibetan friend Gyalwang Drukpa Rinpoche, a Mahamudra master and yogi, saying, "I enjoy and appreciate everything, as long as it's not harmful. And even the negative has to be included, accepted, known, and dealt with—not denied, ignored, or neglected outright. Everything has its own karma, its own logic, its own momentum or reason for being."

What does it mean to be sagaciously balanced on this level? What's involved in creating an inner state of equanimity and inclusiveness? The most important element is getting beyond the notion of a separate egotistic self and instead becoming one in our hearts and minds with the world around us, with all its myriad forms and dreamlike manifestations.

As human beings, we can't help but experience individual sorrows and joys throughout the innumerable twists and turns of life. We also inevitably form our own intellectual opinions and beliefs. The point is not to indulge in these emotions or thoughts to the exclusion of everything else. In addition, we must remain in reasonable control of our emotions and thoughts, rather than allowing them to control us, for the mind is a good servant but a poor master. Finally, we must always remember that we are interconnected with everyone and everything else in the universe through karma. The more we train ourselves to think and feel along these lines, the better balanced our inner life and, as a result, our outer life become.

St. Augustine of Hippo offers one of the best descriptions of inner-self patience that I've ever encountered. "That virtue of the mind which is called patience," he writes,

> is so great a gift of God, that even in Him who bestoweth the same upon us, that, whereby He waiteth for evil men that they may amend, is set forth by the name of patience.... The patience of man, which is right and laudable and worthy of the name virtue, is understood to be that by which we tolerate evil things with an even mind, that we may not with a mind uneven desert good things, through which we may arrive at better. Wherefore the impatient, while they will not suffer ills, effect not a deliverance from ills, but only the suffering of heavier ills.

Let me provide a more colloquial example of the same attitude. The other day I asked Joseph, a Haitian-born cab driver I know here in Cambridge, how he defined peace of mind. He replied, "Taking everything that comes in stride.... Not letting the pressure build up in your head. Roll with the punches, man."

Tulku Thubten Rinpoche gives us an excellent Buddhist insight into what patience means on the inner level of our being. "Patience," he tells us,

> is being in the natural state of mind, being in this very moment. Then we don't have to try to be patient or react to any conditions. That is patience. Patience is also the understanding of courage. The Buddha says to understand the nature of reality, the great shunyata [emptiness or absence of separate forms], one has to have a unique patience or Dzogpachenpo [great patience]. Patience means fearless courage to understand. Egoless wisdom. This is a threatening subject, to comprehend the nature of reality, because the ego has to die. Concept has to die.

As we work to develop this ideal inner state, we draw support from the truth of our secret, innermost, peaceful Buddha nature. At this third and deepest level of our being, which is our true nature, patience exists in its purest form. Here we let go of everything selfish and place all our trust in the universe, in the fact that everything is already fine, at rest, and at peace. In the words of the ancient Chinese sage Lao Tzu:

The master sees things as they are
Without trying to control them.
She lets them go their own way
And resides at the center of the circle.

My lama friend John Makransky shared with me a true story about an individual who reflected this kind of ultimate, innermost secret patience and revealed its power to everyone around him. When Makransky was a graduate student at the University of Wisconsin, long ago, one of his teachers was the Tibetan Buddhist master Geshe Sopa (*sopa* actually means "patience" in Tibetan). One day Geshe Sopa received word from India that the Dalai Lama had accepted his invitation to come to Wisconsin and publicly offer the rare and precious Kalachakra Empowerment (Wheel of Time Initiation), which requires extensive preparations. Knowing it would be the first time that this special esoteric initiation had been given in the Western world, Geshe Sopa was determined to handle all the complexities associated with the event, even though he had no idea how he was going to do so. He had complete trust that, with the blessings of the Buddha and the auspiciousness of this opportunity, all things were possible.

For starters, he had to find or build a pristine new house where His Holiness and his entourage could stay. Afterward, the house would have to be kept as a shrine, since it had been blessed and consecrated. He also had to acquire land for the large outdoor ceremony, land that likewise would have to be preserved and maintained as a peace park and temple grounds so that others in the future could benefit from the accumulated energy of the scared ceremony. On this land, he would need to construct a partly covered pavilion, a teaching throne, and a three-dimensional Kalachakra mandala. And during the week of the ceremony he would be required to host thousands of attendees at numerous prayer services, teachings, and related events.

Geshe Sopa lived in a small house. He resolved to sell it to start raising money for the preparations. He then located a beautiful piece of parklike land for sale and set about the arduous process of trying to buy it. As the complicated negotiations dragged on, somewhat to his surprise, he had to work assiduously to satisfy building inspectors, the town zoning board, land-use permit officials, and fire and sanitation regulators. None of these difficulties would have occurred in his native Tibet, where such an event would have been welcomed with delight, total cooperation, and much assistance.

Meanwhile, Geshe Sopa had to raise a great deal of money to cover the many other related expenses, as well as recruit people to do all the skilled labor and other tasks involved. His students, for example, were thunderstruck when they realized that he expected them to construct the entire temple by hand. He needed to placate committees of citizens who were leery of having shaved-head foreigners in red robes wandering around the neighborhood. He even had to hammer out a difficult compromise with local environmentalists, who were concerned about the effect of the event on the surrounding terrain.

Through it all, Professor Patience (as he was called) remained indomitable, never once considering the idea of giving up, or doing things on a smaller scale, or even renting a place instead of buying it. In his own words, he "knew beyond all knowing" that the event had to happen in the right manner, for the benefit of peace in the world and the spiritual enlightenment of all sentient beings. Eventually, the Dalai Lama came, the event was a great success for thousands of people; today others can enjoy the site. Now a forest sanctuary, it is known as Deer Park, after the sacred grove in Sarnath, India, where the historical Buddha gave his first teaching.

STEP-BY-STEP PATIENCE

Once in the early 1970s in Darjeeling, India, I asked old Lama Thubten: "When you were escaping from Tibet, how did you ever manage to walk through the snowbound Himalayas all the way to India with no maps, compasses, weapons, tents, sleeping bags, or even food?"

"One step at a time, Surya," he said with a smile. "Just one step at a time."

I think this is a good way to describe not only how Geshe Sopa went about making preparations for the Dalai Lama's ceremony but also how each of us needs to practice the daily challenges to our patience that we experience: step-by-step, always going forward, never stopping. And managing to stand up again and keep going, even when we fall down and flounder around.

Let's look at a worldly example of a real-life situation calling out for patience. Rob is very much in love with Pamela, his girlfriend, and would like to marry her. The only thing standing in his way is Pamela's fifteen-year-old son, Tyler. Rob feels as though he never gets enough time alone with Pamela because Tyler is always around. Remembering how rambunctious he was himself as a teenager, Rob is also not sure whether he can tolerate living in the same house with an adolescent male. Tyler seems like a good kid, but Rob can't help suspecting that some of Tyler's behavior toward him is motivated by feelings of competition or even rebellion. As it is, Tyler's friends come to the house often, and they're very noisy and messy. Pamela tells Rob that Tyler will most likely be leaving home in a few more years, and she wants to cherish the little time she has left with her son under her roof. She doesn't understand why Rob can't be more patient.

Whenever we're impatient with another person in our lives—whether it's a mate, a lover, a child, a parent, a friend, a neighbor, a boss, an employee, or a colleague—I think we need to recognize that the fundamental problem is our own. It is *we* who are deciding, whether consciously or unconsciously, to react to the other person with impatience. We need to remind ourselves that we always have the choice to respond to any situation positively rather than negatively, constructively rather than destructively. We don't have to be at the mercy of our most selfish, unrefined emotions, especially such a potentially destructive one as impatience, which is, after all, a form of anger. Other people can't cause us to be impatient unless we let them do so. In other words, others don't make us impatient. We make ourselves impatient, through our expectations and demands, fixated attachments and stuckness.

If I were to counsel Rob, I would try to get him to focus on how to skillfully modify his own negative reactions, rather than on how to change Pamela's mind or Tyler's behavior. If Rob concentrates on improving the way he thinks, speaks, and behaves in regard to both Tyler and Pamela (since he exhibits impatience toward each of them), all three individuals are bound to get along in a much better fashion. In fact, this strategy is the only way Rob can effectively influence Pamela and Tyler to cooperate with him in the genuine, heartfelt manner that he wants. It's clear from just this short case description that a happy, healthy, loving marriage with Pamela will have to include developing a harmonious relationship with her son so that all three can live together peacefully, whether or not Tyler is sharing their home.

First, I would ask Rob to accept the premise that he has to take at least one step forward in being more patient with Tyler and Pamela as individuals. This step is for his own good as well as everyone else's. Impatience is his problem, and acting out of this impatience will get him nowhere.

Then I would ask him to think for a few minutes about each of the people who are going to be the recipients of his patience. I would advise him to ask himself the following questions: "Who is this person?" "How can I identify with him or her?" "Why is he or she deserving of my patience?" With Tyler in mind, for example, Rob's answers to each question, respectively, could be as simple as: "He is my girlfriend's son," "We both love Pamela, and she loves both of us," and, "I love Pamela, and she loves him." Of course, Rob's answers could also be more detailed, which would be even better. He might help himself appreciate, for example, that Tyler is a gifted artist, or that Tyler shares his own interest in sports cars, or that for many years Tyler hasn't had the benefit of an older man's example and guidance. It is always useful to be able to empathize with others, trying to feel what they feel and see things through their eyes.

Finally, I would suggest that Rob decide on one specific way in which he could demonstrate active patience with the other person. Continuing with Tyler as the recipient of his patience, Rob might choose to initiate a conversation with Tyler about his art or about sports cars. If Rob is especially ambitious about improving his relationship with Tyler, he might think of a few other ways in which he could change his own thoughts, words, or deeds so that they are less determined by impatience and more motivated toward exercising wise and compassionate patience. The important thing, however, is for Rob to come up with actual steps he can take, rather than relying on a vague and general plan that's too imprecise to work well.

Rob also needs to be prepared for the possibility that his steps toward patience and forbearance may falter. For example, Tyler might reject Rob's efforts to start a conversation, or he might respond sullenly. Facing such possible outcomes, Rob needs to remain aware that the whole purpose of the activity is for Rob himself to cultivate patience with *whatever* response he gets, not for Tyler to do anything in particular. Similarly, Rob needs to be patient with himself. If, for example, he feels that he passed up an opportunity to talk with Tyler or actually botched a conversation, he needs to forgive himself, objectively accept things as they are, and try again.

Alternatively, Rob may find that a step he has taken works better than he anticipated. For example, a conversation with Tyler may create an opening for Rob to address more directly, but still tactfully, some of the complex issues clouding their relationship. Perhaps Rob will use the occasion to talk with I-statements about his own feelings and difficulties, revealing some of his own personal likes and dislikes in a casual way that doesn't bring up anything Tyler did or didn't do, just so that Tyler is more aware of these things. Rob may also gain information about Tyler that makes him more eager and equipped to develop a better relationship with the teenager.

Now I recommend that you try this same "step-by-step patience" activity with someone in your own life who triggers your impatience. Here again are the directions:

1. *Accept* it as a given that your impatience is the problem and that you need to take at least one step toward being more patient.

2. *Ask:* "Who is this person? How can I identify with him or her? Why is he or she deserving of my patience?"

3. *Decide on*—and commit to—at least one specific step you can take toward this person to demonstrate your active patience.

THE SACRED PAUSE AND THE SIX STEPS TO ANGER MANAGEMENT

Patience means not retaliating with anger for anger, or harm for harm, and voluntarily bearing up under difficulties in order to progress on the path of spiritual awakening. How do we actually do this? How do we slow down our conditioned, knee-jerk reactions while speeding up and sharpening our conscious, mindful, moment-to-moment awareness? How do we broaden the gap between stimulus and response so that we have time to give the situation a proper amount of consideration? This takes clarity, resolve, meditation, and practice.

I call this gap the Sacred Pause, because it is the only possible source of peace and harmony in our interactions with people or events. By consciously minding and utilizing the Sacred Pause, we can master ourselves and assert leverage over our clumsy, semiconscious, often unwarranted conditioned reactions.

Begin the process by taking a deep breath, smiling, and relaxing. Much of the accumulated pressure and tension may begin to dissipate right away, thus providing more space and clarity for mindful work. Breathe, smile, relax, and center yourself.

Then apply what I call the Six Steps to Anger Management, which also could be called steps to mindfulness, freedom, and authentic responsiveness. Collectively, they are like cool, fresh breaths of mindful awareness that can help you let go of negativity and keep you from falling into regrettable outcomes. To remember these steps, think of them as the Six R's:

1. *Recognizing:* Noticing with objective equanimity a familiar stimulus—like harsh words—that pushes a hot button for you, triggering an unskillful retaliatory response.

2. *Recollecting:* Remembering the disadvantages of returning anger with anger, negative with negative, and the advantages of practicing patience, forbearance, tolerance, and acceptance.

3. *Refraining by restraining and reframing:* Seeing things from alternative points of view, including that of your antagonist (if the situation involves a button-pushing person); cultivating compassion; acknowledging the law of karma (what goes around comes around); and considering the situation an opportunity to develop patience or the person a teacher who can help you do this.

4. *Relinquishing:* Letting go of habitual reactivity and impulsive urges in favor of more consciously chosen and intelligent courses of action.

5. *Reconditioning:* Going back over what you have done and learned so far—the entire dynamic—to help you

substitute a healthier response process for your old knee-jerk conditioning. Repetition is crucial.

6. *Responding:* Addressing the person or situation patiently, appropriately, intelligently, and proactively (rather than reactively). Let spiritual intelligence be your guide.

Applying the Six Steps of Anger Management is an adult version of kindergarten's counting to ten in order to give yourself time to think before you act. Keep in mind that it is not other people or external circumstances that determine our karma, our character, our experience, and our destiny. It is how we relate to these other people and circumstances that makes all the difference. It is not what happens to us but what we make of it that makes all the difference; this is the secret of autonomy and spiritual self-mastery.

The gift of patience is truly the gift of yourself, but not in any way that diminishes you, the giver. Instead, you share your strength with someone and become stronger yourself in the process. Please keep in mind these wise words on patience from the Dalai Lama:

When we talk about patience or tolerance, we should understand that there are many degrees, starting from a simple tolerance, such as being able to bear a certain amount of heat and cold, progressing toward the highest level of patience, which is the type of patience and tolerance found in the great practitioners, the Bodhisattvas. One should not see tolerance of patience as a sign of weakness, but rather as a sign of strength coming from a deep ability to remain steadfast and firm. We find that even in being able to tolerate a certain degree of physical hardship, like a hot or cold climate, out attitude makes a big difference.

During strenuous extended retreats, my mentor Tulku Pema Wangyal Rinpoche always used to say so sweetly and at the same time implacably, "You can get used to anything." I often hear his voice in my head whenever I feel discouraged and want to complain. You can get used to anything. That is the secret of kshanti, peace paramita. Here is an ancient Chinese proverb to help you recall it:

Grant yourself a moment of peace, and you will understand
how foolishly you have scurried about.
Learn to be silent, and you will notice that
you have talked too much.
Be kind, and you will realize
that your judgment of others was too severe.
Hasten slowly,
and you will soon arrive.

FOUR

THE POWER OF HEROIC EFFORT

*May I perfect the noble virtue of enthusiastic effort
and fearless perseverance, which selflessly strives
for the ultimate benefit of all.*

A young American journalist moved to Israel and rented an apartment that had a view of Jerusalem's famed Wailing Wall. Every morning before leaving for work, she looked out her window at the sacred wall and saw an elderly man standing there wrapped in his prayer shawl and praying with great zeal. Every noontime she returned home for lunch and saw the same man there, intently praying. Every evening she came home after work, and there the same man stood, rapt in prayer.

After several months of noticing this fervent soul, the young woman went outside and waited for him to pause in his prayers. When he did, she introduced herself and asked him, "How long have you been praying like this, every day, and what is it you pray for so earnestly?"

The man told her, "I have come to this spot every day for more than twenty-five years. In the morning, I pray for world peace, and then for the brotherhood of man. I go home briefly for a cup of tea, and then I come back and spend the rest of the day praying that there will be no more illness, disease, hunger, or suffering in the world."

The young woman was astonished at his answer. She asked, "How do you feel, after coming here for twenty-five years and praying for these things?"

The elderly man looked at her with profoundly sad eyes and said, "As if I'm talking to a wall."

Can you identify with this elderly man? When you think about your own prayers and spiritual practice, your own attempts to speak up for what your heart tells you is right—your own social activism perhaps—do you sometimes feel as though you are talking to a wall?

Many of us have deep pockets of spiritual resolve, and we dedicate ourselves to act accordingly, even though we don't always get an immediate payback or, for that matter, any discernible payback at all. Heroic effort, the fourth paramita, refers to maintaining a continuity of practice without expecting such rewards. Instead, we exercise our willpower and persistence toward the higher good and never give up even when we have to battle despair or discouragement in our own minds. There is actually another version of the last line of this prayer story, where the end is a little different. The old man says, "Just imagine how much worse it could have been without these prayers."

On a personal level, it can be spiritually distressing to turn on the television at night and face the amount of havoc and misery, so much of it unnecessary, in the world today. It's especially upsetting when we consider all the good-hearted souls and well-meaning efforts that are regularly ignored and even trampled on. I think of the Dalai Lama's heroic efforts for peace and human rights. How discouraging it must sometimes be for him and for all the dedicated peacemakers whose praiseworthy endeavors seem to go unheeded, while war and violence continue raging around the globe. Yet they keep on keeping on, and for the most part they radiate peace and even joy as they do so. Admirable, remarkable—inspirational.

How can we better navigate those days when the morning finds us disheartened by all the suffering around us and yearning just to roll over in bed, to stay in our familiar rut, warm, cozy, and oblivious? How can we restore our determination and excitement about living a good life and following our joy-path, whatever may happen? That's when we have to reach deep within ourselves and reconnect with our highest purpose and motivation. Fyodor Dostoyevsky, the wonderful Russian novelist, wrote,

"A new philosophy, a new way of life is not given for nothing. It has to be paid dearly for and is only acquired with much patience and great effort."

Yogis have a special, energizing Wake Up practice designed to help us through exactly this kind of morning-time situation. You can try it yourself, provided you don't have a sleeping partner who would be disturbed by the noise. As soon as you awaken, sit up in bed and take three deep breaths. With each out-breath, look upward and chant, "AAAAH!" It's a good way to rouse your energy and, as a result, your whole frame of consciousness, so that you can once again draw power from your innermost convictions while tapping into the deepest source of universal power. Actually, I'd recommend doing the Wake Up practice whenever you feel spiritually down, worn out, or tired. It reassures you that you are a vibrantly alive being with awesome reservoirs of energy and innate powers of self-renewal. It also reinforces your spiritual awareness as well as your energy body. You can practice raising yourself and waking up at any time of the day.

Buddha himself, the paragon of yogis, taught that the greatest motivation in awakening energetic effort is the mental factor of interest, without which it is very difficult to continue to do anything. When something appears to be meaningless, don't we easily feel enervated, bored, and ready to quit, finding any number of plausible reasons (or even flimsy excuses) to be able to do so? I myself have noticed that when I am bored or simply disinterested, I fall asleep at an early hour, almost anywhere; on the other hand, if I am passionately engaged, fascinated, challenged, inspired, in danger, or required by some sort of emergency to maintain alertness and presence of mind, it is relatively easy to stay up all night. Therefore, intentionally raising the interest factor, spiritually speaking, is the best way to arouse, maintain, and further develop the inner energy necessary for persistent effort and significant accomplishments, whether worldly or spiritual.

Making any heroic effort is very much connected to faith, trust, commitment and intention. We have to sustain the belief that we can make a difference in the world, whether we can always see that difference or not. Norman Vincent Peale, the twentieth-century Protestant theologian, spent his career developing and refining the message that any of us can put the principles of positive thinking into practice and improve our own lives dramatically. He insisted, "If you want to get somewhere, you have to know where you want to go and how to get there. Then never, never, never give up."

It's so easy to rationalize not taking a proactive interest in the unfortunate things that happen to others or even, if we're really pessimistic, to ourselves. We need to ignore this self-defeating logic. For the good of humanity and ourselves, we need to tap into a greater wisdom, the one reflecting our own Buddha-ness, our innate, inexhaustible spiritual nature. It tells us that we must take action to alleviate suffering and promote well-being for all if we're going to live full, honorable, and meaningful human lives. The Roman Catholic activist Dorothy Day, herself a tireless Bodhisattva in service to the poor, once said, "No one has the right to sit down and feel hopeless. There's too much work to do." Without this kind of courage and inspired commitment, it is very difficult to practice any of the far-reaching paramitas, or even to accomplish much in a worldly way.

This greater wisdom is joyous and expansively buoyant. Not only does it direct us toward a profoundly satisfying sense of fulfillment, contentment, and aliveness, but it also serves as the only antidote to the despair we can often experience when we consider the dire social, political, and economic straits of today's world. Heroic effort on our part depends on, and generates, a true enthusiasm for life. Literally, the word *enthusiasm* means "infused with God" (from the Greek roots *en* and *theos*). In Buddhism, we would translate this to mean "filled with our good-hearted best selves," our Bodhisattva within, our will to merge with and save all sentient beings. As the Beatles might sing, I am you and you are me and we are one and we are all together.

THE THREE KINDS OF EFFORT

The Sanskrit term for "heroic effort" is *virya*. Essentially, *vir* means "hero" (as in the English word *virile*), but it also implies the dynamic forces that go into creating a hero: courage, zest, vigor, exertion, and enthusiastic zeal on a continuing basis. The very nature of heroism suggests a persistent movement forward, an ever-ready campaign to realize a noble vision of things. In his book *The Hero's Journey*, mythologist Joseph Campbell likens this lifestyle to the legendary quest of King Arthur's knights for the Holy Grail, the vessel used by Jesus for communion during his last supper with his disciples. Like those shining, chivalrous knights, a person engaged in the kind of heroic effort associated with this paramita is seeking the eternal, the infinite, the ultimate communion of all sentient beings. Accordingly, the endeavor itself is never-ending and always beginning anew. The late Korean Zen master Seung San Sunim, mindful of the many lifetimes through which a serious Buddhist practitioner must sustain this search, this enlightenment quest, eloquently summed up its spirit in his broken English: "Ten thousand years, only go straight ahead." The first two lines of Shantideva's chapter on virya paramita are, "With patience I will bravely persevere; through zealous effort I shall reach enlightenment."

Wise effort is step six on the Buddha's Noble Eightfold Path to enlightenment. It implies balanced, appropriate effort, not simply straining and striving mightily. It includes knowing when to relax as well as when to push. It understands the necessary connection between work and vacation and includes balance as well as excellence and intensity. Buddha taught that there are four Perfect Exertions comprising the six-step Wise Effort, on the Eightfold Path. They are the exertion of restraint, in order to avoid unwholesomeness; the exertion of overcoming negativities; the exertion of developing wholesomeness; and the effort of maintaining and further developing these positive factors.

According to my Tibetan teachers, there are three kinds of virya. The first kind is the armorlike effort of diligent perseverance. This kind of effort protects the Bodhisattva against laziness, complacency, weariness, fear, and discouragement. It is said to be like a fine steed to carry us to the so-called other shore of enlightenment. It is the antidote for belittling yourself by thinking, for example, "I am such a small, insignificant, powerless person. There's nothing I can really do. I can't accomplish anything that's truly worthwhile."

The other night, while watching the Red Sox and Yankees baseball teams fight it out in virya style, I channel-surfed during a commercial and came across Kyle Maynard, who was appearing on the interview program *Larry King Live*. Maynard was talking about his recent book, *No Excuses! The True Story of a Congenital Amputee*. A larger-than-life motivational speaker, Maynard was born with mere stumps for arms and legs, yet managed to rise above his disability to become a champion in wrestling as well as in life. I watched Maynard use his arm stumps to sign a copy of his book for King: he was even able to wield his pen with a graceful flourish in front of the cameras! If you think your limitations are keeping you from accomplishing your dreams, think about people like Kyle Maynard.

The second kind of virya is the joyous effort that comes with acting virtuously and accumulating meritorious karma. It involves cultivating all the paramitas as practices. It also serves as an antidote to procrastinating, for example, with thoughts like, *I know I have to do this, but I don't have to do it today. It can still be done tomorrow or, really, any time in the near future.* Joyous effort anticipates what needs to be done and takes it on actively, as if it couldn't wait to express itself. The Buddha said that if we truly realized the angst of the human condition, we would practice as if our hair were on fire and our hands could not help but be busy putting out the fire.

The third and highest form of virya is the tireless, wise effort to serve others. Scriptures tell us that the Bodhisattva benefits others through four forms of liberating effort in Bodhisattva activity: through generosity, through interesting discussions about truth and reality, through encouraging others to implement what they have understood, and through embodying and modeling the teachings in action. This kind of virtue is an antidote to distraction. Like laziness, distraction can keep us from getting our proper work accomplished. We can be very active throughout each day, keeping ourselves constantly busy, and yet all this effort may be simply a means to distract ourselves from more serious matters that sometimes tend to daunt us, such as our quest toward enlightenment. We must always remember that this life is a rare, precious, and brief opportunity to attain true liberation and that our effort must be focused on making progress toward that most meaningful goal.

OUTER, INNER, AND SECRET EFFORT

Now, let's consider virya on the outer, inner, and secret levels. On the outer or behavioral level, heroic effort translates into hard work, however enthusiastically we may embrace it. As the old adage says, whatever is worth doing is worth doing well, and this means taking extra pains to ensure greater benefits. Every moment of every day we could and even should challenge ourselves to manifest brilliantly our best and clearest

Bodhicitta-inspired intentions in the world of samsara. As the peerless football coach Vince Lombardi once said, "The price of true success in life is hard work, dedication to the job at hand, and the determination that whether we win or lose, we have applied the best of ourselves to the task." Sometimes I feel like a spiritual coach to my students as I exhort them to practice hard, train well, and be all they can be, far beyond me. I want people to learn to exercise their critical faculties and spiritual intelligence, their hearts and minds, in evaluating their goals. I also wish they could manage to strive as hard as they can to develop themselves. This is where wisdom (prajna—the sixth transformative practice) must inform effort, just as it necessarily guides and pervades each of the paramitas, making them virtues-that-have-gone-totally-beyond rather than ordinary positive qualities.

As we become more and more engaged in heroically activating our best intentions, we increasingly appreciate that we cannot serve these intentions well without conscientiously and industriously keeping each of the ten paramitas in our thoughts, words, and deeds. For example, on the inner level, heroic effort is obviously related to patience, the third paramita, because we must persevere despite our inevitable moments of doubt, discouragement, resistence, or fatigue and regardless of interference or opposition. In addition, heroic effort relies on high ethical standards, which help us formulate our good intentions. It also requires a generous spirit, which gives us the flexibility to be responsive to others as well as proactive on their behalf, assuming their burdens just as Jesus tried to do. The same interdependence characterizes each of the other six paramitas we have yet to examine. The ten paramitas are like the spokes of a single wheel—connected at the center and supporting the entire world all around.

My Bodhisattva ordination name, given to me by His Holiness Dudjom Rinpoche in the mid-1980s, is Urgyen Tseundru Yeshe: The Lotus of Diligent Awareness. Tseundru (the "diligent" part of my name) is, in Tibetan, virya paramita. Thus, in a sense, my vow name represents an internalization of virya, an authentically edifying name to grow into. On the internal level of our being, heroic effort means cultivating the overall courage, fortitude, steadfastness, enthusiasm, and inspiration that make heroic effort possible in the first place. These qualities form the basic character of what Chögyam Trungpa Rinpoche calls "the spiritual warrior," the one who completely and fearlessly devotes himself or herself to realizing the Bodhisattva ideal. We rely on these fundamental traits to coach ourselves to victory and to heal the wounds we get along the way. Shantideva, the master Bodhisattva, says:

> Do not be downcast,
> But marshal all your strength.
> Take heart and be master of yourself. . . .
> Secure the welfare of beings
> Through aspiration, firmness, joy, and moderation.

At the innermost, secret, level of our being, we remain connected to the eternal energy flow of the universe, the indefatigable, dancing rhythm of life. Realizing this inexhaustible higher power within fills us with trust and confidence. Heroic effort at this level keeps us in touch, through prajna wisdom, with the bigger picture, the long-term view, and helps us avoid getting hooked into dualistic reactivity and taking too hard the momentary disappointments and setbacks and obstacles along the way. Effort at this level is goalless, aimless, effortless, even—like a bird catching and riding an updraft—but nevertheless totally committed. It is from this indomitable source that we draw the essential energy for our heroic effort on all the other levels.

HEROES FOR ALL:
PAST AND PRESENT BODHISATTVAS

> When we do the best that we can, we never know what
> miracle is wrought in our life, or in the life of another.
>
> —HELEN KELLER

When I consider heroic effort as a special type of journey during which the three levels of being—outer, inner, and secret—function in complete harmony, I automatically think of five great Americans who are famous for the heroic journeys they undertook, both literally and symbolically. The first is Harriet Tubman, probably the best known of all the "conductors" on the Underground Railroad, the secret network of hiding places that southern slaves used to escape to the free northern states in pre–Civil

War America. Born into slavery herself in Maryland around 1820, she ran away (or, more accurately, walked away) to freedom in Philadelphia, traveling mainly at night while using the North Star as her guide. By 1856 this intrepid, uneducated, impoverished woman with a $40,000 bounty on her head had made nineteen perilous trips back and forth across the Mason-Dixon Line to rescue slaves, without losing a single one along the way.

Altogether Tubman liberated three hundred slaves, including her own parents, in a manner that graphically illustrated what the Buddha said long ago—that intrepid Bodhisattvas should become like rafts, like sea captains, like guides to deliver people from suffering. During the Civil War, she worked for the Union army as a cook, a nurse, and even a spy. Frederick Douglass, the great nineteenth-century orator who devoted his life to promoting fair treatment for black people, called Tubman "one of the bravest people on the continent, who had willingly encountered more perils and hardships to serve our enslaved people than anyone else."

Imagine the heart and the guts Tubman must have had to sustain herself and her intrepid "passengers" during those lonely, scary treks through hostile territory, often while being chased by dogs, lawmen, and angry posses! Think of the bountiful courage and hope she must have given to others during her lifetime, including people who never met her! Even today her heroism and determination inspire everyone who cares about human rights. The same can be said for all the brave and diligent people who worked for the Underground Railroad, especially those selfless slaves who deliberately stayed behind on their plantations to assist other slaves in escaping. These heroes not only gave up their own chance for freedom, becoming Bodhisattvas in the most literal sense of the word, but also risked certain death if their activities were ever discovered by their masters.

A second, more recent American I associate with virya is Wilma Rudolph. She demonstrated superlative effort in overcoming childhood polio to become an Olympic winner of three gold medals in track. With armorlike effort, her mother drove Rudolph to distant doctors twice a week for two years until she was able to walk. Then her mother underwent professional training so that she could administer physical therapy to her daughter on a daily basis. At age twelve, Rudolph decided to become an athlete, and so she did—one of the most celebrated female athletes of all time. She broke gender barriers in previously all-male events and color barriers in her native Tennessee. In 1960 she received the United Press Athlete of the Year Award. She is an inspiration. How she must have struggled and what she must have endured to accomplish her goals and help open the way for others!

Rudolph's story is closely related to that of another American whom I associate with the hero's journey—Lance Armstrong. A six-time winner of the Tour de France, Armstrong returned to championship bicycle racing after conquering testicular cancer that had spread to his lungs and brain. This physical, mental, and spiritual feat alone demonstrated his personal stoicism, grit, courage, and tenacity, but he also applied the same qualities to a more humanitarian mission. Responding to what he called a "special wake-up call to activism" when he received his cancer diagnosis, he formed the Lance Armstrong Foundation to benefit cancer research, promote urologic cancer awareness, and aid cancer survivors. Today he travels tirelessly as a spokesperson and fund-raiser for this rapidly growing foundation, all the while exemplifying that generosity of spirit that is inseparable from true heroism. We can see his charitable cause's "Live Strong" yellow bracelets on people all around the world.

When I ponder the notion of maintaining a heroic effort against the odds, of setting myself the task of doing the inconceivable without any "reasonable" expectation of success, I think naturally of the Bodhisattva Vow. Beginning with a promise to save all sentient beings, however numberless they may be, and to renounce entry into nirvana until all may likewise join in, it commits us to a path that defies logic. As a result, it compels us to proceed solely according to our intuitive heart, spirit, faith, and trust.

An outstanding exemplar of this particular aspect of heroic effort is Milarepa, the eleventh-century hermit and yogi who is one of the most venerated superheroes of Tibetan Buddhism. Intent on achieving enlightenment despite a past history of violent behavior, motivated by fear of infernal rebirth, he devoted twenty years of his life to solitary meditation in a cave above the snow line after undergoing an extremely arduous apprenticeship with his guru Marpa. Milarepa wore only the white cotton clothes appropriate for an ascetic (his name in Tibetan means "Mila who wears the white cloth"), keeping himself warm with what we in the Tibetan tradition call the "yogic heat of samadhi," or intense meditative concentration. Because he was forced to rely solely on wild nettle soup for nourishment, his skin eventually turned green, and he was sometimes mistaken for a wild animal by local hunters.

What a heroic effort Milarepa made, and what a glorious outcome it produced! He not only achieved full enlightenment, progressing from sinner to saint in a single lifetime, but also realized diamondlike teachings—compiled in his renowned *Hundred Thousand Songs of Milarepa*, a classic of world literature—that brought about the founding of the Kagyu lineage of Tibetan Buddhism, personified today by such estimable tantric teachers as the Karmapa Lama, the Gyalwang Drukpa, Chögyam Trungpa, Situ Rinpoche, and Thrangu Rinpoche. Kagyu lamas insist that it is because of Milarepa's great diligence, or virya, that the wheel of Dharma practice is still rolling today, a thousand years after his lifetime. For this reason, he is widely considered the paragon of virya paramita, the practice of energetic effort.

In this same category of heroes persevering against impossible odds for the benefit of all humankind I include Helen Keller and Ram Dass. Both of these remarkable individuals refused to let extreme physical limitations thwart their inner drive to spread hope, joy, and inspiration to others.

In 1882, at the tender age of nineteen months, Keller suffered a bout of rheumatic fever that left her permanently blind and deaf. With the help of a gifted teacher, Anne Sullivan, she was able to overcome these enormous handicaps by mastering the manual alphabet, reading Braille, and even using the typewriter. By the time she was sixteen years old, she could speak well enough to go to preparatory school, and eight years later she graduated cum laude from Radcliffe College. She went on to become one of American history's most notable and admirable women. Keller devoted her entire life to improving conditions for blind and deaf people throughout the world, lecturing virtually nonstop on all of the five major continents. In the process, she brought new courage and resolve to millions of individuals, whether or not they shared her so-called disabilities. We can still hear her hard-won speech on old audiotapes today.

Ram Dass continues to perform the same kind of service to the world. In the early 1960s, when he was still known by his birth name, Richard Alpert, he left his position as a psychology professor at Harvard University to pursue Vedanta spiritual studies in India. There he received the name Ram Dass ("Servant of God") from his teacher and forged his commitment to "live a simple life, love everyone, feed people, and see God everywhere." In 1969 he wrote and published *Be Here Now,* his groundbreaking message of higher awareness. It earned millions of dollars in royalties, all of which he donated to charitable foundations.

Like Keller, Dass traveled ceaselessly, raising funds to help the underprivileged, lecturing on the value of living in harmony with others by engaging in what he termed "applied spirituality," and generally helping to introduce Eastern philosophies, religions, and meditative practices to the Western world. His slogan, or mantra, was "Love, serve, and remember." He eventually cofounded the Seva Foundation (to foster many different humanitarian campaigns, including the fight against curable blindness in India and Nepal), the Hanuman Foundation (to promote spiritual well-being), the Prison-Ashram Project (to assist prison inmates in pursuing spirituality), and the Living/Dying Project (to help terminally ill people face death). In addition, he wrote numerous other books to encourage people to work for positive social change under the banner of *seva,* Sanskrit for "selfless service" or service to God through serving humankind.

On the personal front, my dear old India friend Ram Dass assiduously practiced what he preached. When skeptics in the media threatened to expose his homosexuality—thinking that such a revelation, in the homophobic climate of our culture at the time, would ruin his career—Dass called a press conference and simply announced his sexual orientation. In doing so, he inspired many other closeted, tormented gay people to perform similar acts of self-liberation. When his estranged father, who had criticized his unconventional life choices, became physically incapacitated, Dass provided full-time personal nursing care for over two years, right up to the day his father died.

In 1997, at the age of sixty-five, Dass suffered a stroke that left him half-paralyzed and wheelchair-bound. Nevertheless, after two years of physical rehabilitation, he persisted in making regular lecture tours, even though his speech remained slow and labored. He also produced a powerful book, *Still Here,* to record his arduous recovery from the stroke and help others cope with similar challenges. "Stroked by the guru, by God," he says. "Have to learn to accept it, tho' not always easy."

Now the tables are turned: Dass no longer has the physical stamina to work so actively and must usually remain at home in Maui, accepting constant help from others merely to sustain his existence. And yet he remains a champion of spiritual growth by taking every opportunity he can to speak out on its behalf. He is actively engaged in teaching on the Web through streaming video. In a recent interview with Virginia Lee, former editor of *Yoga Journal,* Dass talked about his unanticipated new mode of continuing to serve his lifelong cause:

> Before my stroke, I was very much into helping others. Just read my book, *How Can I Help?* It's about the power of being a helper. And now I am experiencing the opposite, the powerlessness of being a dependent person. I am the one being helped. At first, I was freaked out by that and then I got used to it. I've found that the heart-to-heart resuscitation goes both ways. I've found that in the role of a dependent person, I can contact the heart space and the soul of another human being. I get to make people feel really good.

THE EVERYDAY HERO: WHAT DOES IT TAKE?

> When you first begin to practice, you must be like a deer
> locked in a pen, or a prisoner in jail, urgently seeking a way
> out of samara. In the intermediate stages of practice, you must
> be like a farmer during the harvest.... Just as a farmer works to
> make the most of the crop he has grown, we who now have
> opportunities and conditions which are so valuable to our
> practice, should use them immediately, understanding that
> there is no time to be wasted.
>
> —GAMPOPA

How do we overcome and even rise above the many struggles we encounter each day in order to sustain heroic effort? How do we go about making that key change in our lives—from being worriers to warriors, mere survivors to active champions?

Not long ago I stopped by my friend June's home office. Her part-time assistant, Eve, arrived shortly afterward and apologized for being late. Eve looked agitated, so June asked, "What's the matter?"

"Can I just vent for a minute here?" Eve replied. It was hard to tell whether she was going to laugh or cry. It turned out that her car battery had died while she was driving her two children to school, and she'd had to wait for the service truck for a long time by the side of the road. "What's really bothering me," she continued, "is that the car stopped right near the parking lot for an express bus stop. I saw all these men and women leaving their cars behind and taking the bus into the city. Most of the people were dressed in expensive clothes, and their cars were shiny new SUVs, Porsches, and Volvos. Meanwhile, I was wearing my usual faded old duds and sitting in my ten-year-old wreck of a car. My husband and I knew for some time that we probably needed a new battery, but we put it off. You know why? Money. You know, I went to a good college. I expected that I would have an easier life. Don't get me wrong: I love my husband, and I love my kids, but I still feel so pathetic! I feel I have to start doing something with my life to make it better! What do you think, June?"

"It depends," June replied. "Slow down a minute. So—what are your goals?"

Eve became surprisingly thoughtful. "I'm not sure," she finally said. "I've got to think about it." She went back to her desk in the other room. Soon we could hear the clacking of her computer keys as she typed. About twenty minutes later, she returned. "Well, I've been working on my goal list," she said. "You want to know what my goals and dreams are?"

"Yes," June and I said simultaneously. We were both trying to be supportive, yet we were also quite interested. I expected Eve to start rattling off a life plan that included a better job and more money. What she actually said startled me.

"I want to be a better person," Eve told us, reading from her list. "I want to be a better mother to my children and a better wife, a better friend, and, yes, a better employee. I want to be kinder, more loving, more giving, more accepting, and less impatient. Those are my goals because nothing else really matters." She smiled at us and went back to work.

I well understand how easy it is to be discouraged, even by comparatively minor events, just as Eve was upset by the circumstances around her car's breakdown. Occasionally, I too can get a bit blue thinking that others, like my very successful and accomplished brother and sister, are doing better than I am in some worldly way or another. Over the years I've learned to remind myself that I have invested in different goals and that the results show up in different ways. Any effort I can make to be grateful for what I do have and what I've been able to accomplish instantly helps me recover peace of mind and inner strength. After all, I have a certainty about the value of what I'm doing that no one can take away, as well as a love that is greater than death. I'm convinced that if and when I'm true in following the direction I've chosen, I need never feel lonely, bored, meaningless, or hopeless. Recalling my own values, goals, and ideals—especially my Bodhisattva commitment—helps me to keep going, take things more lightly, and maintain a joyous heart, even when the going gets tough.

I knew an old lama, Palden Gyatso, who was tortured and imprisoned for decades in Communist-controlled Tibet merely for the crime of being a monk. He taught me to count my blessings and recall with gratitude all that I have, which is what Eve did in turning her mind away from her troubles and back to her happy marriage and loving family. The lama explained that he was able to endure torture, imprisonment, and starvation with equanimity because he kept thinking about how much worse it would have been if he had not had the internal security of mature wisdom, faith, and endless patience. He amazed many of us by stating that he actually felt glad it was he who was being tortured rather than his parents and siblings, who would have been much less prepared to endure it. Meanwhile, he continually reflected on the many other people who were going through similar hardships at the time without such valuable supports. This activity caused Palden Gyatso to develop even more compassion and empathy, which, in turn, helped fuel his resolve to triumph over adversity. He survived for three long decades in the Communist Chinese prison system in eastern Tibet and lived to escape China to tell the tale.

The first and foremost thing we need to do to recharge our inner heroism is to reconnect with our basic goals. What objectives mean the most to us and to the world around us? In addition to our Bodhisattva Vows, if we've taken them, what are the most important commitments we've made with our hearts and minds? Maybe we've pledged ourselves to our familial loved ones, like Eve, or to a special humanitarian campaign, or even to a vital personal improvement project, like a healthy dietary or exercise regimen. Restating our core intentions is the best way to motivate ourselves through those periods when we temporarily lose our will or our way.

We also must acknowledge that heroic effort takes a considerable amount of courage, and so we need to coach ourselves through the rough times. The author and columnist Anna Quindlen spoke beautifully of this type of courage and coaching in her June 2005 commencement address to the graduates of Barnard College in New York City:

> Here is what awaits you: You will be offered the option of now becoming exhausted adults, convinced that no achievement is large enough, with résumés as long as short stories. But what if that feels like a betrayal of self, a forced march down a road trodden by other feet, at the end of which is—nothing you truly care for? Fear not. Remember Pinocchio? There is a Jiminy Cricket on your shoulder. It is you, your best self, the one you can trust. The only problem is that it is sometimes hard to hear what it says because all the external voices and messages are so loud, so insistent, so adamant. Voices that loud are always meant to bully. Do not be bullied.

It helps me to recall the traditional Zen saying about never abandoning the fight: "Six times down, seven times up." Specifically, when faced with a setback or a disappointment, I like to recall my childhood "Joe Palooka" punching bag. It was an inflatabl e, four-foot-tall plastic figure with a big, beachball-shaped bottom half and a top half with the upper torso, raised fists, and smiling, confident mug of a boxer. No matter how hard I walloped Joe, he just rocked right back for more—unharmed, ever smiling, and always confident. That old softie had a great deal of backbone and was always ready to bounce back from whatever blows life struck him—reminiscent of the patient forbearance and indomitable effort of the Bodhisattva. He never stayed down for long.

Besides cultivating courage and perseverance, we also need to combat laziness. Looking at this issue from the opposite perspective, heroic effort is the antidote to laziness. In essence, laziness comes when our attachment to the sensual pleasures of worldly life causes us to lose our inner clarity and the active sense of a higher purpose. Gampopa, a student of Milarepa's, warns about the dire results in his masterwork, *The Jewel Ornament of Liberation,* and urges us to receive the precious Dharma teachings of virya paramita as a special uplifting hand. "By laziness's power," Gampopa tells us,

> this precious human life with all its excellent opportunities is wasted. If utilized properly, it could have been used to accomplish the ultimate—

Buddhahood. If we don't receive the precious Dharma teachings, our lives will not be much different from those of animals. Some animals work very hard to collect wealth and make a comfortable place to live, but they don't have the special wisdom mind that can know about samsara and nirvana, so their suffering is endless. We who have precious human life need to wake up from the sleep of delusion, wear the armor of commitment to purify all our mental conflict, and actualize the primordial self-awareness.

Once, as I was sitting in a group gathered around a campfire, I heard a Native American story that captures perfectly the kind of moral, effort-related choice that Gampopa describes and that each of us faces on a daily basis. A Cherokee elder was instructing his grandson about a battle that goes on inside every human being. He said to the young man, "The battle is between two wolves. One wolf is slothful, cowardly, vain, arrogant, and full of self-pity, sorrow, regret, envy, and anger. The other wolf is diligent, courageous, humble, benevolent, and full of compassion, joy, empathy, and faith." Then there was silence.

The grandson thought about the two wolves for a moment and then asked his grandfather, "Which wolf wins?"

The Cherokee elder replied, "The one you feed."

Whether you feed your good wolf, your source of diligence and courage, or your bad wolf, your source of sloth and fear, is a true test of your sincerity about becoming a Bodhisattva. In the spirit of this kind of testing, I recommend doing some serious self-assessment right now, even though it may require more time, energy, and thought than you prefer to expend. Have courage, and consider this activity a step forward in your effort to be heroic! Honestly ask yourself the following questions and answer them as best you can at this moment. If possible, record those answers in writing. Then return to these questions for reconsideration whenever you need some extra motivation.

1. What are my most important goals in life—the things I truly believe, with all my heart, are worthwhile? What is my greatest dream and highest aspiration? What am I or could I be most passionate about?

2. How does each goal relate to specific aspects of my life right now?

3. What past moments of heroic effort on my part toward achieving each of these goals do I recall? What circumstances or factors at the time helped me to make such an effort?

4. What circumstances or factors keep me from making a more heroic effort to achieve each of my goals? How are my own thoughts, beliefs, and habits holding me back? How, specifically, can I remove, counteract, or overcome these obstacles?

5. What steps could I take *each day* toward achieving each of my goals? Who might be willing and able to help? Whose example can I emulate?

Always remember that heroic effort does not necessarily mean doing big things. What makes an effort heroic is that it is insistent (you are committed to doing it), consistent (you stay focused on your goal), and persistent (you don't give up), and it is wise, appropriate, and dedicated to something beyond yourself. Even very small actions, done faithfully and wholeheartedly day by day, can result in heroic progress. In fact, that may be the only way true heroism manifests itself.

SOTO ZEN CHANT

May all awakening beings extend with true compassion
their luminous mirrorlike wisdom.
May the merit and virtue of these considerations
of the Bodhisattvas,
both of the words herein and in the readers' hearts,
be extended to all beings,
that all may find their unique, sparkling place
in the way of awakening;
and may the practice of awakening go on endlessly.

FIVE

THE LIBERATING POWER OF MINDFULNESS AND MEDITATION

May I perfect the subtle virtue of concentration
and alert mindfulness, which clarifies the heart
and mind, body, and soul, and allows awareness and discernment
to dawn within.

If the primary goal of the budding Bodhisattva is to edify and deliver all sentient beings, why do so many Buddhist teachings revolve around meditation? What does the solitary, still, and silent act of meditation have to do with alleviating suffering, helping others, making a positive difference in the world beyond ourselves? The short answer is that the fifth paramita, meditation (in Sanskrit, *dhyana*), leads directly to wisdom, the sixth paramita, which pervades all ten transformative practices, providing much of their dynamic power. Meditation in itself is a wakening up. The Bodhisattva is the Awakener who, while coming to fuller consciousness, has begun the process of awakening others as well from the deep sleep of separateness, delusion, and confusion. Meditative mindfulness is the main ingredient in the Buddha's recipe for attaining enlightenment, for awareness is curative.

When I first returned from Asia after many years away, people often asked me to explain why meditation isn't just an exercise in self-indulgence. "How can you help anybody by sitting for hours with your legs crossed?" they would say. More than once my Jewish mother inquired, "Tell me again, why exactly are you staring at your navel?" The Buddha himself was asked similar questions by curious natives of ancient India who came to hear him teach.

Buddhist teachings tell us that a Bodhisattva never forsakes the rest of the world. Even when he or she prays or meditates alone on a mountaintop in the Himalayas, this act is never a selfish one, precisely because it is done for the benefit of all sentient beings, with their plight and ultimate welfare in mind. Meditation is an intense form of spiritual training that develops mental clarity, spiritual awareness, and cosmic insight, so that the meditator becomes all the more empowered to function wisely and compassionately for the benefit of the world at large. How can we serve others as effectively as possible without first cultivating the highest form of consciousness possible—the mind of enlightenment?

The incandescent inner awareness discovered through practicing meditation gives us access to the entire totality, just as it is, right here and now. As the Buddha said after becoming enlightened under the Bodhi Tree, "When I was awakened, all beings were awakened, even the rocks and the trees." When we see with clarity, everything becomes clear. This is universal truth. We can attain enlightenment in this lifetime and discover the kingdom of heaven here and now, not just after we die or after many dedicated lifetimes of trudging to bliss and schlepping toward nirvana. Thus, we ourselves can help usher in the kingdom rather than waiting for some kind of messiah, savior, or answer-man to come and do it for us. Meditation is our "Imitation of Buddha," analogous to the Imitation of Christ—the spiritual program for Christians outlined by the theologian Thomas à Kempis. Through meditation, we realize profound wisdom and become Buddhas ourselves. And as we're meditating, we are already expressing our Buddha-ness. There is no other Buddha outside oneself to be sought.

The process of meditation is the best way we humans have yet devised to free our minds from clouds, cobwebs, illusions, confusions, defilements, and bad habits so that eventually they remain totally open, alert, collected, and composed. The awakened mind illuminates everything, not only while we are meditating but also during every moment of our experience, no matter how busy or quiet those moments may be. Tibetan masters say that this kind of consciousness can persist even during our sleep, when it results in what Western science calls "lucid dreaming" (or conscious dreaming) and Tibetans themselves call Luminous Dream Yoga. What's more, these masters teach that we can retain this alert meditative consciousness throughout the death process and into our next rebirth.

Whether or not our own meditation practice allows us to achieve a high level of conscious luminosity during sleep or death, it can definitely improve the way we navigate our waking life, giving us increasingly more inner tranquillity and attentiveness. We need these qualities if we're going to have the wherewithal to realize our Bodhisattva intentions—and given the social, political, religious, environmental, and economic woes of our time, the world desperately needs us to act now on these sterling intentions.

Meditation can also have significant physical, mental, and emotional health benefits, which can only make us more fit to do the work of a Bodhisattva. It can lower stress, tension, blood pressure, and anxiety. It can help relieve chronic pain and insomnia. It can elevate energy, level out our obsessions, and help us track and tame self-destructive patterns of thinking and feeling. Over the past few decades, Harvard Medical School, the Massachusetts Institute of Technology, the National Institutes of Health, and other prestigious research facilities have been studying the effect of meditation on brain activity using trained meditators (including the Dalai Lama himself) as both fellow researchers and subjects. Their discoveries verify that meditation can significantly increase our sense of happiness and well-being by increasing levels of serotonin and other endorphins in the brain. Thus, meditators can come to experience naturally what Dr. Herbert Benson of Harvard dubbed "the relaxation response." The findings of the University of Wisconsin researcher Richard Davidson, a leader in this field, suggest that if we can train ourselves to become more mindful, we can learn to monitor our moods so that they don't handicap our proper mental and emotional functioning or spiral us into negativity and depression. In other words, we can make ourselves happier and live more joyfully. Modern neuroscience confirms much of what yogis and meditation masters have known for centuries about the hidden powers of the mind. For example, recent research on meditators verifies that the learning, insight, and experience acquired through contemplative practice helps structurally reorganize the brain and its functioning, allowing us to consciously transform the mind as well as changing the brain. This is known as neuroplasticity, or brain malleability, which offers tremendous beneficial potential.

Master Tsong Khapa said, "Concentration is a king with sovereignty over the mind. Once placed and immovable, it induces bliss as well as malleable body and mind. Meditative stabilization defeats all mental agitation and distraction." The dhyana paramita bids us to place meditation in our lives and make it immovable, so that we can realize our full Bodhisattva potential and attain enlightenment. If there are physical, mental, and emotional side benefits along the way, all the better—and all the more appropriate for living the good life in every sense of the word *good*.

WHAT BUDDHISTS BELIEVE: VARIETIES OF MINDFULNESS AND LEVELS OF MEDITATION

Basically, meditation means the intentional use of attention as applied to this very moment: to whatever is arising in the body-mind field of consciousness. According to Tibetan Buddhist tradition, there are four kinds of mindfulness. First comes average mindfulness—the attention that springs naturally and spontaneously through our own interest in a particular person, situation, or phenomenon. For the most part, it's concerned with worldly matters and lasts as long as the interest itself. The second kind is cultivated or generated mindfulness—the type that we intentionally apply to particular objects of awareness in order to stabilize or deepen our understanding of them. This can be considered the general practice of mindfulness: a highly focused and alert presence of mind free from judgment, evaluation, reactivity. The third kind is abiding mindfulness: the well-trained mind is sufficiently tamed to rest naturally, without wavering, wherever it is focused. Accomplished meditation masters can sustain this kind of concentrated or one-pointed mindfulness for hours, days, or even longer, uninterrupted by distractions. The fourth is Dharmakaya mindfulness, or innate wakefulness, where awareness itself remains undistracted from its own nature. In other words, there is no observer "I" noticing awareness within our consciousness, nor can anything within or outside our consciousness diffuse its energy. My teacher said that there are "no arisings, alterations, or conditioning in this pristine state of innate awareness. All is luminously clear and serene."

This fourth and ultimate kind of mindfulness is not acquired through practice. Instead, it is already present within us, and we come to realize it as a result of cultivating the other three kinds of mindfulness. As the true essential nature of the mind, it is regarded as being the ground as well as the fruit of practice. The other parts are the growth or the pathway connecting the ground and the fruit. The catalyst for this growth, the force that moves us along the way, is meditation.

In the paramita wisdom literature of Buddhism, it is said that dhyana paramita, the transformative practice of meditation, has three levels. The first level involves meditative concentration on an object, without regard to purpose, motivation, or any moral issues. This level is called worldly concentration, and it's not unlike the concentration developed by a sharpshooter or the focus demonstrated by a watchful cat perched in silence near a mouse hole. Buddhists might cultivate it, for example, by concentrating on a candle flame, a mantra, or the breath. The second level is called altruistic concentration. Here the intention and attention are directed toward benefiting others through compassion and selfless service. Buddhists cultivate it not only through being simply mindful of other people's welfare but also through focusing on acting mindfully and compassionately to help others. The third and most profound level of meditation is called wisdom meditation: at this level, the mind sees both the unconditioned, unconditional emptiness of everything (sunyata) and the vividly apparent, dreamlike nature of reality, the true nature of things. This is the naked awareness that brings with it pure presence. It's not directed toward anything, and it's not going anywhere. In wisdom meditation, awareness is at its most wholehearted and wholeminded—fully capable of functioning at its best. Wisdom meditation is therefore the transcendent union of all meditative levels, beyond notions of oneness or nothingness, and the supreme gesture of awareness: Mahamudra—the Great Seal, or Ultimate Totality—the nondualistic outlook that includes and appreciates everything, just as it is.

In the Tibetan Buddhist tradition of Mahamudra, the mind is considered to be sheer lucidity. Many of our Western concepts of mind accord with this notion of the mind as clear light or brilliancy. When we meditate, we learn to concentrate our scattered mental energies in a manner not unlike using a magnifying glass to focus the sunlight so that it can start a fire. Samadhi, or mental concentration, also represents a burning fire of mental absorption. It can act as a laser beam cutting through the thickest fog of illusions and penetrating right to the truth of things. Experienced meditators sometimes experience the blissful heat of samadhi, which suffuses the body and mind, purifies and refines our energy, and blissfully uplifts the soul.

Regarding concentrated samadhi, which is the essence of the meditation paramita, Tibetan meditation manuals explain that there are three levels of focused absorption. First is the mundane concentration of mental stabilization, such as through well-developed one-pointedness, which is a slightly immature type of concentration; like a sharp tool, it lacks insight or skill. Second is supramundane concentration, with all its concomitant superpowers, divine experiences, and psychic abilities, known as effective samadhi because it is well endowed with extraordinary powers and abilities far beyond those of mortal monks (to echo the original *Superman* theme song). Third and highest is the Bodhisattva's supreme samadhi, which is concentrated on reality in both its absolute wisdom (nondual emptiness) and relative (unconditional compassion) forms. The trained and focused mind is the most potent force in our world.

When we align ourselves with all the enlightened ones who have gone before and shown the way by summoning and crystallizing our own Bodhisattva intentions, inexhaustible energy and blessings can be ours. There is nothing that can limit our effectiveness. Such is the promise of the Buddhas and Bodhisattvas of the past to you and me today. I have seen this to be true. I've filled the preceding chapters with guidelines designed to help you put yourself on the Bodhisattva path by cultivating generosity, patience, ethics, and heroic effort in your day-to-day life. When it comes to meditation, however, you need to do more introspective work to help yourself. I can still offer some suggestions, but the whole point of meditation is to take it upon yourself to teach yourself about yourself.

In meditation, you focus more intently on how your particular mind works. What thoughts and feelings clamor for the spotlight? What layers of past training and conditioning reveal themselves? Where does your mind want to go, despite your efforts to be still? The more you simply sit quietly and register the ongoing activity of your mind, without allowing any particular detail to snag your attention and divert it from your main enterprise, the more deeply you can see into its nature, until eventually you awaken to its fundamental essence—your inherent Buddha nature. As Lao Tzu wrote, "Knowing others and the world is knowledge; knowing oneself is wisdom.... The master knows himself through and through, and thus understands all things." The profound wisdom and certainty of authentic self-knowledge answers all questions and doubts.

This is a journey that each person must take for himself or herself because it's an internal journey. In Zen it's called "taking the backward step." Rather than facing forward and getting the truth from any teacher in the outside world, you turn within and realize the truth within yourself. The Tibetan master of old called Dampa Sangay, the Buddha of Tingri (a village on Mount Everest), said, "It is all within, all that we seek is within." This does not mean all is solely within our own selves, for what we discover when we look within is in fact within everyone and everything. Meditation ultimately helps us bridge the gaps between the knower, the known, and the act of knowing, revealing the wholeness that underlies all. Meditation done with our whole heart and mind occurs at the great crossroads of self and other, being and doing, time and timelessness. It brings us to the place beyond past, present, and future known as the eternal now, what the American writer and self-described Buddhist Jack Kerouac called "the golden eternity."

Some schools of Buddhism believe that the activity of meditating in itself is the activity of an enlightened mind, and so it is said that meditation equals enlightenment. In other words, while you are meditating, you are living the enlightened life. As I've said, I like to think of it as "being there while getting there." It's a wonderful, seemingly paradoxical, and therefore mystical law of practice: we can achieve enlightenment as we practice enlightenment. In a similar way, since we are participating in the oneness of everything, we are liberating all as we liberate ourselves. As Suzuki Roshi said, "It is Buddha meditating on your seat."

The Tibetan Buddhist teachings that most appeal to me are the Dzogchen (Natural Perfection) teachings that arose in India around 200 BCE and arrived in Tibet some nine hundred years later. According to Dzogchen texts, if we practice meditation today, we awaken today. At the same time, we need to work hard and persistently in our practice to reach our greatest capabilities, even if that seems contradictory. Another way of putting it is this: we are already perfect Buddhas as we are, but we have to practice diligently for an extended period of time—maybe over many lifetimes, maybe only within this lifetime—to realize our perfection *completely,* to experience the *total* freedom it gives us, and to manifest it *fully* in the world around us.

The kind of meditation I've been describing so far is the basic awareness practice that most people associate with meditation: sitting for a certain length of time and remaining silent, motionless, and mentally focused (in any one of a wide variety of ways), all the while being aware of how your mind is functioning. In Dzogchen meditation, for example, you simply register and appreciate each thought and feeling as it passes by from moment to moment, noting how things rise and fade away, like ripples on a stream, without any need for a reaction. You don't suppress any of these distractions, nor do you allow yourself to be carried away by any of them. You simply let them come and go without stopping them. Over time you become increasingly aware not only of the workings of your own mind but also of the insubstantial, fleeting, miragelike nature of thoughts, perceptions, and feelings.

The basic awareness practice of meditation can be accompanied by a host of complementary practices that follow different formats. I'll mention just a few to give you some idea of the range: guru yoga (in which you meditatively unite with a master or the Buddha himself); visualization or contemplation meditations (in which you focus your mind on a particular sublime quality, thought or issue, utilizing guided imagery); tonglen (the generosity-related sending-and-receiving meditation outlined in chapter 1); chanting meditations; koan study (a Zen meditative technique in which you focus your mind by attempting to resolve an apparent paradox); physical yoga, dance, movement and walking meditations; music meditations; healing meditations; nature meditations; couples meditations; chakra meditations; and what is perhaps the most widespread meditative practice among the world's contemplative traditions—prayer. In fact, there is a magnificent world of meditations out there for those called to savor and appreciate meditations for different times, places, people, and purposes. The best practice is the one that suits you, and that you can keep doing and deepening over time.

Meditation teachers worth their salt are familiar with at least a few traditional forms of meditation and are accomplished in at least one.

Moreover, they are familiar with the kinds of outer and inner experiences that can occur as meditative experience deepens and old habitual mind patterns start to loosen and dissolve. They can spot with alacrity healthy evidence of insightful inner development as well as warning signs of deviation and pitfalls, like drowsiness, dullness, boredom, agitation, overexcitement, extreme views, spiritual pride, or attachment to feelings or experiences of any kind—good or bad. For this reason, they can help you immeasurably along your way.

Beyond awareness meditation and its supporting practices is mindfulness itself. Our goal as Bodhisattvas must be to bring the same awake and finely tuned consciousness that we develop during the practices I've just listed to everything we think, say, and do in the everyday world. As we learn through meditation to recognize the kinds of thoughts that distract, mislead, anger, or otherwise trouble us, we can then let go of them earlier and more efficiently during the times when we're not meditating. We can exercise more conscious control over our moment-to-moment desires as well as our moods, and best of all, we can interact with other people more smoothly, skillfully, compassionately, and constructively.

This kind of mindfulness, or meditation-in-action, makes me think of cats blissfully doing their morning yoga stretches or birds singing at the first light in the morning. We too can experience this happy opening up to each moment of the day. That is why the great master of old, Lord Atisha, exhorts us to "always cultivate a joyous heart-mind." He doesn't mean that we should wear a false smile on our face while suppressing our darker emotions. Instead, he is reminding us to face life as much as we authentically can with positive, open-minded, benevolent interest, whatever other feelings we might have.

The more formal act of sitting meditation itself encourages and assists meditation-in-action by stabilizing, balancing, and fueling our overall mental energy, giving us greater clarity, vigilance, objectivity, and discernment in every aspect of our existence. It helps remedy our everyday absentmindedness, scatterbrained thinking, obsessiveness, hysteria, bias, and ignorance. By enabling us to focus more intently on what we are thinking, saying, and doing each minute, meditation ensures that we derive more knowledge and enjoyment from the world around us. We don't miss out on life simply by not paying attention to it. We also learn not to be so afraid of things, because we stay in the present rather than mourn the past or worry about the future. The peerless French essayist Montaigne captures this sense of moment-to-moment alertness in his famous statement "When I dance, I dance; when I sleep, I sleep; yes, and when I walk in a beautiful orchard, if my thoughts drift to far-off matters for some part of the time, for some other part I lead them back again to the walk, the orchard, the sweetness of this solitude, to myself."

The truly meditative mind is a calm one that can rest in open, clear, nonreactive attentiveness at all times, not solely during certain periods of meditation practice. Having this kind of mental presence in life—which, for most us, can result only from continuous training and practice—is the mark of someone who is genuinely enlightened. In the words of contemporary lama Mingyur Rinpoche, "The Buddha said that all sentient beings possess Buddha nature. Because of that we have this natural purity, peacefulness, and power. We can rest the mind naturally because we are already in possession of these qualities. If one can rest the mind naturally, that's the best meditation. Nonmeditation is the supreme meditation."

MEDITATION: OUTER, INNER, AND SECRET LEVELS

> As a fletcher straightens his arrows and perfects his aim,
> the meditator straightens his concentrated attention and
> perfects his mind.
>
> —MAHASIDDHA SARAHA,
> A TANTRIC YOGA ADEPT OF ANCIENT INDIA

Meditation is the central concern and core practice in all schools of Buddhism because it most directly works toward the positive transformation of our entire consciousness, waking us up to our Buddha nature at all levels of our being. Only in this state of enlightened integrity, of whole body, heart, and mind synchronization, can we realize our full potential as human beings, and as Bodhisattvas, for the benefit of one and all. Meditation paramita concerns itself with unified and total awareness, beyond dualities like self and other, meditator and meditation activity, the relative world of different things and the absolute world of emptiness or no-things. It is this oneness and nothingness that makes the practice of dhyana transcendental rather than ordinary, as it would be if we practiced meditation just for the sake of a specific goal like relaxing or gaining the concentration to play a better game of golf.

On an outer level, meditation involves practicing specific meditative techniques that are effective in bringing us physically and mentally to what Buddhist teachers call "the still point." Breath by breath, moment by moment, we sit motionless, training ourselves not to fixate on transitory distractions such as bodily discomfort, emotional turmoil, and our virtually ceaseless mind chatter. Eventually we work free of these entanglements that cause so much anxiety and suffering in our day-to-day lives and begin to experience stretches of pure awareness. To our amazement, refreshment, relief, and even enlightenment, we stay focused clearly and totally on the present, unencumbered by past baggage or fantasies of the future—just totally, unequivocally, wholeheartedly here and now. How delightful!

Outer-level meditation also includes transferring this same kind of present-moment mindfulness, as best we can, to our activities in the outer world: the realm of karma, or cause and effect. This is what I call meditation-in-action. We take care to meet each person and circumstance with openness, clarity, and benevolence. We don't allow ourselves to become preoccupied, depressed, agitated, or otherwise caught up in our own fixed mode of perception. We don't let laziness, perversity, or simple self-absorption trigger our negative patterns of thinking, acting, or speaking. Instead, we strive to remain awake in every sense of the word.

Padma Sambhava had a wonderful teaching (or, as it's called in Tibetan, "pith instruction") about meditation-in-action. Alluding to many people's mistaken belief that meditation is an exalted state of quiet mind incompatible with life in the real world, he says, "Though my view is higher than the sky, my actions regarding cause and effect are as meticulous as finely ground barley flour." What he means is this: Yes, his meditative practice has given him rare insight into the great mystery of things, the infinite sweep of time and space, the *mahashunyata*—the luminous void. That doesn't mean, however, that he no longer takes note of the myriad details of daily life. Indeed, he is all the more keen on respecting each detail as a fulcrum of karmic importance, and he takes extra care that every one of his thoughts, words, and deeds is aimed at achieving the most positive possible effect.

Of course, we don't have to wait until we're fully enlightened to begin practicing more mindfulness even in the tiniest events of the day. During the *Ango* (peaceful dwelling) periods of intensified Zen Buddhist retreat practice that typically occur in the spring and fall, many Zen students formally commit themselves to focus on one small, habitual activity, making sure that they engage in it with as much mindfulness as they can. They may choose, for example, brushing their teeth, climbing stairs, getting out of bed, or feeding the dog—anything that they do regularly but often mechanically rather than attentively, or sloppily rather than skillfully. As they note the positive difference it makes to perform the chosen task with greater awareness—an improvement not only in the quality of their consciousness but also in their experience of the actual event—they are persuaded of the potential value of being more mindful at *all* times.

On an inner level, meditation is a matter of developing greater overall self-awareness and expanding our general powers of contemplation, concentration, introspection, and intuition. We don't direct our minds toward a specific task that becomes the focus of our attention. Instead, we pay ongoing attention to the way our mind displays its innate capabilities. We're not so much concerned about *what* the mind does as *how* it does it. Whenever I walk by the former Cambridge home of the American philosopher William James, I recall his famous words "Most people live, whether physically, intellectually, or morally, in a very restricted circle of their potential being. They make use of a very small portion of their possible consciousness and of their soul's resources." It is meditative self-awareness accompanied by inner-mind training that helps us grow into our full Bodhisattvic potential.

Suppose we come to realize that we have a short attention span. This is a personal inner-self issue. Just being more conscious of the problem at all times and taking responsibility based on that consciousness can help to resolve it. The sooner and more clearly we see that the monkeylike mind is jumping around from one train of thought to another and not effectively settling down to the matter at hand, the more easily and competently we can bring it to rest. Attention can be refined and trained.

If we want, we can also do what is popularly called "inner work" to lengthen our attention span. For example, we can deliberately take on projects that require extended periods of patient mental application, like completing challenging crossword or jigsaw puzzles (activities recommended by doctors to their patients with attention deficit disorder). We can also schedule at least an hour of reading a day or regular ten-minute periods of contemplating a single image, whether it's a famous painting, a holy card, a flower, a lake, or a quilt design. This is working on the outer level of our being to benefit us internally.

The effort that pays off most, however, is simply remaining observant of the inner workings of our mind, always watchful over its predisposition to slip out of our control, like a mischievous monkey. It doesn't matter whether we suffer from a short attention span, a quick temper, weak willpower, a compulsion to lie, an addiction to drugs, or a habit of zoning out in front of the TV or numbing ourselves with booze or food. Our basic inner-self alertness or meditative mind monitoring, all on its own, can do wonders to nip the problem in the bud.

At the same time that we keep internal guard over our negative mental patterns, we also need to look more deeply into what triggers positive mental activity on the inner level of our being. Perhaps the most important such catalyst is our intuition. It gives us our most direct, nonverbal perception of the truth. It's also the source of our most authentic (or "gut") feelings and our most creative impulses. Modern civilization puts such a high premium on intellectual thinking that we tend to devalue our more original, instinctive, nonrational, and holistic ways of knowing things. As a result, we underutilize and even lose touch with this precious dimension of our inner selves. Albert Einstein, despite being the most highly regarded scientific thinker in modern history, often deplored this sad state of affairs. He once said, "The intuitive mind is a sacred gift and the rational mind is a faithful servant. We have created a society that honors the servant and has forgotten the gift."

To help revitalize this inner-being gift in our own life, we could put more of our time and energy into creative forms of self-expression on an outer level, like poetry, drawing, music, dance, and photography. We could also investigate the many books and workshops on the market today that are designed to help us exercise and develop our intuitive powers. No doubt they are continuing to grow in popularity because people are increasingly feeling the need to counteract our culture's overemphasis on rationality at the expense of the creative, sacred spirit trapped within us, just waiting for the chance to come out. I sincerely believe, however, that the single most effective thing we can do is simply listen more closely to our inner genius so that we have a better ear for what it is trying to say.

On the secret, innermost, level, our Buddha nature, our mind is inseparably at one with the universal mind. This is the very essence of dhyana paramita, which cannot be either obtained or lost. Our own innermost wakefulness and incandescent presence pervades all forms of consciousness that exist, whether we're aware of it or not, whether we're feeling concentrated or distracted. The universal mind reflected in the secret level of our being is whole, coherent, incorruptible, luminous, and fundamentally unalterable, just as the ocean is all one and the same entity, regardless of the fact that our rational mind sees it in the various forms of wave, current, whirlpool, tsunami, iceberg, tidal basin, bay, mist, rainbow, cloud, or rain. As we strive to cultivate meditation and mindfulness on both the outer and inner levels, we open ourselves up to this infinite universal mind, our prime source of equanimity, attentiveness, and enlightened vision. We realize that the transcendental perfection of meditation is innate wakefulness itself, the Buddha within.

SAKYAMUNI BUDDHA:
OUR MODEL OF MEDITATION

> Meditation is not a means to an end. It is both the means and the end.
> —J. KRISHNAMURTI

The supreme exemplar of dhyana paramita, or meditation as a transformative practice, is without a doubt Sakyamuni Buddha. He is the original meditation master, who discovered and realized the path to enlightenment that meditation offers and passed this knowledge down to us—his greatest gift. We can say that his self-generated mind training and conscious evolution as a Bodhisattva took place over countless lifetimes as various kinds of animals and then human beings, during which he consistently reached higher and more evolved levels of consciousness. Finally, at his birth into the Sakya clan of northern India in 563 BCE, Prince Siddhartha (as his parents called him) was primed to achieve full enlightenment and to enlighten the world for millennia to come.

After straying outside his palace and unexpectedly taking in the Four Revealing Sights—or, in other words, being struck by the profound reality of aging, sickness, death, and the pure monastic ideal—the young Siddhartha forsook his royal destiny and became a *sadhu* (mendicant holy man) seeking to solve the mysteries of life. Inevitably, in his place and time, this spiritual quest led him to become a student of various types of mental and spiritual discipline. His first teacher, Alara Kalama, was a Brahmanic yogi who taught him, through intensive concentration exercises, to rise above the confusion of emotions and remain in a state of pure objective consciousness. When Siddhartha became adept at this practice, he still felt that something was lacking, so he moved on. Next he studied with another Brahmanic yogi, Udraka Ramaputra, who trained him to cultivate a mental state that was neither conscious nor unconscious, thus avoiding the two extremes of mind activity. Again, Siddhartha mastered the process but realized its limitations. He studied and practiced with other masters, yogis, ascetics, wizards, and gurus, always feeling compelled to find an immutable truth beyond the vagaries of birth and death. Finally, striking out on his own, he sought to rise above egotistic self and worldly matters by practicing extreme fasting along with a strict ascetic regimen akin to what we now know as hatha yoga.

Six years later came a pivotal turning point. Near death from his lifestyle of brutal austerity, Siddhartha fainted and fell into a river that swept him downstream, where he chanced to hear a lute player tuning his three-stringed instrument. One string was so loose that it could produce only a dull, ugly twang; another was so tight that it just squeaked before breaking. Only a third string, neither too taut nor too slack, gave forth a clear, resonant, perfectly pitched tone. From this simple observation, Siddhartha suddenly realized the importance of the Middle Way: namely, that one can achieve enlightenment, as well as live an enlightened life, only by avoiding the self-oriented extremes of both worldly indulgence and other-worldly asceticism. Another mind might never have made this intuitive leap, but his mind had been well prepared to do so when the right moment came.

After Siddhartha's near-fatal mishap in the river and his insight about the Middle Way, a kind cowherdess brought him a bowl of fresh yogurt and he ate it, breaking his grueling fast. Then he sat down beneath a tree to ponder the next step. What would that step be now that he had tried everything else? Immediately he recalled a moment early in his childhood when he had in fact experienced the eternal, absolute nature of deathless nirvana. It happened one glorious spring day when his father took him to watch the ceremonial plowing of the fields. Left alone by his nurses under a rose-apple tree, he suddenly felt suffused with pure joy. Instinctively, he folded his legs in the classic meditative posture and fell naturally into a calm, deep trance. He was still mentally alert to the real world underneath and beyond that rose-apple tree, but simultaneously he was aware of dwelling in a boundless and blissful world beyond the limitations of separate selfhood. The sensation lasted only a short time. Afterward, the child Siddhartha apparently forgot about the experience, yet the memory reemerged in his adult mind precisely when it was most needed.

Today we might refer to the child Siddhartha's transcendent state of consciousness as a peak experience, or a moment of ecstasy—a child's spontaneous expression of natural spirituality. In Siddhartha's case, it became much more: a catalyst for the most famous meditation in history, the one that brought Siddhartha to enlightenment and made him the Buddha, the Awakened One. Remaining under what was later called the Bodhi (enlightenment) Tree, he meditated all through the night. During the first watch (in ancient India, the night was divided into three equal time periods called "watches"), he wrestled in his mind against terrors and temptations inflicted on him by the evil god Mara: tidal waves, lightning storms, attacking armies, and Mara's own bewitching daughters. Siddhartha withstood them all. Eventually, he achieved a profound level of meditative calm that opened up his innate visionary powers. During the second watch, these powers allowed him to witness and reflect on the suffering he had endured and the wisdom he had acquired during all his previous lives. During the third watch, he came to realize what would later become his core teachings: the Four Noble Truths and the Noble Eightfold Path.

In this story of how the Buddha came to be enlightened, we find inspiring testimony to the power of mindfulness in its many different forms and at every stage of life and spiritual evolution. We see not only the magnitude of what meditation itself can deliver but also the potent possibilities that lie within every act of intuition, attentiveness, mind training, wonderment, memory, and introspective realization.

All of these elements work together to bring one to a full heart-mind awakening. The secret lies in continuous practice of dhyana paramita so that our minds are slowly but surely purified, freed from habitual karmic conditioning, and ripe for breakthroughs to occur. Just as the Buddha really attained full enlightenment not in one night or even one lifetime but through the course of this entire path, we cannot expect miracles of mindfulness in our own lives without preparation, commitment, and continuing to energetically progress along our spiritual way.

When I consider this key factor—the work we need to do, especially in terms of meditation—I can't help but remember the story of Milarepa saying good-bye to his pupil Gampopa, when the latter had completed his training. Milarepa, as I mentioned in the last chapter, was renowned for spending twenty years of solitary meditation in a high Himalayan cave. Gampopa, motivated by his teacher's example to go on a similar retreat, made his farewell bows, crossed a small stream, and walked away. Milarepa called after him, "Hey, Gampopa!" and Gampopa looked back at him, hoping for one more teaching. Milarepa then turned around, lifted his robe, and exposed his bare butt, heavily callused from all those years of seated meditation on a hard stone floor. "Just do it!" Milarepa cried.

I'd like to offer a cautionary note here: Milarepa's example of continuous, marathon-like practice is definitely something that we can admire and use to fuel our own aspirations, but it is not a feat we can immediately challenge ourselves to replicate. Too many people take on the impossible task of trying to leap, like Superman, from zero to perfection in one bound, with unhappy results. Nor should we feel bad about ourselves if our own meditative practice, sincere and commendable though it may be, seems insignificant compared to Milarepa's monumental dedication. Milarepa is an example of a world-champion meditator; we too can gradually follow in his footsteps.

Bodhisattvas come in all sizes, shapes, forms, and capacities. We each have to do what we can and keep on doing it with patience and diligence until we attain enlightenment, just as he and so many others have done. There is simply no other way. We have to begin where we are, take our training step by step, and keep our eyes, minds, and hearts wide open so that we can learn and mature as much as possible along the way. Meanwhile, as we persist, we are Buddhas-in-the-making. That is why Zen masters say that "sitting meditation is sitting Buddha; walking meditation is walking Buddha." We just have to do it, gain trust in the process, and see what happens.

A LIFETIME OF MEDITATION:
MOMENT BY MOMENT

> Our being is silent, but our existence is noisy.
> —THOMAS MERTON

Okay, so we can't all be Milarepa and devote our entire day, day after day, to formal meditation. How much time *do* we need to devote to some sort of formal meditative practice in order for it to work effectively in our lives? What specific practice should we undertake? If our daily schedule is inclined to be busy or unpredictable, how can we sustain a regular formal practice over time?

These are all good questions, which we must each answer for ourselves. It's up to you to experiment and learn the amount of time you need to devote to meditation each day in order to feel that it's being effective. You may also need to take it upon yourself to explore different formal practices so that you can discover on your own the one or more particular practices that work best for you. And above all, you must figure out how to sustain practice on a daily basis, given your specific needs, scheduling concerns, aspirations, and disposition. All these responsibilities—evaluating, exploring, looking deeper—are part of what is involved in mindful living.

Before I suggest some steps you can take, let's restate the basic issue in simpler, more universal terms: how does one go about combining a hectic life with a regular contemplative practice? This conflict plagues both newcomers and longtime meditators. Now let's consider a hypothetical case of this type that reflects many real cases I encounter among my students. Jennifer and Troy are both American Buddhists who meditate daily. Their walls are lined with shelves of books on mindfulness, meditation, compassion, psychology, and engaged Buddhism. Until their daughter Molly was born, they spent ten days each year at a silent retreat with an insight meditation (*vipassana*) group.

Now Jennifer is seven months pregnant with their second child. She wakes up one morning to discover that little Molly has a fever and a sore throat and needs to see a pediatrician. Jennifer has been experiencing some premature contractions lately and was planning to spend the day in bed after going out only long enough to visit her obstetrician. Her sister was supposed to pick up Molly this morning and take her home to play with her little cousins, but now this plan has to be changed.

Jennifer feels forced to call Troy at his small computer firm to tell him he needs to come home and help out. She really doesn't want to do this because Troy is completely backed up with orders. Lately, clients have been calling him every five minutes wanting to know when he's going to show up to fix their ailing PCs. To make matters worse, both Jennifer and Troy are worried about this pregnancy, which hasn't been an easy one. They are also concerned about money, especially since it's becoming increasingly apparent that Jennifer is not going to be able to return to work anytime soon, and their finances are stretched to the breaking point.

Jennifer and Troy are dealing with a variety of stressful situations. At this important time in their lives, as they are approaching the birth of their second child and trying to be good parents to their first, they want to stay mindful and aware. They want to be conscious and awake, but they're not residing at a calm meditation center that would support this goal. Nor are they living alone in the country like hermits or artists. Life is throwing problems at them with machine-gun rapidity. How can they integrate meditation more effectively into this tumultuous period of their lives?

The first thing I would ask Jennifer and Troy to do is to reexamine what they think meditation means. Many people knowingly or unknowingly believe that meditation is something that can be practiced only under idyllically peaceful conditions. I've even heard people say, "I'm too tense to meditate," or, "There's too much noise for me to meditate." Although these are perfectly understandable concerns, they represent limited thinking. Meditation as a way of wakeful being can fit in anywhere.

Practicing mindful awareness and presence of mind in any form is certainly more challenging in these kinds of situations, but it's also more necessary and valuable. Mindfulness is what can allow us to stay focused, healthy, and true to our inner Buddha nature even while strong storms rage around us. For this reason, training ourselves to maintain our equilibrium, harmony, and balance in the midst of chaos is, in my opinion, the finest possible way to begin or revitalize our appreciation of meditation's value.

For example, I discovered my own "American One-Minute Instant Meditation" method long ago while commuting to my job as an English teacher at a college in Kyoto, Japan. I often teach this method these days at public lectures as a way to begin incorporating meditation more naturally into daily life. First I guide the audience into breathing, relaxing, and centering themselves. Then I loosen them up by exhorting them to meditate as fast as they can, or joke that Buddhism is more fun. This is the spirit I wish to inculcate in a brief teaching encounter—lightening up while enlightening up. From the outset I want to dispel the grim, burdensome atmosphere of religiosity and expectation that some people attach to learning how to meditate. Then we just sit together and breathe for a couple of minutes—breathing, relaxing, and smiling. Attentiveness seems to be naturally included when genuine interest is there.

Sometimes I tell a joke, such as this one I heard on the Buddhist circuit, in lieu of a more formal Laughter Meditation.

Four monks were meditating in a monastery, when all of a sudden the prayer flag on the roof started flapping. The younger monk came out of his meditation and said, "Flag is flapping." A more experienced monk one-upped him and said, "Wind is flapping." A third monk, who had been there more than twenty years, added, "Mind is flapping." The fourth and eldest monk exclaimed, annoyed, "Mouths are flapping!" I think this nicely points out the outer, inner, and secret levels of things, worth being aware of.

It's good to have a formal seated meditative practice that you do for a distinct twenty- to forty-minute period each day, but as Jennifer and Troy are now realizing, it can be even more beneficial if you can also teach yourself to weave meditative moments into the warp and woof of daily life. Think of it as taking meditation practice into nonmeditation, beyond the dichotomy of practice and afterward. You can do this, for instance, simply by taking one intentional breath, relaxing, and letting yourself smile while waiting for a stoplight to change or an elevator to arrive. It provides you with fresh air, mental energy, and inner lightness that can help transform a heavy mood or an oppressive day, just as a longer meditation period can. Through this "American One-Minute Instant Meditation," I've often been able to clear my mind, open my heart, relieve stuckness or obsessive preoccupations, and connect with something meaningful beyond myself at the precise time when it was most necessary. When we've taught ourselves how to achieve such moments of mindfulness, such Sacred Pauses, we can realize them whenever and wherever we want. This is the ever-present joy of meditation.

Essentially, meditative mindfulness is a matter of guiding our full attention to focus on the present moment instead of letting our mind get carried away, this way and that, by discursive thoughts and fluctuating emotions, interior monologues, or concerns about the past and the future. I would advise Jennifer and Troy to engage in this small practice whenever, and as soon as, they begin feeling overwhelmed by or dissociated from circumstances around them. Mindfulness is a great way to tune in rather than to give up and merely tune out.

When either Jennifer or Troy has anything to say to the other person, or when there's something they need to discuss together, I would suggest, if possible, that they first spend a few quiet moments alone just clearing their minds of all mental chatter, breathing together, and settling into the moment at hand. They might even try doing the Sky Gazing Meditation I describe later. During their times together, whether or not they have a prior period of meditative alone time, I would advise them to take turns listening to each other with the fullest nonreactive attention possible: one person speaking at a time, and the other not responding until the speaker has finished. In Buddhist terms, this is a relational mindfulness practice called Just Listening. It helps two people join and find themselves together as well as alone in themselves and in each other. Listening is the essence of the art of communication. It greatly enhances meaningful connection on many levels.

If Jennifer and Troy can learn to open themselves completely to each other, the rest will have a much better chance of taking care of itself. In time, they'll come to interact with other people and engage in other events with a similar sense of inner composure and strength. Relational mindfulness is one of the basic tantric (or special teaching) practices in both Buddhism and Hinduism that is now being explored by Westerners. I consider it particularly significant and instructive for the Western world, where monastics are rare and most spiritual practitioners are laypeople for whom intimate relationships must be part of a truly integrated spiritual path.

The common thread in each of my suggestions for Troy and Jennifer is making the effort to be fully mindful of what is happening *right now,* rather than losing themselves in some interior drama or agenda with a timing all its own. Thich Nhat Hanh said, "The most precious gift you can give to the one you love is your true presence. What must we do to really be there? Those who have practiced Buddhist meditation know that meditating is above all being present: to yourself, to those you love, to life."

People often ask me what kind of meditation I do. The short answer is Dzogchen meditation, but almost daily I supplement it with various other practices, such as devotional chanting, praying, breath and energy yoga, compassion meditation, tonglen, and self-inquiry. It took a while for me to learn how to meditate anywhere, anytime—that is, to integrate meditative awareness into regular daily activities. With constant application and attentiveness, however, over the years I gradually succeeded in spreading the principles of openness and letting-be into all the nooks and crannies of my life. An individual meditation period for me might last an hour, a half hour, five minutes, or a moment, depending on how the day is going, but I try to keep myself always vigilant. "Anywhere, anytime" is the best approach to cultivating your own inner atmosphere of concentration and wisdom awareness. Natural Meditation is fully paying attention to the task at hand. Surrendering totally to simply doing what you are doing is the best samadhi, revealing the extraordinary power of nowness.

For novice and experienced meditators alike, I recommend the Sky Gazing Meditation as an easy, highly adaptable practice for training the mind to focus on the moment at hand. You can begin doing it now without any other instructions than the following:

1. Sit any way that's comfortable for you in an outdoor or indoor place where you can see the sky. Rest your body so that it can remain pleasantly motionless for a while, close your eyes, and take a couple of deep breaths to put yourself mentally and physically at ease. Then continue breathing in a natural manner, with full, relaxed breaths.

2. Still keeping your eyes closed, let any thoughts, emotions, and physical sensations pass by like waves in the sea or clouds in the sky, just observing their impermanent, dreamlike, rainbowlike nature, and then coming back to rest in the present moment. When you find yourself mentally pursuing a particular thought, feeling, or sensation, let go of it and gently return to an open awareness of simply sitting and

breathing right now. Allow yourself to smile slightly with the assurance that there's nothing else you have to do right now but relax. The three essential elements in this initial phase of sky gazing are breathe, relax, and smile.

3. When you feel settled in a calm alertness, open your eyes and, keeping them in a soft focus, gaze evenly into the space of the sky. Like the mind, this space is beginningless and endless, with no inside, outside, shape, or size. Each time you exhale, follow your out-breath into this emptiness until you become spacious awareness itself. Allow individual thoughts, feelings, and sensations to float freely away and dissolve, like clouds in the infinite sky.

4. Continue breathing freely into space, letting everything go. Breathe the sky in and out. Keep the process flowing until you feel you are resting evenly in luminous, empty awareness, and dissolve into that.

Besides practicing different kinds of meditation exercises, I often read, create, or ponder poetry in order to put my mind into a more meditative, unedited, present-moment state of consciousness. To close this chapter, I'll give you a poem of my own that you can use as a meditation tool. The word *Emaho* in the title of my poem is Tibetan for "wondrous," "fantastic," "far out." "Emaho!" in itself is the most concise Dzogchen teaching. To say "Emaho!" either silently or out loud is to express the joy of realizing within ourselves the freedom and radiant splendor of our innate natural state, our oneness with all that is, the universal Buddha-mind.

EMAHO: THREE POINTS OF MEDITATION—
OPEN ARMS, OPEN MIND, OPEN HEART

Stay put, seek nothing.
It is all within.
What we seek
we are.
Externally, just sit and relax.
Internally, breathe, drop everything, let go
and let be.

Secretly, nothing doing,
everything happens.
Nakedly aware, recognizing,
penetrating and releasing;
looking, seeing through, letting go and letting be;
nondoing,
noncontriving,
nonreacting,
remaining undistracted.
These are the four
steps to freedom and
peace of mind.
Emaho!

SIX

THE PANACEA
OF WISDOM

May I perfect the profound virtue of transcendental
knowledge-wisdom, which knows how things
actually are, as well as how they arise and appear,
interrelate, and function.

What would it be like to be wise, really wise? What would it be like to
see things as they actually are, to grasp reality directly, and to understand how things arise, interrelate, and function? What would it be like
to distinguish with certainty true from false, right from wrong, real from
unreal and intuit underlying patterns and universal principles?

Do you know anyone whom you consider to be wise in this manner?
What exactly makes them seem so wise? Where are the spiritual elders
and wise ones this world needs today?

I've lived with these questions all my life. They popped up immediately in my mind when I first heard about the Buddha and his main
disciples. Shariputra, for example, was known for his brilliant wisdom,
and I wondered exactly how he acquired that quality. So I asked one of
my Tibetan Buddhist teachers, himself a very learned and erudite lama.
I expected him to talk about a lifetime of meditating and practicing

the teachings. Instead, my teacher told me an amusing little story about Shariputra, the Buddha's wisest follower.

Legend has it that Shariputra was a tailor in an earlier lifetime who did two things in particular that contributed to his later incarnation as the Buddha's wisest disciple. First, he made a gift of needles and thread to the local monastic community. Second, when he sewed late at night, he placed a candle in front of a holy image of the Wisdom archetype, Manjusri, on a nearby altar. He did this as a practical means of providing light for seeing, not as an overt devotional act. Nevertheless, his persistent if inadvertent illumination of the holy image had far-reaching karmic consequences. It actually helped facilitate his becoming spiritually illuminated and later being reborn as the Buddha's wisest disciple.

How are we to interpret this anecdote in terms that make *rational* sense? We can't really do that, because the process to which it refers is not a logical one, such as the intellectual mastering of a particular body of information. Instead, it's a process of *illumination* through faith and blessings, which, in this ancient story about Shariputra's life as a tailor, is represented both literally and figuratively.

By diligently engaging in his craft while at the same time remaining in an environment conducive to spiritual enlightenment, Shariputra—already a devout person—gradually developed transcendental wisdom. It was as if the candles he lit functioned as a type of sun, stimulating profound growth within his mind. In other words, he put himself in a better position to "see" and to experience inner illumination, and these are essential steps in becoming wise.

The sixth transformative practice involves learning to recognize, appreciate, and activate this kind of wisdom, or, in Sanskrit, *prajna,* which can be translated as "the best knowledge," or "the highest knowing." We can all do this because prajna is ever-potential within us as a key aspect of our Buddha nature. It inevitably emerges as we strive to engage in the other transformative practices that are part of the Bodhisattva's path, for prajna wisdom pervades all the paramitas and raises them above the level of ordinary virtues. Also, we can cultivate it by engaging in the specific wisdom practices explained later in this chapter.

What is prajna wisdom? How do we define a vast and profound concept such as transcendental wisdom—the wisdom beyond ideas and intellect—in only a few words, or, for that matter, in any amount of words?

All we can do with words is use them to point in the direction of prajna wisdom, giving clues as to what it's like. The ancient Greeks, for example, divided wisdom into two broad categories: *sophia,* representing what we would call mystical, holistic, intuitive, synthesizing, right-brain, principle-oriented wisdom, and *phronesis,* representing rational, conceptual, linear-sequential, particularizing, left-brain, fact-oriented wisdom. I think of these as the two wings of wisdom: deep discernment coupled with un-common common sense. Prajna wisdom includes all this as well.

When I asked my own Dzogchen master, the late Nyoshul Khenpo Rinpoche, "What is prajna wisdom?" he replied, "Wisdom is realizing truth unerringly. Wisdom is like the inner sun and is more for oneself. Compassion, unselfish action, and altruistic service are its inevitable, spontaneous rays, reaching out for others. Wisdom is like an inner lamp by which we see. Heartfelt warmth and compassionate caring are its nat-ural radiance."

The basic definition of wisdom in Buddhism has two parts. The first is *right view,* or seeing things as they really are: absolute truth beyond conceptual thought. The second is *right understanding,* a selfless compre-hension of interconnectedness, right intention, and karma: relative truth, practical and learnable, about how things operate in the ever-changing world. Prajna wisdom as a whole can be said to be a Middle Way wisdom, in that it negotiates between the absolute and the relative. It is being able to see through things to their empty, radiant nature while simultaneously seeing them clearly in the context of their form and function.

I once heard a very interesting Native American elder claim that these days people seek only knowledge, which is about the past, and not wis-dom, which is about the future. The ancient Talmud says that wisdom is kindness. Some theists say that wisdom is found while loving God, while others maintain that wisdom is oneness and unity of vision. Lin Yutang, author of the classic *The Importance of Living,* writes that wisdom is get-ting rid of nonessentials and that the wise one reads both books and life itself. Philo of Alexandria, an early religious philosopher, said that the goal of wisdom is laughter and play—even becoming laughter itself. All of these interpretations point in the direction of prajna wisdom.

I like to think it is wise to live justly, truthfully, and peacefully in har-mony and love. I agree with the saying of the ancient Roman philosopher Epicurus: "It is impossible to live pleasurably without living wisely, well, and justly." Wisdom implies deep understanding about patterns and relationships, causes and origins, as well as insight into the future implications of all our thoughts, words, and deeds. The more we truly understand, the more we grow into a state of objective nonattachment, integration of the various parts of ourselves, and transcendent connection with all that lives.

How can we become wise? The Buddha said that insightful wisdom is understood through recognizing the three characteristics of existence: all conditioned things are impermanent, ownerless, and dissatisfying in the long run. To think otherwise is delusion. Wisdom and delusion of any kind are antithetical. Bodhisattvas who have prajna do not proceed out of ignorance or incomplete understanding, nor do they traffic, knowingly or not, in deception or half-truths. In addition to a highly objective understanding of themselves and an uncommonly high level of common sense in approaching life as a whole, prajna has developed in these Bodhisattvas the powers of discernment and discrimination that enable them to grasp the truth at the heart of any situation. Wisdom is the universal panacea. Ignorance and delusion confine us and drive us into all kinds of craziness; misunderstanding and misconstruing things brings all kinds of problems. Wisdom is the answer, the antidote, the single medicine that relieves all ills and afflictions. Thus, many say that prajna wisdom is the most important paramita.

Prajna is the capacity to see the forest as well as the trees, the big picture as well as its individual images, the collective patterns within the myriad specific details of existence. Think about all the delusions, fantasies, prejudices, misconceptions, and narrow points of view that pervade our own lives. Think about the ways in which we rationalize questionable behavior, engage in denial, and manipulate the truth—not just with others but also with ourselves. Cultivating prajna trains us away from these destructive habits of thinking, speaking, and behaving. It's a remedy for overcoming not only selfishness, stupidity, and unfairness but also feelings of confusion and meaninglessness. Often problems arise not just through what we don't know or comprehend but due to knowing wrongly. Seeing things clearly, as they are, helps at every step of the way.

Tibetan Buddhist teachers generally teach six paramitas, culminating with prajna, the ultimate virtue that caps and enfuses the other five transformative practices leading up to it. As I said in the introduction, certain Mahayana sutras expand the list to include ten paramitas, and I find it useful for my own practice and teaching to use this expanded list. Still, prajna remains just as crucial on both lists. When it comes right down to it, all of the paramitas—whether they total six or ten—are equal in value and completely interdependent, so that each paramita contains the others within it.

Not long ago I was visiting Khenpo Karthar Rinpoche at the monastery in Woodstock, New York, where I used to reside. I noticed a new addition to the main temple: a large, spontaneous, black-and-white calligraphy by the Seventeenth Karmapa, the official head of the monastery, who is now twenty years old and living in Dharamsala, India. Entitled "Prajna Pervades All the Paramitas," the calligraphy shows the paramitas as interrelated spheres joined together with swirling, swooshing brushstrokes. One big energetic stroke links and carries them all along, like a river current through space. This dazzling image captures beautifully my sense of the inseparability of prajna—or, for that matter, any one paramita—from each of the other paramitas.

Shantideva said that prajna extends throughout all the paramitas and, in doing so, makes them transcendental and not just ordinary virtues. One of my own teachers told his students that the wisdom of understanding reality is like a sighted and experienced guide capable of leading the otherwise blind practices of generosity, ethics, effort, patience, and meditation—the other five paramitas in the scheme of six. His imagery reminds me of Helen Keller's statement reflecting a similar attitude toward wisdom: "To be blind is bad, but worse it is to have eyes and not to see."

Wisdom is often called the Third Eye, or the Wisdom Eye, as in the Dalai Lama's first book, *Opening the Wisdom Eye*. This name can be taken to refer to the subtle or mystic eye said to exist in the middle of the forehead, between the two eyebrows. This "special" third eye perceives unity, while the other two "normal" eyes see dualistically. The transcendental practice of wisdom aims at developing such a clear, holistic, third-eye vision of the cosmos. This is what I call BuddhaVision: seeing particular things just as they are as well as how they fit into and affect the entirety.

OUTER, INNER, AND SECRET WISDOM

Supreme wisdom is the eye for seeing profound suchness.
It is the path, which totally uproots worldliness.

It is the treasure of knowledge praised in all scriptures.

Renowned as the finest lamp

To dispel the darkness of confusion.

Knowing this, the wise who seek liberation

Cultivate this Bodhisattva path with every effort.

—TSONG KHAPA

Externally the paramita of wisdom is seen as uncommon common sense, sagacity, and having a large-minded perspective. Outer wisdom includes reading between the lines; exercising discernment and discrimination; knowing right from wrong, true from false, vice from virtue, just from unjust, real from unreal.

Inner-level wisdom is seeing things just as they are and as they take form through interdependent origination and karmic causation. The inner level of wisdom includes simultaneously seeing absolute truth and relative truth. Wise people internally understand how to regulate their emotions, body, and intellect. Sometimes wisdom simply consists of knowing what to focus on and what to ignore. One of my early Indian Dharma teachers, Anagarika Munindra, used to say that wisdom is non-attachment and nonclinging, since nothing is ultimately worth getting tied to or stuck on. I find a great deal of wisdom in getting out of my own way, in trusting things to proceed without interference. This has been called the wisdom of allowing, and it often involves not only acceptance and nonresistance but a sense of humor!

The secret, or innermost, level of wisdom is pure intuition, clarity, lucidity, innate wakefulness, presence, and recognition of reality. This transcendental wisdom is within all of us—it just needs to be discovered and developed, unfolded and actualized. The contemporary lama Tulku Thubten Rinpoche says, "We are already like Buddhas, endowed with the Buddha qualities or perfections the moment we are born; this is the main message of Mahayana and Vajrayana Buddhism. The only problem is that our wisdom is obscured like a sun behind the clouds."

Transcendental knowledge-wisdom, or prajna, is the wisdom heart and wisdom mind of all Bodhisattvas and the will or intention of the Buddhas. This wisdom mind is called *Dharmakaya*—ultimate reality—and is also what Tibetans call *rigpa:* supreme knowledge, total awareness, and incandescent presence. There is no more profound wisdom that we can attain. The Buddha called it transcendent wisdom because it transcends duality, samsara (worldliness), and concepts. I have found this wisdom to be the ultimate guide and best friend, ally, and protector. Innate wisdom is like the higher power I can always rely on.

In basic Buddhism, having wisdom means having an intuitive understanding of the Four Noble Truths, dependent origination, and the law of karma. Insight-oriented (or vipassana) meditation is the means to attain such wisdom. In Mahayana, the motivation underlying the perfection of wisdom is Bodhicitta, the aspiration to realize enlightenment for the benefit of others—the Bodhisattva path. Mahayana Buddhism balances prajna with *karuna,* or compassion. When prajna and compassion are joined in us, we attain supreme wisdom. We then express this compassionate wisdom spontaneously, along with all the other paramitas, which are simply wondrous ways to conduct ourselves in life.

WISDOM-GIVERS TO THE WORLD

Wisdom does not mean knowledge but experiential understanding.
Wisdom helps you to change radically your habits and perceptions,
as you discover the constantly changing, interconnected nature
of the whole of existence.

—MARTINE BATCHELOR

Throughout the ages, people who are truly wise have inspired others to tap more deeply into their own wisdom. In making such a valuable contribution, these exemplars of wisdom have functioned according to the famous adage of the British statesman Benjamin Disraeli: "The greatest good you can do for another is not just to share your riches, but to reveal to him his own." This wisdom-exchange inevitably breeds others, as those people whose lives have been illuminated wind up shedding light on the lives of innumerable others who encounter them, either in person or through their works. Potent wisdom is like active yeast that can leaven an entire loaf of bread. Thus does wisdom travel beyond all barriers of space and time.

The world's great religious movements have all arisen from dynamic wisdom energy set in motion by particular individuals who have simply—but not always easily—awakened to their own inner genius. I think, for example, of the Chinese sage Lao Tzu, a contemporary of Sakyamuni Buddha's and a founder of Taoism. Following his own intuition that all things in nature are completely interrelated and flow rather than remain static, Lao Tzu spent many years wandering through rugged natural landscapes in China while keeping his mind as open as possible to what those landscapes revealed to him about his own innermost self. In this manner, he opened the Book of Nature and learned its lessons by exercising his inherent wisdom as if it were some kind of muscle that grew stronger with each step he took.

Lao Tzu's hard-won wisdom by its very nature contained a great deal of compassion and ultimately directed him to reveal what he'd learned to others. When he later retired from his post as royal librarian, the western border's gatekeeper stopped him as he was riding away and requested the old sage's final words of wisdom. It was only then that he extemporaneously penned his timeless *Tao Te Ching* ("The Way and Its Power/Virtue"), which is still profoundly influential as a spiritual text classic twenty-five hundred years later. In this work, he restates the theme we've been exploring so far in this chapter: "Knowing others is knowledge. Knowing oneself is wisdom."

Another ancient model of wisdom is connected with my own Jewish heritage and with Christianity: Solomon, the ancient king of Israel. One of the best-known stories of Solomon's wisdom, found in I Kings 16–28 of the Bible, features two mothers who come to Solomon with a baby and ask him to judge which of them is the rightful mother. The previous night, the two women were sleeping next to each other with their babies when one of them rolled over and smothered her child. Grief-stricken, this mother exchanged her own dead child for the living one while the latter's mother continued to sleep. Now, in Solomon's presence, they both claim to be the living baby's mother. Solomon calls for a sword, saying, "Divide the child in two and give half to each of these women!"

The real mother cries out, "Oh, no, sir! Give her the child—don't kill him!"

The other woman says, "All right, it will be neither yours nor mine. Divide it between us!"

Solomon replies, "Give the baby to the woman who wants him to live, for she is the mother!"

In this story, Solomon looks into his own heart-mind of wise compassion to arrive at the best way to resolve a tricky decision-making challenge. From his empathetic understanding, he spontaneously stages a means of triggering each woman's innermost feelings: the real mother's selfless love and the other woman's grief-induced jealousy and rage. He doesn't need to study each woman's background, collect evidence from midwives and neighbors, or closely examine similarities between the baby's physical attributes and those of the two women. In short, he doesn't need to look outside for the answer. He draws on his own inner wisdom in making his decision.

Solomon's intimate connection with this potent source of truth did not go unremarked by those who witnessed its results. As I said before, such illuminating wisdom can't help but be seen by others. According to the biblical account, "Word of the king's judgment spread quickly throughout the entire nation, and all the people were awed as they realized the great wisdom God had given him." Of course, in Buddhism we would characterize this same great wisdom in different terms—namely, as a virtue that pervades the universe and is innate within each of us. But how did Solomon come by his vaunted wisdom? The Bible tells us that God came in a dream and gave him the wisdom to know right and wrong. May we all experience such a dream!

Another renowned wisdom-bearer in the world was my favorite saint, St. Francis of Assisi, founder of the Roman Catholic Franciscan order, the monks who are dedicated to living simple, humble lives and serving the poor. As a wealthy young man in the late twelfth century, St. Francis devoted his life to pleasure, wenching, consorting with troubadours, and forsaking all responsibilities. Then, stricken with a serious illness, he had a mystical epiphany and began to have compassion for the suffering of others. One day as he was praying for the sick in the dilapidated Church of St. Damian, he heard a voice within himself that said, "Francis, go and repair my house, which you see is falling down."

In complete obedience to what I interpret to be his own inner prajna, which he called the Lord, St. Francis began his life of reparation by literally stripping himself of his worldly goods: when his father confronted him in public and threatened to disinherit him if he didn't give up his spiritual quest, St. Francis took off all his fancy clothes, gave them to his father, and walked away naked. He went on to lead a life of singular simplicity, joy, social compassion, and reverence for nature. He rebuilt churches that had fallen into disrepair, and in a similar manner he helped shore up Christianity as a religion at a time when more and more people were forsaking it. One of St. Francis's most respected biographers, G. K. Chesterton, dubs him "a man of supreme wisdom made flesh" and adds, "From him came a whole awakening of the world and a dawn in which all shapes and colors could be seen anew. The mighty men of genius who made the Christian civilization that we know appear in history almost as his servants and imitators."

Surveying more recent times, I would cite Albert Einstein as an icon of wisdom, not because he was smart enough to develop his famous theory of relativity—which revolutionized modern physics—but rather, because he realized in a very fundamental and active way that what he called "cosmic religious feeling" functions as "the strongest and noblest incitement to scientific research." His original and penetrating genius was to see that true knowledge-wisdom transcends mere intellectual mastery of facts and figures and even a very gifted imagination. With this wisdom, he grasped the underpinning of both the material and the immaterial universe.

Einstein's powerful intellect was related to the kind of wisdom we've been examining, but in a secondary rather than a primary way. His intellect didn't make him wise in every aspect of life. Instead, his wisdom helped release and guide his intellect, so that it could shine forth in the especially striking way that it did. He despaired over the widespread tendency among people to confuse wisdom with smartness, and he complained that modern educational systems place far too much value on learning as opposed to wisdom. He once said, "It is, in fact, nothing short of a miracle that the modern methods of instruction have not entirely strangled the holy curiosity of inquiry."

Another person I consider to be an exemplar of prajna is Eleanor Roosevelt. Certainly she was a well-educated and articulate woman, but strictly speaking, she's not known today for her intelligence. Instead, what impresses us about her legacy is her preeminently wise approach to dealing with grave personal challenges and with some of the thorniest social, political, and economic issues of our time. When her husband Franklin was stricken with polio early in his career, she became active in the New York State Democratic Committee, not only to keep his ideas alive in politics but also to further her own humanitarian causes. While her husband was governor of New York and then president of the United States, she put aside her private grief over his marital infidelity to serve as one of his most astute advisers and ambassadors. She traveled tirelessly to places where her husband could not go to meet with political leaders and investigate the plight of America's disenfranchised. Her sincerity and acumen, obvious to everyone wherever she went, earned the respect of all kinds of people: rich and poor, great and humble, white and black, male and female, old and young, Republican and Democrat. Breaking precedent for a first lady, she skillfully communicated what she learned in groundbreaking press conferences, lectures, radio broadcasts, and even a syndicated daily newspaper column, "My Day." After her husband's death and the end of her White House years, she headed the committee that drafted the United Nations Charter and continued to campaign vigorously and insightfully for human rights until her death in 1962. I have enjoyed visiting her hermitage in upstate New York (now a museum and conference center), where John F. Kennedy personally sought her blessing before he ran for president and where UN committee members often came to get her advice.

Throughout Eleanor Roosevelt's long career of public service, one incident stands out as a sterling example of her prajna wisdom. In 1939, during her husband's second term as president, the Daughters of the American Revolution (DAR) refused to let African American soprano Marian Anderson sing in their Constitution Hall because of her race. As soon as Eleanor Roosevelt heard of this outrageous decision, she resigned her membership in the DAR and arranged for Marian Anderson to perform an outdoor concert at the Lincoln Memorial on Easter Sunday. It was an inspired strategy on Eleanor Roosevelt's part to rectify a great wrong and, at the same time, strike at racism and provide a symbolically rich occasion for promoting interracial harmony. Speaking years later of her secret for success in life, she uttered words that relate directly to what she did for Marian Anderson and what prajna wisdom is all about: "Do what you feel in your heart to be right." To know oneself makes this possible.

PUTTING WISDOM INTO ACTION

Blessed is the man who finds wisdom,
who gains understanding;

for he is more profitable than silver
and yields better returns than gold.

—PROVERBS 3:13

Too often we regard life from the perspective of our emotions rather than our wisdom, and the resulting view is usually gloomy. Beset by greed, anger, jealousy or depression, we moan to ourselves, "Why can't I be happier? Richer? Luckier? Better? Where can I find love? Peace? Justice? Paradise? Why can't I have as much fun as my friends? As the people I see on TV? As I had last year? As I want and deserve?"

The Buddha's First Noble Truth states that to live is to suffer. Some people interpret this to mean that life is inherently filled with suffering and that is why we let so many of our negative emotions—our thoughtless, automatic responses to provocation—have the upper hand. Others claim that it's the other way around: life becomes filled with suffering precisely because we so frequently let ourselves get carried away by our conflicting emotions instead of leading with our wisdom and we come to grief from seeking what we want in all the wrong places.

The truth lies somewhere in the middle. Life is undeniably *difficult* and often dissatisfying because of all the challenges, choices, illusions, misknowings, and interrelated karmic stresses and strains involved. It's also true that in many cases this difficulty causes and is caused by suffering. Suffering diminishes, however, the more we train ourselves to meet life with our best wisdom instead of our unbridled emotions. I call this kind of existence wisdom-in-action.

In contrast to the worldly life, the enlightened life is not dissatisfying or full of suffering, although pain and difficulty may be part of it. Buddhist scholar Mu Soeng, author of *Trust in Mind,* writes, "The foolish and the ignorant are bound to emotional choices that in turn attach them more fiercely to their ignorance. The wise person, on the other hand, walks through life unswayed and nonreactive, yet free to act compassionately and with equanimity."

So how can we wisen up? How shall we go about making this transformation to active wisdom in our own lives, not only to help us develop and achieve better, more fulfilling long-term goals but also to help us think, speak, and behave more meaningfully on a daily basis? Who can help us to gain insight, clarity, and the highest forms of knowledge? What do we need to do in order to start turning things around *right now?* How can we start climbing out of our emotional ruts, where, wallowing in darkness and confusion, we have little choice but to hurl rhetorical questions out into the universe? How can we begin asking ourselves the right, productive questions—ones that move us forward toward enlightenment? Can the wisdom of each of the paramitas guide us into the authentic lives we long for?

People often ask me to advise them. What many of them really want is for me to make decisions for them or to simply validate and bless their own decisions. It's much too easy to tell people what to do, but also much too foolish and even irresponsible. Taking the decision-making process away from people disempowers them. It also makes them much less likely to buy into the decision, however right it may be. One's own conscience remains the ultimate arbiter.

Rather than endeavoring to produce answers, I prefer to ask people questions and see whether together we can't come to understand the root causes of the situation at hand and the ultimate consequences of all possible courses of action. I try to point people in the direction of developing better powers of inquiry and discernment so that they can generate wiser and more informed choices on their own. Most of all, I wish to empower and guide them toward developing a greater clarity of purpose. We have to know who we are and what is real in the world around us and, in the light of this understanding, intuit what it is we truly want and need. Otherwise, we have no hope of accomplishing or attaining anything worthwhile. We end up constantly, as the song goes, looking for love in all the wrong places. This helps no one and leads nowhere. A Tibetan Buddhist abbot and professor once said, "The whole problem is that everyone thinks that happiness and difficulties come from outside, from possessions, from other people, and mere circumstances and conditions. True happiness is not found there." This is Buddhist wisdom in a nutshell.

Buddhist texts tell us that prajna wisdom, the kind that leads to wisdom-in-action, comes through three traditional forms of wisdom practice. Learning, reflection, and meditative experience are phases of what we can consider truly "higher" education; they are analogous to filling your mouth, chewing and swallowing, and then digesting. *Learning* involves much more than merely gathering information from the outside world. It is also, and more importantly, an examination of our inner world: looking into what afflicts or limits us as well as what truly inspires and nourishes us. In *reflection* we thoroughly analyze and process all that we've learned and investigated through contemplative self-inquiry and meditation. The Zen master Bassui said, "When you understand the nature of your mind, delusion will change into wisdom." *Experience* is the final step of realizing, or "making real," what we've learned and reflected upon—actually applying what we've now mastered to the way we live. Eventually we get used to integrating learning in both theory and practice, and it becomes part of who we are. Having learned well how to learn, there is no end to it.

But where can we find these three phases of a truly higher education in our schools today? Where are wisdom classes offered, taught by someone proficient in such a subject, language, outlook, and way of life? I failed to fund much of it in college philosophy classes I attended.

Our main objective in this three-phase effort to develop prajna is to determine what best motivates us to actualize our finest and truest self, so that we can repeatedly actualize dynamic wisdom—moment after moment, crisis after crisis, opportunity after opportunity. The Dalai Lama often says, "Everything depends on motivation," and his words echo all the ancient Mahayana Buddhist texts on the heroic Bodhisattva's way of living and benefiting the world. We also need to be honest with ourselves about our talents, limitations, practical needs, and emotional flexibility. Once all these factors are acknowledged for what they are—and can become—we have a good chance of living creatively and proactively rather than simply reacting semiconsciously or even unconsciously to circumstances. Through cultivating greater conscious awareness that extends both inside and outside ourselves, we can choose how to respond effectively to what life brings us, rather than dwelling in what Buddhists call the "animal realm" of blind instinct, knee-jerk reactions, and sleepwalking through life.

For starters, one very important thing we need to know when making significant decisions is what we need to undertake *and* what we need to abandon. This is often the most essential question involved in determining the right choice for us individually and for everyone around us. We have to make sure that we're being mindful and attentive to all dimensions of a situation—including what to do and what not to do, what to reach for and what to let go of; why we're doing it as well as how—before taking a leap into action. This conscientious approach to making a decision is especially critical in today's social and political climate, which is increasingly characterized by short-term thinking, blurred values, ambiguous truths, media hype, and partisan facts. In the words of journalist Dorothy Thompson, "One cannot exist today as a person—one cannot exist in full consciousness—without having a showdown with one's self, without having to define what it is that one lives by, without being clear in one's mind what matters and what does not matter."

Then, of course, we need to take that leap into wisdom-activity very clearly and strongly. Being decisive in itself produces magnetism and a will to succeed. This is true even when we're off the mark, so how much better when we know we're on it! The Buddhist scriptures and some of my own lamas' magnificent dynamism have taught me that a genuine Bodhisattva should have great plans and then execute them grandly. As Goethe famously said, "Boldness has its own power and magic." Thus the Bodhisattva stretches his or her wings to embrace the whole world.

The sagacity of prajna wisdom results in the kind of right and assured decision-making that works most successfully to release our own best potential and to benefit the world. Because Bodhisattvas are committed to both of these goals, they continually strive to awaken and be enlightened leaders in everything they do. Even the smallest, most humble gestures, if inspired by prajna wisdom, can make very potent contributions to the general good.

With this in mind, we need to be compassionate toward others in our decision-making and actions at all times, whether we're dealing with our own personal concerns or acting in our roles as leaders, representatives, teachers, mentors, parents, colleagues, or team members. We need to remember that everything we do affects all that lives and that our seemingly individual existence is inextricably linked with countless other lives. In the early 1990s, when the Dalai Lama met privately for the first time with Bill Clinton in Washington, D.C., he told the president, "You are the most powerful man in the world. Every decision you make should be motivated by compassion." Whether or not we are, or become, such a powerful person in the worldly sense, I think we need to approach our lives with a similar commitment to active compassion.

It is wisdom that seeks wisdom, as the Zen master Suzuki Roshi famously said. We need to awaken the sage within, gathering what wisdom we can muster and passing it on to the next generation. We must become the wise ones and the visionary leaders we wish to see in the world today. We can do that in innumerable ways, great and small, through modeling a wise, healthy, balanced, and beautiful way of life. Among these ways are teaching, parenting, mentoring, inspiring, motivating, volunteering, healing, and helping—that is, being of service wherever, whenever, and however we can.

An authentic and effective spiritual practice not only helps us to cultivate wisdom but also transforms how we live, think, and act. Regular, ongoing practice forms the basis for developing prajna wisdom, which leads to enlightenment. Discussion, introspection, life planning, and learning to deal with uncertainty and ambiguity also help in what I lovingly dub "the Wisdom Project," a path of sagacious discrimination.

The Talmud says that the wisest among people is the one who learns from all. I have found that we all have lots of potential learning experiences, but not everyone digests their lessons and becomes a wise elder over the years as a result. Some simply become old fools—jaded and cynical, bored and disillusioned—because they don't reflect on, comprehend, and learn from what they've lived through. As Plato says, "The unexamined life is not worth living." Wisdom tells us that it is not what happens to us but what we do with it that makes all the difference. We can't help our past negative conditioning, but that doesn't mean we have to remain at the mercy of it. Magician Eliphas Levy's words are well worth taking to heart: "Wisdom may be summed up [as follows]: to know, to will, to love, and to do what is good, true, beautiful and just."

Here are activities I recommend for developing prajna wisdom:

- *Read wise words every day.* You can use a book or calendar of daily readings or you can subscribe to daily words of wisdom online.

- *Walk through a cemetery on a regular basis,* preferably once a week or month. As you do, contemplate impermanence, mortality, the brevity of life, and the vital need to prioritize your goals and values. Read the inscriptions and dates on the tombstones and consider this: *The persons buried here lived on this planet and are now gone, just as I shall be one day.*

- *Meditate daily on a selected portion of wisdom scripture.* For example, you might choose the Heart Sutra, the best-known and
  most-often-recited sutra in Mahayana Buddhism; Lao Tzu's
  Tao Te Ching; or the long poem by Seng Ts'an (the Third Zen
  Patriarch), "Trust in the Heart" (also known as "Faith in Mind").
  Intentionally reflect on individual lines as they become luminous during the course of each day.

- *Spend time with those who have genuine wisdom.*

We can't simply study and swiftly acquire wisdom, but we can gradually become wise. And we must do so, not only for our own sake but also
for the sake of everyone else in this sorely troubled world. Many can utter words of wisdom, but few can actually practice them. Henry David
Thoreau believed, "To love wisdom is to live, according to its dictates, a
life of simplicity, independence, magnanimity, and trust." Timeless wisdom is practically useless unless we personally confirm it for ourselves
and the world. Everyone has the beauty of enlightened wisdom within
their own mind.

SEVEN

THE UNIVERSAL TOOL OF SKILLFUL MEANS

May I perfect the multifaceted virtue of skillful means
and resourcefulness, which makes all things possible
and swiftly accomplishes all that is wanted and needed.

The first five paramitas can be seen as virtues leading up to perfect, enlightened wisdom, or prajna, the sixth paramita. As I mentioned in the introduction, the original Buddhist list of paramitas ended there. With the advent of Mahayana Buddhism and an expanded concept of the lay Bodhisattva and the ideal of enlightenment actively engaged in the world, four more paramitas were added, partly to counter the quietist, individualistic tendencies of early Buddhism. We can regard these last four sublime virtues as Bodhisattvic applications of the first six—further dimensions of fully realized prajna wisdom expressing itself outward into the world to relieve the sufferings of all sentient beings. Some gradualistic Mahayana teachers say that the first six paramitas lead up to the wisdom of enlightenment, and the next four are expressions of it.

Skillful means (or, in Sanskrit, *upaya*), the seventh paramita, refers to being resourceful and appropriate in benefiting others, so that our thoughts, words, and deeds effectively serve the specific individuals and circumstances involved. The development of perfect wisdom, or prajna, which comes only with the constant practice of each of the preceding five paramitas, gives us sublime understanding of how things function and interrelate, of what fundamentally matters and what doesn't, and of the relative costs and advantages of all the available options. Discriminating wisdom reveals to us how things actually are and what truly needs to be done, and this profound knowledge leads naturally to the sacred know-how of skillful means. Wisdom knows clearly how things are and can be; skillful means are required to accomplish what needs to be done.

Another way of putting it is that Bodhisattvas, by relying on their clear, all-seeing Wisdom Eye, always know the most effective ways to think, speak, and act. This way of knowing is not merely a mechanical, logical process but a spontaneous, organic one. Their ability to be flexible, adaptable, and creative in serving the world around them is part and parcel of their spiritual genius, which knows no bounds but represents an inexhaustible wellspring of blissful Buddha-activity, enlightening for one and all. Skillful means engage and even enhance whatever worldly talents the individual Bodhisattva may possess—anything from psychological insight and language facility to an aptitude for fixing toasters. Skillful means do not, however, *originate* with these talents. The virtue of using skillful means arises from the concurrent practice of each of the other paramitas, all of which shine with the brilliance of prajna wisdom.

There is an old Buddhist story that illustrates the indispensability of wisdom's guiding light in each and all of the other paramita virtues while providing insight about the cyclical nature of conditioning in the vicious cycle of samsara (or unenlightened life). Once there was an illiterate villager who heard that saving life was a meritorious practice resulting in longevity and better rebirths, and vowed to save at least one hundred fish each day from drowning. Yet the more he netted and pulled out of the water, the more died after flopping around on the riverbank. This simple soul could not stand the suffering of the poor fish, and concluded that he simply wasn't saving them from drowning fast enough, so he tried harder to work faster, concluding that so far he had been too late to save them. He also bought a better net, used a faster boat, and so forth. Don't we too often try to accomplish good things without comprehending the entire picture, often even continuing to do the same things over and over again while expecting different results? The dull but kindly fisherman obviously had good intentions and fine aspirations, energetically exerted himself in his efforts, was focused on helping others as well as accumulating good karma for himself, and felt compassion in his heart, but without the indispensable paramita virtue of clear-sighted wisdom, of which intelligence and common sense are necessary parts, he accomplished more harm than good.

In life, there are always problems we need to address, our own as well as those of others. Often we look at these problems and know not only what is wrong but also what needs to be accomplished to improve the situation. We may even have all the tools required (whether we realize it or not). The sticking point is that we don't know with any satisfying certainty exactly *how* to do the accomplishing part. Instead, we handicap ourselves with questions: *What if I'm wrong? What if there's some better way I'm not considering? What if I make a mistake and things turn out even worse than they were before? Who am I to take this on?*

Let me give you a couple of examples of the kind of dilemma I'm talking about. Tom's son Mark, a freshman in high school, is failing in math. Tom knows that Mark is a smart kid, and he is fairly certain that Mark is failing because he doesn't like his teacher, who has often made him feel awful. Tom also realizes that his son needs help in bolstering his self-esteem. What Tom can't determine is how to deal with the situation, and so he remains perplexed about it. Should he talk to Mark's teacher? If so, what should he say? What if it backfires? Should he tell Mark about going to his teacher beforehand, or afterward, or not at all? What can he do in his own relationship with Mark to improve his son's self-esteem? Suppose his intervention only makes the situation worse?

Meanwhile, Tom's sister, Brianna, works in an office that can best be described as a war zone. Her immediate boss, the vice president in charge of sales, and his superior, the marketing supervisor, are having a power struggle that has given her work environment a tense, hostile atmosphere. Her boss expects her to be on his side, to share his antagonism for his superior. He's even asked her to stop having lunch with anybody from the marketing department because he would consider such an act disloyal. How should she handle the situation? Should she do what she wants? Should she obey her boss, according to the corporate code? What's the smartest thing to do?

The seventh paramita, in cooperation with the other paramitas, offers the key to achieving the best possible solution to such dilemmas. It's about seeing each problem in its totality, recognizing fully our potential to handle it, and then handling it with decisiveness and the utmost skill, trusting in our Buddha nature to guide us. It's the inevitable follow-through on wholeheartedly practicing the spiritual virtues of generosity, patience, ethics, heroic effort, meditation, and wisdom.

In the examples I've just given you, Tom and Brianna are confronting difficulties that require both psychological and practical solutions. As we continue to develop all of the transformative practices in our lives, we become increasingly more capable of meeting any challenge with an approach that combines metaphysics and practicality as skillfully as possible. Remember that the objective of the Bodhisattva is to awaken and to help others to wake up as well. Spiritual know-how gives us the moment-by-moment, day-by-day, problem-by-problem resourcefulness to do precisely that. The more we progress along the Bodhisattva path, the more adept we become at reaching out to others in a wholesome, positive, and fitting way. The Bodhisattva is a spiritual hero, an Awakener, a door-opener. He or she is capable of becoming the right person in the right place at the right time, in order to do the right thing.

Now let's revisit a classic example in Buddhist history of an individual Bodhisattva, Patrul Rinpoche, applying this kind of skillful means to an especially serious problem he encountered (see chapter 1). One hundred years ago, Kham, a large province in eastern Tibet, was a virtual wilderness inhabited by a few tribal clans, some of whom feuded with each other. In his travels in Kham as a wandering yogi, Patrul Rinpoche often walked along a dirt trail through a high and narrow mountain pass connecting two warring villages. He repeatedly passed armed fighters on horseback riding from one direction or the other to attack the opposing village. The sensitive Patrul responded to the violence surrounding him with compassionate prayers. He wanted to help the people of both villages avoid anger and bloodshed, and his intense devotion to this cause prompted an ingenious plan. He decided to lie across the path and stay there, next to a campfire.

For the next few days, every traveler going from one village to the other came up to Patrul Rinpoche and felt compelled to step over him rather than disturb him. As each traveler approached, Patrul prayed for him or her individually, hoping in this way to pacify any angry emotions the traveler harbored.

One time three armed riders came upon the weathered old lama lying next to his campfire. Forced to halt their horses abruptly and dismount, they demanded, "Are you deranged? Are you sick? What is wrong with you that you're lying across the path like this?"

The wise master replied, "Don't worry. You won't catch my disease. They call it lovingkindness, and it is hardly contagious for healthy young fighters such as yourselves." The three warriors were so ashamed and confused that they simply remounted their horses, turned around, and rode back.

Another time two fighters came by from the opposite direction, and a very similar exchange took place, but before the fighters turned back, Patrul added, "Perhaps my disease *is* contagious, this impartial loving-kindness, for it is said you can catch it from the greatest spiritual prac-titioners known as Bodhisattvas. These days, however, although many claim to have the disease, few develop its symptoms of unconditional love and selfless compassion."

After a few days, as if by a miracle, the ongoing blood feud between the two villages came to an end. The local folks claimed that the young fighters must have caught the infectious disease of peace from the non-violent witnessing of the anonymous Enlightened Vagabond obstructing the mountain pass. Once the feuding stopped, Patrul Rinpoche was not seen at the trail again.

Being a master of skillful means like Patrul Rinpoche does not de-pend on training ourselves in particular problem-solving disciplines like conflict resolution, crisis management, negotiation, or psychotherapy—as helpful as these kinds of training can be. Exercising skillful means primarily involves drawing on our total reservoir of knowledge, creativity, and experience in the ways of benefiting others as well as ourselves, both in practical, relative terms and in spiritual, absolute ones. This is a truly remarkable characteristic of Bodhisattvas that sets them apart from other do-gooders: Bodhisattvas have arrived at their singular effectiveness in being beacons in the world by progressing all the way from their initial, Bodhicitta-inspired vow to the development of each and every one of the transformative practices described in this book about the Bodhisattva's tenfold code and altruistic way of life. This spiritual effort and advanced inner evolution gives them exceptional capacities for knowing the right thing to do in the right way for the specific time, place, people, and cir-cumstances at hand. As they enlarge these capacities, they rise above the internal obscurations, biases, inflexibility, vacillation, doubts, and feelings of helplessness that can otherwise keep a person from seeing and doing the right thing. A Bodhisattva thus becomes like a wish-fulfilling jewel.

How do we go about developing our own potential to utilize skillful means? In the sutras, Sakyamuni Buddha explains that we must focus on the following Seven Arya Wealths beyond all others:

1. The richness and wealth of faith and devotion
2. The richness and wealth of self-disciplined ethical conduct
3. The richness and wealth of critical analysis, learning, and attentiveness to the teachings
4. The richness and wealth of generosity and charity
5. The richness and wealth of modesty, honesty, purity, and sincerity
6. The richness and wealth of conscience, decorum, shame, and moral dread
7. The richness and wealth of discriminating wisdom

Keeping our focus on the Seven Arya Wealths does not compel us to reject altogether any other endowments, or "treasures," we may have, such as health, beauty, a good family life, or power and positive influence. Many New Age spiritual people in particular tend to fear or look down on such endowments as being dangerously worldly. True, we can get overly attached to these resources in the mistaken assumption that they're essential to our personal happiness. However, if we have large, heroic Bodhisattva aspirations, we can learn to utilize these treasures skillfully in the service of others. A Bodhisattva has the wisdom and fearlessness to wade right through the swamp of worldliness and doesn't have to live as cautiously as a person carrying a full bowl of hot soup.

In Buddhist tradition, the Bodhisattva of skillful means is also one who needs to be well endowed with the Four Vastu (or virtuous attributes), previously described as beneficial speech, which gathers and motivates people; generosity, which includes giving of our own time and energy; altruism and helpfulness; and the ability to embody the exemplary virtues we talk about—in other words, to practice what we preach.

All of these different lists of qualities and virtues represent a variety of skillful means—multiple ways of communicating spiritual values efficiently and effectively so that all sorts of people with different mind-sets and lifestyles can have access to spiritual truth and further their development. The Buddha himself said that all his teachings were just like toys laid out in front of the burning house of samsara (or worldly, impermanent things) to entice the children inside to come out and be saved. He never claimed that the teachings as such had ultimate importance or eternal reality of any kind. Instead, he emphasized time and time again that they were temporary expedients that could be left behind once the journey to enlightenment was achieved, like medicine that is necessary only as long as the illness lingers. He compared his teachings to a make-shift raft that could be left behind after being used to cross the torrent. He also said, "Like the leaves in the forest compared to those I am now picking up and holding in my hands, thus more there is to know in this universe than what I have taught. I really never said a word of teaching or instruction; everyone simply heard what they needed to hear in the language and way they needed to hear it."

SKILLFUL MEANS ON THE OUTER, INNER, AND SECRET LEVELS

> Try not to localize the mind anywhere, but let it fill up the whole
> body, let it flow throughout the totality of your being. When this
> happens you use the hands where they are needed, you use the legs
> or eyes where they are needed, and no time or energy will go to waste.
>
> —ZEN MASTER TAKUAN,
> GIVING ADVICE TO A SAMURAI WARRIOR

The grand ascendant Bodhisattva exemplifying the infinite skillful means of inexhaustible Buddha-activity is called the Thousand-Armed Avalokita (Kuan-yin in Chinese), a cosmic archetype who it is said sprang ten heads out of compassion for the cries of the world and myriad arms to reach down and help. Each of her many hands holds an implement useful for accomplishing her mission, such as a lotus, book, jewel, bell, prayerful gestures, shepherd's staff, mirror, diamond scepter, wisdom-sword, star, and other tools of the Bodhisattva's trade.

Perhaps the person who has taught me the most about the three levels of upaya paramita is my last living Tibetan mentor, Tulku Pema Wangyal (whose name means Dynamic Lotus), now residing in France. Not all realized masters are gifted teachers. Tulku Pema, however, seems to embody skillful means as a master Bodhisattva and a teacher and can relate to anyone wherever that person is at the time, helping him or her to move swiftly forward on the path to enlightenment.

Like the Buddha himself, who could reportedly be understood by listeners of all kinds and in all languages, Tulku Pema has the sacred teacherly gift of being able to speak on several different levels at once to large groups of people from different backgrounds while simultaneously seeming to speak directly to each individual person. He lights others' lamps without gathering light, or credit, for himself—a truly selfless, humble, Bodhisattva—and exemplifies the adage from the Diamond Wisdom Sutra: "Cultivate a mind that fixates nowhere and holds to nothing." His inner freedom, lightness, and spaciousness help Tulku Pema to see every situation as workable and no problem as insurmountable.

True Bodhisattvas are not rigid dogmatists who can instruct people to do things only the way they themselves do it, as if they were some sort of answer man or fix-it woman. Having the attitude "my way or the highway" is antithetical to the resourcefulness associated with upaya paramita. From Tulku Pema Rinpoche, I have learned to embody a great deal of flexibility in my own teaching style. Thus, I don't experience much difficulty handling questions from my students, no matter where they are coming from or how learned, thoroughgoing, aggressive, challenging, confused, willful, or resistant they may be. As Tulku Pema taught me, effective teaching is a matter not of always having the correct answer to every question but of remaining open, clear, attentive, patient, and adaptable enough to keep things moving in the right direction.

Tulku Pema also models for me how upaya paramita functions on all three levels of a Bodhisattva's being. On the outer level, upaya manifests itself as knowledge, competence, effectiveness, and experience in various worldly sciences, arts, language and communication skills, trades, leadership modes, family and social roles, and so on. On the inner level, upaya consists of being unselfishly altruistic in our inexhaustible and unimpeded capacity to help others attain their goals—in other words, a true Bodhisattva orientation. Upaya on our innermost, secret, Dharmakaya level represents our clear, all-embracing understanding of the pervasive oneness of absolute truth (sunyata) and relative truth (karma, interconnectedness, and interdependence). With this realization, we can discriminate between what is valid and what is not.

To sum it up, outer-level upaya is skill in the means and methods of spiritual practice. It involves knowing how to do what prajna wisdom tells us to do, effectively, efficiently, and harmoniously. Inner-level upaya is our power to be open, resourceful, flexible, and adaptable in doing what we do. Secret-level upaya is actually *being* the right person in the right place at the right time—and being this person in all places and at all times, like an all-accomplishing, wish-fulfilling jewel, knowing nothing more need be done. Thus, advanced Bodhisattvas have the power of multiple emanations.

BODHISATTVAS OF SKILLFUL MEANS

> May I be a wishing jewel, a magic vase,
> Powerful mantras, and effective medicine;
> May I become a wish-fulfilling tree
> And a vessel of plenty for the world.
>
> —SHANTIDEVA

One day Helen, an elementary school teacher I know, had her first-grade class draw with pencils and crayons. She was walking around the classroom looking over her students' work, encouraging here, helping out there, enjoying and appreciating the entire show, when she came to little Camilla, who was furiously working on her picture. "What are you drawing, Camilla?" she asked.

Camilla replied, "I'm drawing a picture of God."

"But, Camilla," Helen said, "no one knows what God looks like."

"They will in a minute!" exclaimed Camilla, and she got back to work.

To invoke the motto of the U.S. Naval Construction Force—the "Seabees"—Camilla's "can-do, will-do, am-doing" attitude is exactly the spirit of the fearless Bodhisattva. It knows no limits and proceeds with the boundless energy and confident resourcefulness of a spiritual hero, an Awakener intent on awakening the world. Like water that is unstoppable in finding its way to fall or flow downward and eventually rejoin the source of all waters, the Bodhisattva of skillful means is totally committed to solving problems and accomplishing goals that benefit all human beings.

My uncle Wilbur Miller, better known as Bill or Willy, was like that. He was my father's younger brother, and he always seemed to be engaged in doing or fixing things for people. An electrical engineer by trade, he enlisted in the army during World War II, along with my dad, and played on the traveling baseball team, which included major leaguers, to entertain the troops in the European theater. He played with me from my earliest childhood years, took me to major sporting events, and taught me many sports. But what I remember most about him is how positive, industrious, and ingenious he was in figuring out ways to accomplish things. Rather than being a jack-of-all-trades (who is often master of none), he exemplified the ideal of the modern engineer, for whom every problem has to have a fitting solution. He taught by example that nothing is impossible unless you think it is. We nicknamed him "Can-Do Willy."

When no one in our family could repair the boiler, radiator, car, lawn mower, roof, or whatever, we chanted our mantra, "Call Uncle Willy over." He always entered through the back door and, after hearing the problem, said, "I'll have to put on my thinking cap!" He then grabbed whatever appurtenance was at hand—an actual hat, a doily, or a manila envelope—and made a show of donning it while starting up the machinery inside his brainpan. He even mimicked smoke coming out of his ears. My mother always put up with these antics, having learned through experience that there was real hope of a swift if not simple solution amidst all this *mishigas*.

If the situation was really challenging, Uncle Bill might say to me, "Jeffrey, let's go to the library and look further into this." We would then head out, stopping on the way at the corner soda fountain to get an old-fashioned, hand-mixed chocolate egg cream or a cherry Coke. At the library I discovered, thanks to him, that all manner of things could be learned with comparatively little research. And the library wasn't the only resource to which he introduced me. In that long-ago, more male-dominated historical period of my middle and late childhood, we often had to seek a bit of what was essentially "guys' knowledge" about how something worked—mechanically, politically, economically, or socially. I found out from my uncle that it sometimes helped in this pursuit to put on work clothes, bring a six-pack of cold beer to the local gas station, and discuss matters with the head mechanic, or to pay a friendly sunset visit to the coach of one of my sports teams. One such visit produced the unforeseen side benefit of getting me to play in an especially memorable North-South all-star Pop Warner League football game during a weekend road trip that included a tour around the Civil War battlefield at Gettysburg.

Sometimes Uncle Bill would give me the present of a book, an erector set, or a kit to build a ship or a plane, a favorite pastime for my brother and me. In doing so, he passed along yet more skillful means for learning how things worked. He loved to read and, referring to classic authors, often said, "Some of my best friends lived long ago," a truth that only later came home to roost for me. But I think he preferred to read with his hands, as if feeling through his able fingertips the Braille-like secrets of whatever he was working to understand or fix. His appetite for getting his fingers into a new challenge remained undimmed into his last years. I remember that he was one of the first people in his suburban Los Angeles neighborhood to master a personal computer. "It's only numbers!" he told me once. "I'm like a number myself—just like a computer program."

"I just don't get numbers," I told him. "I'm a word man."

"I know, Jeffrey," he said. "But there's an elegance and a poetry to mathematics too, you know!"

To my mind, Uncle Bill was a Bodhisattva—not only because he was a master of skillful means but also because he always seemed to have time to give himself to others and he was gladly ready to participate, contribute, help, teach, and mentor. Perhaps he is now teaching folks up in heaven about digital wireless and cable while using it himself so he and my Aunt Sally can follow the ball games and keep track of each of us family members still here below. My father is probably next door to him, building a house for us all to come live in, with a garden all around it. Probably I'll still have to mow the lawn when I get there!

Recently I was teaching at a weekend retreat in Austin, Texas, on the subject of the Bodhisattva way of life and the stellar exemplars, both traditional and contemporary, from whom we can learn. Austin is renowned as a capital of live music. It was therefore appropriate that when we were discussing possible modern Bodhisattvas, one student suggested the rock icon Bono of the long-popular U2 band. Bono has certainly demonstrated extraordinary Bodhicitta virtues and skillful means in bridging the gap between the arts and social activism. His messages on behalf of the poor have reached even the ears of the world's highest-level political and governmental figures, moving some of them to engage in uncharacteristically generous acts of outreach. For example, Bono managed to enlist Jesse Helms, the archconservative former U.S. senator from North Carolina, in the fight against AIDS in Africa.

Another, much more widely known, example of a Bodhisattva of skillful means is Oprah Winfrey. No one can begrudge her the success she has attained; after all, she did it by overcoming formidable obstacles, including poverty, neglect, sexual abuse, racism, and sexism. Winfrey reminds us that we don't have to inherit a family trust fund in order to be a light-bearing philanthropist in the world. Instead, we can do it by combining will and character with talent and perseverance.

Aside from being an innovative television and movie star, a media producer, and the editorial director of her own magazine, with a firm commitment in all these endeavors to helping people lead better lives, Winfrey runs a variety of unusually skillful philanthropic organizations with a worldwide scope. To date, her private charity, the Oprah Winfrey Foundation, has awarded hundreds of grants to support the education and empowerment of women, children, and families through the development of schools, curricula, and scholarships. I was especially moved by the foundation's 2002 initiative, "Christmas Kindness in South Africa." Winfrey herself visited orphanages and rural schools in South Africa and handed out gifts of books, school supplies, food, clothing, and toys to over fifty thousand children. She also provided funding for libraries and teacher education in sixty-three South African schools and announced a partnership with the Ministry of Education to build a special academy for girls. I especially honor her for putting her boots on the ground in South Africa rather than just sending a check.

In addition, Winfrey has established a public charity, Oprah's Angel Network, featured on *The Oprah Winfrey Show* and also on her Web site, Oprah.com. Designed to inspire people to make a difference in the lives of others, this charity has raised over $27 million in donations to benefit schools, scholarships, women's shelters, youth centers, and other nonprofit humanitarian organizations.

Of course, millions of Americans recognize how skillfully Winfrey uses her television program to promote reading through her book club and to encourage self-development among her viewers through her own sharing of personal experiences and the advice of guest experts. What is often not appreciated about Winfrey, however, is that her commitment to serving others extends well beyond her television program and that she demonstrates an unusual level of pioneering skill in fulfilling that commitment. More recently I was pleased to see that Warren Buffett and Bill and Melinda Gates were joining their substantial forces to further important charitable causes in new and imaginatively effective ways.

Within the Buddhist religion there are many individuals whom I could cite as outstanding models of skillful means. Tibetan Buddhism (or Vajrayana), technically known as the Path of Skillful Means, is replete with relevant inner and outer transformative practices, energy transmissions, empowerments, wise pith instructions, and personal exemplars. Among the modern masters of Tibetan Buddhism, I remember the late lama Chögyam Trungpa Rinpoche as a particularly inspiring icon of upaya paramita. Born in Tibet, where he achieved spiritual realization, he left that country after the Chinese occupation and studied in India and England, quickly becoming fluent in English. He founded the first Tibetan monastery outside Asia—Samye Ling in Scotland—and the first Buddhist university outside Asia—Naropa Institute in Boulder, Colorado, now a fully accredited university with undergraduate and graduate programs. He also wrote many books that introduced millions of Westerners to Buddhism.

To my mind, Trungpa Rinpoche was the greatest of all modern Buddhist pioneers in foreign lands. He was psychologically astute, creative, fearless, iconoclastic, and freewheeling, without losing his grounding in the timeless spiritual tradition into which he was born. Besides being adept at Tibetan Buddhism's many methods of furthering inner development, he became a master of photography, calligraphy, and flower arrangement and was interested in the martial arts, too, skills he put to the service of helping others to help themselves. He established several retreat centers, a theater troupe, a therapy institute, and a spiritual magazine.

Trungpa Rinpoche was the first lama to make a film and, through his friendship with Suzuki Roshi of the San Francisco Zen Center, one of the first to bridge the gap between Tibetan Buddhism and Zen. In 1974 he brought the Sixteenth Karmapa to the West for the first time, a significant landmark for Buddhism in its encounter with modernity. Later he visited and taught us at the Karmapa's monastery in Woodstock, New York.

I knew Trungpa Rinpoche personally three decades ago, when we occasionally had drinks or meals together as well as some valuable teaching and meditation time. I remember one time when he was publicly criticized for some personal improprieties; he immediately fell into a prayer mode and said aloud, "May whoever has contact with me and my lineage receive its blessing and make an auspicious connection. May whoever hurls harsh words or even stones at me hit me and thus make an auspicious connection. May my life be beneficial to all beings."

This response to a tricky, confrontational situation is a terrific example of skillful means, upaya. Trungpa Rinpoche acted like an expert sailor meeting a storm and tacking upwind instead of letting himself be blown away; or like a martial artist using the strength of his adversary as an ally or as an asset, like an aikido master tripping and flipping a charging opponent without doing him serious harm. He always seemed able to lean into the difficulties posed by unwanted situations rather than overreact, contract, hide, or run away. He skillfully used everything at his disposal as part of the path of awakening, what he called "the ever-rising Great Eastern Sun." When I think of him now, with his cheery, British-inspired speaking style and manners, I recall the great Bodhisattva Atisha's adage "Always maintain a joyful mind."

BARRIERS AND GATEWAYS TO BEING SKILLFUL

> When you become detached mentally from yourself and
> concentrate on helping other people with their difficulties,
> you will be able to cope with your own more effectively.
> Somehow the act of self-giving is a personal power-releasing
> factor.
>
> —NORMAN VINCENT PEALE

Just as the key to enlightenment is breaking through the illusion that we are solid and separate from the rest of the universe, and just as the prime characteristic of a Bodhisattva is going beyond his or her own self-interest to serve others, so the secret of developing skillful means is overcoming self-involved patterns that stand in our Bodhisattvic way. In his masterful *The Way of the Bodhisattva*, Shantideva identifies these patterns as Eight Qualities That Limit One's Potential.

As you review each of these negative qualities, think about how it may pose problems for you in your own life, making you unskillful not only with others but also with yourself. Jot down memories of specific times when you exhibited each quality. For each incident, ask yourself:

- What did I actually think, say, and do that demonstrated this negative quality?

- What were the negative results?

- How could I have risen above this negative quality to handle the matter more skillfully?

The Eight Qualities That Limit One's Potential are

1. Being confused and lacking in discernment and understanding
2. Being distracted by emotional conflicts, or having a fondness for unproductive, unwholesome, negative, or crude ways
3. Being overly influenced by others, or under the power of others
4. Being lazy, dull, numb, or complacent, and thus impervious to an awareness of suffering
5. Postponing and procrastinating, or lacking inspiration, aspiration, or devotion
6. Being distracted or unable to break from habitual patterns, reactions, or preoccupations—uninterested in wholesome, positive, and sublime ways
7. Being fearful in regard to survival or livelihood, or selfish and lacking in altruism
8. Being overly concerned with worldly gain and loss, ambitious, or hypocritical and unfaithful to vows and commitments

Once we have studied and made ourselves more conscious of the qualities that limit our potential for being skillful, we can focus more productively on positive, skillful ways of thinking, speaking, and behaving. According to Tibetan Buddhism, there are Four Forms of Buddha-Activity that Bodhisattvas cultivate to enhance their repertoire of skillful means so that they can help advance themselves and all sentient beings *together* along the path to enlightenment. These Four Forms of Buddha-Activity are peaceful, magnetic, powerful, and fierce.

These forms represent the various kinds of skillful means that are appropriate for different situations. Just as one size, one speed, or one flavor does not suit everyone, Buddha-activity has four different dimensions, gears, or styles of energy and presentation from which to choose in order to deal skillfully with different circumstances. Thus, we see in Buddhist mandalas and temple design the Guardian Kings of the Four Directions, each protecting its domain in its own distinctive manner.

As you review each of the Four Forms of Buddha-Activity, think about recent challenges in which you applied that form—or might have applied it—skillfully for the benefit of all.

1. *Peaceful* (in Tibetan, *shiwa*): Pacifying is not a quick-fix sort of activity, like putting a pacifier in the mouth of a crying baby. Instead, it's a proactive and harmonizing approach in which we strive to resolve destructive conflicts on a deeper level and to deal with underlying causes rather than mere symptoms. Jesus's ministry, for example, was largely a sustained message of love, forgiveness, and tolerance that required a great deal of perseverance and courage on his part. Nonviolence, acceptance, forgiveness, and reconciliation are general examples of peacemaking activities.

2. *Magnetic* (in Tibetan, *gyepa*): The Tibetan word for this form can also be translated as "increasing," "gathering," or "enriching." First comes the gentle activity of making peace, harmonizing, reconciling, redressing grievances, or in some way establishing the truth. Then we build more energetically on this base by motivating, inspiring, inciting, exhorting, empowering, inviting, and attracting. Sometimes this kind of dynamic activity can manifest as a miracle, as when saints perform wonders that immediately awaken and powerfully stimulate belief.

3. *Powerful* (in Tibetan, *wangpo*): To be powerful is to display the full natural authority and dignity of the truth without

compromising it. Trungpa Rinpoche often identified this form of activity as "ruthless compassion"—for example, refusing to loan money to someone we have good reason to believe will spend it on illegal drugs, even if we're very close to this person and would love to help him or her out financially. The authentic, divinelike presence of a spiritual master overcomes ordinary mind and its ordinary perceptions and projections, generating a strong state of grace and beatitude.

4. *Fierce* (in Tibetan, *drakpo*): Fierce or wrathful activity is one step more dramatic and aggressive than powerful activity. Instead of displaying authority, we blaze with it to ensure that truth prevails. We exhibit this form, for example, when we shout at little ones who are running into the street. We don't simply speak calmly to them, explaining why they are out of line. Instead, our adrenaline surges and we spontaneously shout at the top of our lungs to arrest their attention before an accident can occur. This ferocious form of love and warning is embodied in the images of the wrathful deities we see in the art of Tibetan Buddhism as well as other religions, such as Hinduism. We can also see it in the story about Jesus wrathfully chasing the moneylenders out of the holy temple. We can appreciate that the same Bodhisattva who can be peaceful (like Jesus in his sermons and his acts of benevolent mercy) can also be intensely wrathful in righting wrongs and bringing things back into balance. It all depends on the Bodhisattva's ability to choose the most skillful means at hand to promote the truth. Sometimes strong or even bitter medicine is required.

The latter two forms of Buddha-activity—being powerful and being fierce—surprise many people, who assume that nonviolence (or *ahimsa*), a key concept in Buddhism, requires that the Bodhisattva always avoid conflict and do nothing actively to defend or fight for a righteous cause. Nonviolence, however, does not imply passivity, complacence, indifference, indolence, or lassitude. Instead, it points to being compassionate and caring rather than crudely violent in our activity. We don't have to be anemic lotus-eaters or societal dropouts in dealing with the difficulties, exigencies, challenges, injustices, and vicissitudes of life. The Dalai Lama himself, perhaps the most pacifist world leader, has maintained bodyguards ever since receiving death threats. When enlightened masters drive a car, they should use seat belts, shouldn't they? Compassion is a powerful force in the world, not a sign of weakness or fear. Protecting and cherishing what is worthy of such care is part of the Bodhisattva's duty.

As a lesson in not being foolishly passive when stronger measures are justified and appropriate, I like the story of a large snake that once approached the Buddha and said, "The village children are constantly harassing me! They throw sticks and stones at me! I want to be kind and gentle, as you advise, but I also can't help wanting to strike at them!"

The Buddha replied, "Do not strike back and harm the children. They don't know what they are doing." Inspired by the Buddha's beatific presence, kind heart, and wise words, the snake vowed to follow the advice and slithered home.

A few days later the snake appeared again before the Buddha. He'd been beaten so much that he was crushed and bloody and could only move with extreme difficulty and slowness. Complaining to the Buddha, he cried, "The children still kept attacking me. They were even more ferocious, but as you instructed, I did nothing in return. I accepted the abuse and barely escaped with my life. Now look at me!"

"Oh, poor, dear, faithful snake!" the Buddha answered. "I did not tell you not to hiss!"

It is said that all Bodhisattvas need two wings to fly to Buddhahood, just as a bird needs two wings to fly through the air. The Bodhisattva's two wings are wisdom and compassion, the wisdom of sunyata and the compassion of skillful means—prajna and upaya inseparable.

Prevent trouble before it arises.
Put things in order before they exist.
The giant pine tree
grows from a tiny sprout.
The journey of a thousand miles
starts beneath your feet.
Rushing into action, you fail.
Trying to grasp things, you lose them.
Forcing a project to completion,

You ruin what was almost ripe.
Therefore the Master takes action
by letting things take their course.
He remains calm
at the end as at the beginning.
He has nothing
thus has nothing to lose.
What he desires is nondesire;
what he learns is to unlearn.
He simply reminds people
of who they have always been.
He cares about nothing but the Tao [the Way].
Thus he can care for all things.

—LAO TZU

EIGHT

THE PROFUNDITY AND VASTNESS OF SPIRITUAL ASPIRATIONS

May I perfect the adamantine virtue of unshakable resolve,
determination, and inspired aspiration,
which has vast vision and universal scope.

Don't we all start out with high hopes for our lives? When I was a kid, I remember my friends and I all talked about achieving fantastic goals. Some of us wanted to be rocket scientists. Others talked about becoming ship captains, jet pilots, firefighters, major league ballplayers, brain surgeons, or presidents. These were our worldly aspirations at the time. The more mature among us may have started formulating spiritual goals even as children, but most of us were concerned with personal, real-life ambitions. The eighth transformative practice, spiritual aspirations, centers on far more evolved objectives.

Pranidhana, the Sanskrit name for this paramita, refers directly to the Bodhisattva Vow, which is, after all, the highest aspiration that any of us can have: to reach toward enlightenment not only for ourselves but for everyone else. As Shantideva summarized it, "Until every being afflicted by pain has reached Nirvana's shores, may I serve only as a condition that encourages progress and joy." Pranidhana can also be translated in more general terms as spiritual resolve, commitment, determination, and inspiration. It's the antidote to common worldly malaises like indecisiveness, lack of focus, passivity, ennui, shortsightedness, discouragement, meaninglessness, alienation, and duplicity. Patanjali, the father of yoga, said when you are inspired, dormant forces, faculties, and talents come alive, and you discover yourself to be a greater person by far than you ever dreamed yourself to be.

The equivalent word for *pranidhana* in the Tibetan language is *mönlam*—literally, prayer-aspiration path—which is more widely understood as spiritual blessings or prayers. In this latter sense, it refers to the accumulated spiritual power, grace, and energy that are believed to be transmitted by a saintly person's highly evolved consciousness and sacred intention. This power is sought or bestowed in various ways involving special ceremonies, initiations, teachings, relics, mantras, pilgrimages, *malas* (or rosaries), flags, statues, protection cords, spiritual pills, and so on.

Among all these blessings and prayers, however, some have the kind of supreme significance I'm talking about in this chapter and others don't. My own late Dzogchen master, Tulku Urgyen-Rinpoche of Karnying Gompa in Nepal, once made this distinction:

> What people usually consider blessings are what I call superficial blessings. Often when people have something they want to get rid of or don't like, they pray, "Please bless me to be free from this." It might be sickness, pain, or an attack by evil spirits. It might be something as mundane as a business not going so well. People also ask for red protection cords to wear around their necks, sacred medicines to eat, rituals to be performed. When they are cured, when the evil spirits have been repelled, when their business is going well again, or whatever, they say, "I got the blessings." On the other hand, the true blessings are the oral instructions on how to become enlightened in a single lifetime, which you can receive from a qualified master.

Here I am translating pranidhana as the transformative practice of spiritual aspirations precisely because it is inextricably linked with this kind of ultimate quest, the constant resolve and determination to become a fully realized Bodhisattva. Just as we need to chant and reaffirm the Bodhisattva Vow every day of our lives in order to keep it fresh, we need to cultivate our individual resolve and determination with the same degree of regularity. Not only must we reinforce over and over again our sterling intentions and their importance in our own lives and for the lives of others, but we must also look into what drives us away from these noble intentions: our petty thoughts, words, and deeds of selfishness, fear, egoism, or low self-esteem.

In addition, I think the practice of spiritual aspirations calls for us to go beyond simply thinking, saying, and doing good. I believe we are further obliged to develop and exercise our capacities for responsible *leadership*. For instance, I firmly believe that being a Bodhisattva on a practical level includes being an informed and active citizen. Most of us are not hermits, nor are we meant to be. We have to know about the world around us: whom and what we're voting for and how best to address the vital social, political, and economic issues facing our communities, our nation, and our planet. No one person can do it all, yet no one person is exempt from participating. We need and depend upon each other.

These days I find that reading the news is just about my hardest spiritual practice. Sometimes I hate doing it. News reports in general tend to be distressing. As the cliché in the newspaper world goes, "If it bleeds, it leads." Part of me would very much like to ignore these reports or separate myself from them, if only to preserve my peace of mind. It is so difficult to cut through the partisan spin of these reports and attempt to figure out what is actually going on.

Yes, it can be frustrating, infuriating, and even heartbreaking, but it's also necessary for my spiritual aspirations as a Bodhisattva, and so I keep bolstering my determination to do it as part of working toward a better future for us all. I try to read the foreign press online for alternative perspectives to U.S. coverage. I go to Amy Goodman's "Democracy Now!" website or Stratfor.com for different kinds of analysis. I read well-respected books on issues that especially concern me. Just recently I was moved by my friend John Perkins's surprise bestseller, *Confessions of an Economic Hit Man,* which chronicles how the American government and corporatocracy have used World Bank loans and international aid to enslave economically poor and developing nations under the guise of helping them to develop. When I start to feel overwhelmed by national and international affairs today, I also seek counsel from wise living masters as well as classic works like the *Tao Te Ching* and the Bhagavad Gita.

As committed Bodhisattvas, we can't afford to give up or give in to despair and cynicism. Nor can we afford to function as so many uninformed, would-be authority figures do, blathering on about things we really don't know much about by making public pronouncements outside our areas of expertise while the spotlight is momentarily on us. Nor can we afford to be rebellious dropouts from, or silent followers of, the status quo. In fact, we need to become more enlightened statespeople and leaders ourselves, if only within our own small circle of family, friends, colleagues, and acquaintances. We must strive to become the wise elders and enlightened leaders this world needs.

That's why I like to think of all ten transformative practices as principles of enlightened leadership. If we want to help awaken and save all sentient beings, we must create a society that is guided by wise men and women who embody these principles rather than by opportunists, extremists, or people who are merely politicians, pollsters, businessmen, and passive focus group members and little else. By following the ten paramitas in our own lives, we can generate this altruistic leadership aspiration in ourselves and foment it among others. As Boris Pasternak claimed, "It is not revolutions and upheavals that clear the way to new and better days but someone's soul, inspired and ablaze."

Robert Greenleaf coined the phrase "servant leadership" to describe this kind of mission in his popular book with the same title. By "servant leadership," he meant, not the ability to lead servants, but rather the ability to be a selfless, service-oriented leader. This latter kind of power and influence is not exploitative or egocentric but compassionate, wise, and enlightened. Instead of the leader being number one, it's the people he or she leads who come first. Like the good shepherd who enters the fold at night only after all the sheep are safely tucked in, the selfless Bodhisattva is the last to enter nirvana, the realm of enlightenment, after everyone else has been delivered.

For this reason, the practice of pranidhana—resolute spiritual aspirations—focuses on developing a heart-mind that is ever more strongly directed toward enlightenment. No matter what is going on in our lives, no matter how stressed, tired, or tempted we might be, such aspirations keep our eyes on the goal of universal enlightenment.

In the many sports I played in my younger years, the ball was usually the most important thing on the field or court. Where and how it went determined the way the game would be played, and we never wanted to drop, fumble, misjudge, throw away, or lose sight of it. The same thing is true of the shimmering "ball" of enlightenment. We need to stay constantly oriented to it—not only for our own sake but also for the sake of everyone else. Keeping our eye on this ball helps get us through the rough patches of life and assists us in helping others to do the same. It also strengthens our commitment to what is truly important in life, which includes never losing sight of the fact that our own peace, harmony, and freedom are inextricably linked with the peace, harmony, and freedom of all sentient beings. As Paul Crafts, one of my amusing Bodhisattva friends, says, "We must maintain our high resolve and good work without slackening until even good old Thelma Finkelstein gets enlightened!"

The concept of the person who is deeply committed to spiritual development of this kind is a critical one in Buddhism, and deserves a great deal of respect and consideration. Such commitment is not always valued in the modern secular world, where people often look askance at faith, virtue, kindness, forgiveness, humility, reverence, and self-sacrifice. Some even fear that these gentle positive qualities might prevent them from achieving their materialistic, competitive goals in life. Those with this attitude, however, are completely ignoring the interconnectedness and interdependence of all beings. No one actually stands alone. As the Dalai Lama repeatedly says, we need each other in order to become enlightened. This is the inclusive Bodhisattva mentality.

One of the main struggles we face in trying to perfect ourselves in an imperfect world is remaining dedicated enough to follow our hearts and stick to our convictions under all circumstances, despite the fact that we sometimes seem to get little or no support from society at large. The practice of spiritual aspirations brings us back to the essence of the Bodhisattva Code, the indispensable Bodhicitta, or goodness of heart—our lodestone, our core belief system, our rock in the ceaselessly shifting sea of daily life. It constantly reminds us that our fundamental purpose is to attain enlightenment for ourselves as well as to lead all others along the path. Everything depends on the strength of this visionary Bodhicitta commitment to our highest spiritual aspirations.

DESIRE VERSUS ASPIRATION:
WHAT IS OUR MOTIVE?

> Although the world is full of suffering,
> it is also full of the overcoming of it.
>
> —HELEN KELLER

Competing with our Bodhisattva Vow—the sacred focus for our heart-mind—are all the worldly desires that arise within us. Shantideva classifies these desires and the suffering associated with them as the Eight Worldly Concerns: praise and blame, pleasure and pain, fame and obscurity, gain and loss.

So how is the kind of aspiration I'm talking about fundamentally different from these desires? Aren't they all matters of striving for something beyond us?

Once during a lecture at Harvard University, not far from where I live, a student asked the Dalai Lama, "Isn't the aspiration for enlightenment just another form of desire or attachment that breeds suffering?" He replied, "I think that a distinction should be made between desires that are due to ignorance and desires that are reasoned. In Tibetan, a difference can be made between 'wish' and 'desire.' For instance, a Bodhisattva is reborn through his or her own wishes, not out of desire. Similarly, it is suitable to aspire toward liberation."

The Buddha clearly stated, in the Four Noble Truths, that life is difficult because of our deluded, desire-based clinging and craving. This being the case, it's possible that even a desire for enlightenment can become an ego-based ambition that gets in the way of our true spiritual development. The late Chögyam Trungpa Rinpoche referred to this misguided state of egocentric ambition as "spiritual materialism," in which self-centeredness and worldly values masquerade in spiritual garb, like wolves in sheep's clothing, co-opting our true path. Still, we should not paralyze ourselves and abandon our spiritual quest by prematurely cutting off striving in itself simply because it seems, on the surface, like desiring. There are already enough obstacles in our way without creating any more for ourselves!

Careful discernment is called for here so that we can discriminate more wisely between ordinary desires and achievement-oriented attachment, on the one hand, and authentic spiritual aspiration, on the other. Keep in mind that genuine aspiration for enlightenment always includes aiming for the welfare of others. If we truly want to liberate ourselves from suffering, we need to appreciate in the depths of our being that we can never do that as long as our loved ones, neighbors, and fellow human beings are still ensnared.

How, then, do we cultivate that understanding? Where do we get the core inspiration needed for all the dedicated effort, perseverance, and energy it takes to journey toward awakening? How do we recognize the basic rightness of our aspiration, so that we can better motivate ourselves to realize it? What brings us the essential grace, blessing, and firm resolve to attain enlightenment and help to awaken all sentient beings?

The secret lies in a realization that takes place so deeply within us that it can't be denied. Some of us wake up one day, perhaps in the course of a midlife crisis or some other disruption of our habitual trance of complacency, and suddenly, poignantly, we feel that we're living what Thoreau calls "a life of quiet desperation." Simultaneously arising with that feeling is a compelling wish to find a truer, deeper, more enlightened way to live.

This kind of inner yearning can help catalyze a truly remarkable spiritual transformation and inner revolution like the one this book advocates. It can also operate more subtly to keep us alert and on balance whenever we get fatigued. My friend Leo, for example, is a very caring parent, psychiatrist, and human being. Last summer, during a bike ride along the Mystic River, he told me that he sometimes finds himself so stretched out as a caregiver that he begins to experience "ratio strain"—too much going out and not enough coming in—and a voice deep inside him cries out, "Who's taking care of *me*?" For years this feeling was a serious problem that he couldn't resolve. But recently, thanks to his maturing Buddhist practice, things have changed. Now when he gets that old, tired feeling and that inner voice asks, "Who's taking care of *me*?" he hears it answer, "God does, Buddha does, and my teacher and community do too." His inner self is then flooded with a feeling of immense gratitude and an inexplicable but inspirational certainty that all is well. "Who would have ever thought of that!" he exclaimed. "I really don't have to take care of everything myself! My work is a lot easier now. Thank God for the Dharma."

Many people can recall breakthrough or "peak experience" moments from their younger years that set them along their spiritual path and that, as memories, still motivate them. Several years ago, an orthodox rabbi named Gabriel came from Israel to Boston to study Dzogchen at my center. He confided to me that he had had mystical leanings since his early teens, but they had almost been drummed out of him by his family, his friends, and the materialistic European society around him. It was only by chance that during the 1980s he encountered a Kabbalistic rabbi who initiated him into that branch of deep Jewish mysticism, a rescue of sorts that helped transform him into a spiritual mensch. Now he is writing a book on Dzogchen and Kabbalah as sibling spiritual paths.

Referring to the start of the whole process, those mystical intimations during puberty, Rabbi Gabriel said, "One day when I was about twelve or thirteen, living in Paris, I had a dreamlike vision in my bed, as if all the divine light in heaven was pouring down into me. Then I was above it all, looking down and seeing everyone and everything, as if with God's eye, and yet I also felt that I was the people I was seeing, that God's eye was gazing through me. It was a more blissful, rapturous, cosmic vision than I could have ever imagined. I had no idea what it signified. So I waited until breakfast time and asked my father, a scientist, what it was all about. For years he had been discouraging me from my yeshiva studies and hoping I would eventually become a doctor or professor like him. He said, 'Son, it doesn't mean anything. Everyone has that kind of thing happen. Don't think about it.' And that was that. It wasn't until much later that I learned what extraordinary grace and blessings had been vouchsafed me at such an early age."

Children are naturally spiritual in nature, but they appear to lose much of it as socialization takes place and they become more worldly. Rabbi Gabriel's dream is similar in spirit to a recurrent dream I used to have when I was little. I would dream that I was on the other side of the world. It felt both like coming home, which was good, and like being far away from home, which was frightening. When I was nine or ten years old, I finally asked my dad about it. Reacting like a typical father wanting to reassure his child about a nightmare, he said, "Aaah, don't worry about it! It doesn't mean a thing. It's just a dream, Jeffrey." A dozen years later, when I landed in the Himalayas and felt immediately that I belonged there, my Tibetan lamas told me that they thought I had Buddhist blood and had probably lived in Tibet and China in previous lifetimes. Only then did that recurrent dream begin to make sense for me. Only then did I understand its role as a precipitator of my internal quest for meaning and, ultimately, the fulfillment of my spiritual aspirations. Now in my fifties, I can feel at home and at rest wherever I am.

When I took the Bodhisattva Vow for the first time, with my root lama, the Sixteenth Karmapa, in 1973, he told me that my obligation included chanting and reaffirming the vow every morning and night as part of our daily Tibetan prayer and meditation routine. This has helped motivate and inspire me over the years. In the beginning, it helped to familiarize me with the vow and its various aspects. Later, it helped to strengthen and solidify my resolve to fulfill it. Discovering Shantideva's Bodhisattva path book at about the same time was extremely helpful.

The discomfiting truth is that it is easier to produce good thoughts and positive intentions than to maintain and fully actualize them. Moreover, it is all too easy to fall into an egocentric outlook and undertake even spiritual efforts and charitable activities with inappropriately limited or selfish intentions. We need constantly to reinvigorate our highest, deepest, and most heartfelt spiritual aspirations—the true life of our best self beyond our worldly, separate, craving ego concerns. Even now I chant the Bodhisattva Vow three times daily, as well as many of the inspiring Karmapa's prayers that I know by heart.

In the Tibetan tradition, the Bodhisattva Vow to be chanted daily is

> I take refuge in and rely on the enlightened Buddha,
> the liberating Dharma,
> and the supportive sangha community;
> For the benefit of all beings,
> From now until reaching perfect enlightenment
> I shall wholeheartedly practice the
> transcendental paramita virtues.

Prayer is a very potent source of inspiration. Praying to stay on the Bodhisattva path reflects the heart of Bodhicitta and the essence of the eighth paramita. It's an act that includes body and mind, speech and breath, devotion and energy, spirit and intention. The law of karma is that every action has a consequence, and so will any prayer. Indeed, could there be anything more efficacious? Scientific studies show that even placebos—substances that patients assume are medicine but that have no medicinal value—are anywhere from 30 to 40 percent effective in treating illness. Why wouldn't genuine faith coupled with earnest and sincere praying work even more powerfully?

There are many different kinds of prayer. Most of them depend on a strongly directed intention, and I believe it is the power of that resolute intention that helps them eventually to become fulfilled. Prayer is also a skillful means of humbling ourselves so that we can open up more easily, knowing that we alone are not the omnipotent lords of the universe and must sometimes ask for help. And it assists us in formulating our concerns and wishes more wisely and compassionately and putting our deepest wishes and hopes into action. As I mentioned earlier, Tibetans call the eighth paramita mönlam, or the prayer-aspiration path.

I have heard some people say that there is no place for prayer in Buddhism, but this makes little sense to me after living for many years in Asia, where prayer is such a dynamic part of traditional Buddhist life and culture. Praying in this context goes far beyond simply requesting things that one wants. There are purifying and confessional prayers, beneficent prayers, healing prayers, peace prayers, centering prayers, praise prayers, obstacle-removing prayers, longevity prayers, empowerment prayers, intercessionary prayers, and so on. All of these prayers lend substance and richness to spiritual aspirations.

Dazzled by all the different prayers and prayer rituals that exist, people often ask me, "How should I pray?" I advise them to begin by taking a deep breath, relaxing, bowing their head, and bringing the palms of their hands together. The next step is to pray from the heart with full attention, humility, and fervency. It doesn't matter what words or language we use to pray; all convey meaning. Oddly enough, I believe that it really doesn't matter much who or what we think we are praying to. It is the heartfelt prayer itself that is important. We pray to become a pure Bodhisattva.

I offer you the following prayer to use as it is and as a model for your own self-generated prayers. One of my favorite prayers came up for me just prior to a candlelight vigil on the cusp of the new millennium: December 31, 1999.

New Millennium Dedication

May all beings everywhere,
with whom we are inseparably interconnected,
be liberated, awakened, healed, fulfilled, and free.
May there be peace in this world and throughout all possible universes,
an end to war, violence, poverty, injustice, and oppression,
and may we all together complete the spiritual journey.

SPIRITUAL ASPIRATIONS:
OUTER, INNER, AND SECRET LEVELS

On the external level of our being, the eighth transformative practice involves vows and dedication. There are many possible outer training vows, like moral codes and ethical disciplines, that are truly behavioral. For example, our external spiritual aspirations may take the form of conscientiously practicing nonviolence, sobriety, voluntary simplicity, vegetarianism, or truth-telling. If we've taken the Bodhisattva Vow, we also aspire to cultivate that vow in practical, day-to-day ways. As Bodhisattvas, we must continually strive to deepen our resolve, strengthen our determination, and recondition ourselves to think, speak, and act in the service of others. To do so, we must at all times discriminate clearly between virtues and vices and between skillful means and unskillful activities. We must also consistently refrain from negativity, harm, and dissipation. My late mentor Nyoshul Khenpo Rinpoche used to say that nothing gets accomplished in either the spiritual or the worldly sphere without effort, intention, and determination.

On the internal level, spiritual aspirations are more attitudinal. They depend on an ongoing inner resolve and unrelenting determination, motivation, and commitment to keep us integrated and focused. Internally we feel inspiration and what I call an opening to grace, blessing, and cherishment, which is uplifting. We are in touch with the sacred, the immaterial, the mysterious, and even the magical in every moment. We can perceive the extraordinary nature of every ordinary person, place, and thing.

On the secret level, we experience spiritual aspirations as a sacred bond, far beyond vowing or striving through actions and prayers to stay meaningfully connected. We sense the connection to innate Buddha nature directly as a communion, a merging, and a blessed oneness. We wholeheartedly embody the paramita's furthest reach. We *are* there while we're getting there, where ego-centered striving, preoccupation, and concern no longer exist. On the innermost, ultimate level, aspiration has truly gone beyond and reached the wondrous place where there's nowhere to go, no one to go, nothing to get or strive for.

THE THREE LEVELS OF SPIRITUAL ASPIRATIONS

In Tibetan Buddhism, there are three traditional levels of spiritual aspirations. On the first level are those aspirations that we make ourselves, such as vows to refrain from killing and harming, or stealing and lying, thus committing ourselves to the benefit of ourselves and others. We need to maintain, reinforce, and strengthen these constantly through repetition and reflection, feeling gratified by their continuance and ever-deepening development.

The next level consists of those aspirations made by others regarding us, both specifically and generally, such as a doctor's Bodhisattva-like Hippocratic Oath to strive to help heal and alleviate the pain and suffering of whoever is before them, regardless of other considerations, such as whether they know the patient or agree with them politically.

It includes the aspirations, dreams, and prayers on our behalf of our benefactors, such as our parents, grandparents, ancestors, teachers, mentors, mates, community elders, and others who have worked, explored, risked, struggled, saved, and sacrificed in order that we might have better lives. We benefit by remembering and reflecting on these individuals and their great kindness, rejoicing in their meritorious beneficence so that we are all the more encouraged to emulate and pass forward their skillful means. When we practice gratefully appreciating the opportunities we have received through their efforts and intentions, we're less likely to squander our potential or overlook the many gifts we have received. We are more inclined to become wise life stewards of earth and the generations to come.

Third and supreme among these three traditional levels of spiritual aspirations are those made by the enlightened ones—the Buddhas of all times. One example is Amitabha, the Buddha of Infinite Light. He made the famous Five Hundred Great Vows, through which he forswore his own nirvanic enlightenment in order to create a blissful ascendant paradise for spiritual practice in the western direction, where anyone who connects with him can swiftly progress toward complete liberation and ultimate enlightenment. These wisdom intentions or timeless aspirations embrace us all, beyond time and space, whether we believe in them or not, just as scientific breakthroughs can benefit us even if we sometimes remain skeptical or ignorant about them.

The historical Sakyamuni Buddha of India said that during his many previous lives as a Bodhisattva, he fervently made five hundred vast and profound aspirational prayers to awaken and free all beings. These prayers resulted in his perfect and complete enlightenment in the sixth century BCE, and they set in motion twenty-five hundred years so far of beneficial Buddha-activity, increasing wisdom and consciousness throughout this world. We need to recall and try to understand the prayers, aspirations, and affirmations emanating from the invisible array of the past, present, and future awakened ones around and within us. We also need to align ourselves with these blessings so that we can catch a great wave of wakefulness that will carry us ineluctably to the far shore, nirvana.

THE BREATH OF BODHISATTVIC LIFE

> Remember one thing only: that it's you—nobody else—who
> determines your destiny and decides your fate. Nobody else can
> be alive for you.
>
> —E. E. CUMMINGS

Speaking strictly in terms of physiology, we refer to the intake of breath as inspiration and the outflow of breath as aspiration. How fitting that the same words are applied to a comparably dynamic process at the core of our psyche. First we fill ourselves with inspiration, and then we transfer this energy into our outwardly directed aspiration. Few things more effectively fuel our resolve to be Bodhisattvas than the examples set by our spiritual heroes, the exemplary men and women who motivate us to want to do the best we can with our lives.

As I mentioned before, Tibetans believe that we get blessings through the subtle yet palpable energy that is directly transmitted to us by great spiritual benefactors. These blessings, most often conveyed from a teacher (master) to a student (disciple), represent inspiration in one of its purest forms. The teacher knows how to step out of the way as an individual person and let a more universal energy or higher power, however it may be conceived, flow through him or her into the world of the student. It is up to us to take responsibility for managing our own karma, but gifted spiritual leaders can certainly help us by interceding, redirecting our thoughts, words, and actions, and bestowing upon us teachings, empowerments, and blessings. They can assume some of our burdens, intentionally share in our karma, and facilitate our conscious evolution.

We can also draw inspiration from other kinds of people who impress us with the strength of their own aspiration. Some of them may be our teachers, but others may be figures from history, heroes in our own era, or even folks we know personally. One of my own spiritual sources of inspiration is Eihei Dogen, the seminal master who introduced Zen to thirteenth-century Japan. When Dogen was only eight years old, his beloved mother died. Stunned with grief at her funeral, he became absorbed in watching a stick of incense burn down to ash. Suddenly, he was so struck by the impermanence of life that he vowed in his mother's memory to seek the true meaning of it all.

Dogen stayed true to his vow by courageously defying the wishes of his own clan leaders and, while still young, becoming a Buddhist monk. Ultimately, he traveled to China—a long, arduous, and perilous journey at the time—to study Ch'an (Chinese for *dhyana,* or meditation) Buddhism. After years of training, he received lineal transmission there and returned to Japan to establish his own branch of Zen (Japanese for Ch'an), which came to be known as the Soto School. Faced with daunting opposition from older, already established Buddhist schools, he was eventually forced to retreat with a few of his monks to a remote mountain where the prospects of sustaining a sangha (spiritual community) were slim. But his strong resolve, coupled with his brilliant intellectual and motivational leadership powers, won out. The monastery he established there, Eihei, became a thriving and powerful instrument for spreading the Dharma in Japan and is still flourishing today.

Always striving to maintain and further develop his spiritual aspirations, Dogen had to battle against mortal illness, buying himself extra years of life through sheer willpower so that he could work on his famous book of spiritual discourses, the *Shobogenzo* (*Treasury of the True Dharma Eye*), now regarded as one of the greatest works of Zen Buddhism, as well as of Japanese literature in general. Death finally claimed him at age fifty-three. He continues to be regarded as one of the most important and influential figures in the long and illustrious history of Zen Buddhism.

I'm similarly inspired by the visionary determination of two more recent historical figures. The mechanical engineers John Roebling and his son Washington Roebling, the creators of the Brooklyn Bridge, may not have been spiritual heroes, but they were boyhood heroes of my handy Uncle Bill. In 1883 John Roebling developed the idea for a spectacular bridge to connect New York City (Manhattan Island) with Brooklyn (on Long Island); such a span would make the lives of millions of working people easier, safer, and more promising. Everyone told him that a bridge of that size, length, and challenging footing was impossible, but Roebling was convinced that it had to be built, and he vowed to do so. Furthermore, he swore to himself that his bridge would be a magnificent work of architecture, one that would "inspire men's minds and stir their hearts, as well as serve their more pedestrian needs to move from one physical place to another." It became the engineering marvel of that era.

The first step in John Roebling's plan was to inspire his son Washington with the same vibrant, all-consuming dream. Together John and Washington Roebling managed to invent revolutionary concepts for making the gigantic suspension bridge feasible. Perhaps even more remarkable, they also succeeded in hiring a crew of men who had faith in the project even though it seemed impossible and dangerous. A few months into the construction process, tragedy struck. John was killed in an on-site accident. In the same accident, Washington suffered a severe head injury that left him unable to talk or move any part of his body except for one finger. Unwilling to let go of the dream he'd shared with his father, Washington worked out a code of communication with his wife by tapping on her arm. She, in turn, transferred his messages to the bridge crew foremen. For thirteen years, he persevered with this strategy, ignoring the many doubts and discouragements voiced by the press and some of his closest associates.

Finally, from a window near his deathbed in Brooklyn Heights, Washington Roebling looked out on the spectacular opening-day ceremonies for the completed Brooklyn Bridge, a landmark in the history of architecture. Evoking the towering style of a Gothic stone cathedral and yet eminently practical for its intended purpose, the Brooklyn Bridge still stands proudly as a tribute not only to Washington Roebling and his father but also to his wife and the crew who believed so strongly in the Roeblings' civic-minded mission.

I also draw inspiration for my aspiration from my neighbor Paul Farmer. After living through many difficulties during his middle-class upbringing, he graduated from Harvard University's medical school and became a professor of medicine. Today he devotes eight months of the year to treating the poorest of the poor in Haiti as he lives among them. His story is told in Tracy Kidder's book *Mountains Beyond Mountains: The Quest of Dr. Paul Farmer, a Man Who Would Cure the World.* It's an inspiring true saga of how the Bodhisattvic aspirations and resulting actions of one person who understands the interdependence of politics, poverty, social systems, the environment, and disease can make a difference in solving global health problems.

Biographies and teaching tales from the world's great spiritual traditions are excellent sources of inspiration. Among the ones I most often read and recommend to my students are Milarepa's *Hundred Thousand Songs* and *The Life of Milarepa,* Shabkar Rinpoche's *The Autobiography of a Tibetan Yogin,* St. Teresa of Lisieux's *The Story of a Soul,* Martin Buber's *Tales of the Hasidim,* Paul Reps's *Zen Flesh, Zen Bones,* Idries Shah's *Tales of the Sufi,* Mahatma Gandhi's *My Experiments with Truth,* and Thomas Merton's *Seven Storey Mountain.* Each of these works provides a multitude of motivational insights into how spiritual aspiration enriches both day-to-day existence and a whole lifetime. For more fantastic personal stories of enlightened masters in Old Tibet, read *Blazing Splendour: The Memoirs of Dzogchen Yogi Tulku Urgyen Rinpoche.*

LADDER OF ENLIGHTENMENT: THE TEN BHUMIS

The winds of grace are always blowing, but you have to raise the sail.

—SRI RAMAKRISHNA

Mahayana Buddhism teaches that a Bodhisattva, or Awakener, on the way to fulfilling his or her spiritual aspirations proceeds through ten stages (in Sanskrit, *bhumis,* literally "grounds"). Gampopa, founder of the Kagyupa School of Tibetan Buddhism, explains them in detail in his twelfth-century classic, *The Jewel Ornament of Liberation.* Mindful of their onward-and-upward progression, I tend to think of them as the ten rungs on the ladder to enlightenment, culminating in perfect Buddhahood. May we all take these steps!

Throughout this conscious evolution or ascent, the Bodhisattva engages in all ten transformative practices. However, each successive stage emphasizes developing and perfecting a corresponding paramita. The first bhumi involves greater focus on the first paramita, generosity, and so on. Only after progressing through all the bhumis does the Bodhisattva attain true enlightenment, which is sometimes characterized in Buddhist sutras and their commentaries as the eleventh bhumi, unexcelled perfect Buddhahood. Meanwhile, reaching each new level brings an exponential—not merely incremental—increase in a Bodhisattva's compassion, wisdom, energy powers, and multiple emanations.

Here's a complete list of the ten bhumis of the Bodhisattva:

1. *Joyous:* The Bodhisattva has glimpsed reality, gone beyond hope and fear, and seen through the illusions of this fleeting world. This brings great joy. The emphasized paramita is generosity (dana).

2. *Immaculate:* The Bodhisattva recognizes all real and possible defilements. With this understanding, he or she works to attain freedom from immorality and other faults. The emphasized paramita is ethics (sila).

3. *Radiant:* For the Bodhisattva at this stage, the vast and profoundly clear light of Dharma wisdom comes to illuminate hundreds of thousands of worlds. Gaining insight from this illumination, he or she, in turn, sheds light for others to see. The emphasized paramita is patience (kshanti).

4. *Luminous:* At this stage, all veils that obscure reality are burned away, and primordial enlightenment, free of attachments, shines forth through millions of worlds and eons. All the Bodhisattva's sorrows are incinerated, making this the stage of glowing wisdom. The emphasized paramita is heroic effort (virya).

5. *Difficult to overcome:* The Bodhisattva works to gain mastery over the most challenging aspects of spiritual practice and then to pass along this more mature wisdom to others. He or she ultimately perceives the underlying continuity of things and surmounts all obstacles and hindrances to taming and refining the spirituality of tens of millions of worldly beings. The emphasized paramita is meditation (dhyana).

6. *Actually transcendent:* The Bodhisattva gains freedom from all dichotomies and does not abide fixedly in either samsara (the world of the relative) or nirvana (the world of the absolute). He or she embraces both light and dark and penetrates billions of highly evolved meditative states. The emphasized paramita is transcendental wisdom (prajna).

7. *Gone far:* The Bodhisattva approaches enlightenment beyond the risk of backsliding and nears the perfection of Buddha-activity—the helping of others—through the realization of oneness and nondifferentiation. The emphasized paramita is skillful means (upaya).

8. *Immovable:* The Bodhisattva becomes perfectly untarnished by notions of being a separate individual or by desires to engage in self-oriented effort. His or her commitment to the Bodhisattva way is total and inalterable. The emphasized paramita is spiritual aspirations (pranidhana).

9. *Excellent discriminating wisdom:* The Bodhisattva has perfect understanding of meaning and significance, patterns and principles, form and emptiness. He or she has an unshakable conviction and confidence in the truth and reality of the Dharma, and with this surety come wondrous capabilities. The emphasized paramita is higher accomplishments (*siddhi*).

10. *Cloud of Dharma:* The Bodhisattva, on the brink of perfect Buddhahood, pervades all time and space like a vast cloud. He

or she has access to limitless powers and omniscient awareness through Buddha-mind. The emphasized paramita is pristine awakened awareness (*jnana*).

It all sounds very mystical, doesn't it? But that is exactly the point and the power of the bhumi schema. To move beyond the dualistic world of self and other, good and bad, birth and death, to a more transcendental connection with the universe, we need to let go of our logical ways of systematizing things. Instead of demanding a tightly wrapped-up, linear-sequential solution to the mysteries of the universe, we need to attune our minds to a more organic, holistic, evolutionary, and revolutionary way of approaching and merging with these mysteries. It's not our intellect that responds—or is meant to respond—to such teachings as the ten bhumis, codified as they seem while remaining mysterious too. Instead, it's some-thing deep in our heart-mind, in our Buddha nature, that spontaneously says, "Yes, I see the truth of this, feel the rightness of this." Naturally, this truth is beyond rational explanation. It's like the Bodhisattvic nondual-istic magic of being there while getting there every step along the way. This path is not simply a linear upward line or ladder but more of a multi-dimensional, ever-widening and deepening, ascending path.

Buddhist sages repeatedly insist that just hearing the names of the ten bhumis can plant seeds of Bodhisattvic generation in the mind that's ripe for their growth. I sincerely believe this is possible. We definitely get a good whiff of what might be in store for us while ascending the ladder of enlightenment if we simply reflect on the bhumi names and descrip-tions on a regular basis, letting them slowly but surely accumulate more significance for us and provide us with greater inspiration as they grow in our consciousness. The Joyous ... Radiant ... Luminous ... Immov-able ... Cloud of Dharma. Yes!

Why not find out for yourself? As a means of elevating and energizing your spiritual aspirations, incorporate this simple but wondrously revital-izing activity into your own life, doing it at least once a week, perhaps as part of a weekly service, or even daily, whenever you seek to bolster your resolve and determination.

Beginning with the first bhumi, "Joyous," and progressing to the oth-ers, follow these guidelines:

1. Silently read the bhumi description given here. Ponder for a moment or two what it means for you, considering your own life and practice right now.

2. When you feel you have some insight about it, say out loud to yourself, "I am, can be, and will be the Joyous One" (or, in turn, "the Radiant One," on through "the One Who Overcomes Difficulties," "the One Who Is Actually Transcendent," and so on). Raise your inner gaze.

3. Go on to state briefly what this title means for you in your own words, based on (or taking off from) the actual words of the description I give for it. For example, in speaking about yourself as "the Joyous One," you might say something like: "I am grateful for the wisdom I am gaining, and I will take care to appreciate more the precious gift of human life. I want to express this gratitude and appreciation by following my joy-path and gladly offering more help to others." You can include specific thoughts and vows if you wish, or you can express your understanding in poetic language that doesn't necessarily even make sense to your rational mind. Simply assume for each bhumi that you *are, can be,* and *will be* that level of Bodhisattva, and speak from that assumption. Pray, and reaffirm your steadfast commitment to actually do so.

Mark Twain, one of my favorite American authors, said: "Twenty years from now you will be more disappointed by the things that you didn't do than by the ones you did do. So throw off the bowlines. Sail away from the safe harbor. Catch the trade winds in your sails. Explore. Dream. Discover."

NINE

THE MAGIC OF HIGHER ACCOMPLISHMENTS

May I perfect the wondrous virtue of spiritual empowerment
and positive influence, which accomplishes unselfish service and
love in action far beyond the limits of mortal beings.

Ten years ago a young American Dharma teacher unfamiliar with the
ways of lamas had the temerity to approach our teacher Tulku Urgyen in
Nepal and say, "I think I am enlightened."

"Can you fly?" our master asked him. "Can you remember past
lives?"

Dumbfounded, the student shook his head no.

The old lama just looked back and remained silent. I interpreted his
bemused expression to mean, "What kind of enlightenment is this?"

Trained in Western rationalism, we tend to think of enlightenment
as a matter of "getting it" intellectually: "Yes," we might say to ourselves
and perhaps even to our teacher, "I understand what is meant by 'emptiness' and 'all is one,' or, 'everyone has Buddha nature.'" It is certainly
possible for us to translate such phrases into concepts that make sense in
real-world terms and then to use those concepts to govern our everyday
behavior. But that kind of translation and application, as beneficial as it

can be, does not indicate that we have become fully and completely enlightened, which is easier said than done.

Enlightenment is an awakening to a state of mind and totality of incandescent being that totally transcends the rational, the intellectual, and the everyday. That is why Buddha himself called it "deathless, utterly peaceful, blissful, radiant, changeless nirvana." As we strive toward enlightenment, we seek to go beyond the limits that our intelligence imposes on our perceptual abilities. We seek to enter into an infinitely vaster and more potent realm of existence, one where we have more power to accomplish higher things. Does this mean that as we advance along the Bodhisattva path we begin to acquire miraculous powers, like Superman seeing through walls and flying or Jesus walking on water? That's one superficial and mechanical way of looking at it.

Traditionally, Tibetan teachers speak of two kinds of powers, or siddhis in Sanskrit: relative and conventional powers, on the one hand, and absolute transcendental accomplishments, on the other. These two types of siddhi powers are also known as worldly and ultimate higher powers or accomplishments. The worldly or mundane siddhis—sometimes numbering eight—include psychic powers and extraordinary abilities that seem to defy our understanding of natural laws, such as telepathy, clairvoyance, clairaudience, telekinesis, divine eye, divine ear, healing touch, levitation, longevity, the power of resurrection, consciousness transference, past-life knowledge, and the ability to shrink or grow large at will or project multiple manifestations in different places at once. The absolute or ultimate siddhis—also codified as eight—include perfect enlightenment, the realization of deathlessness, transcendental wisdom, selflessness, unconditional love, and even omniscience.

Although the Buddha generally discouraged interest in supernatural phenomena, he himself was said to possess innumerable so-called magic abilities that set him well apart from other mortals. In the famous "Miracle at Sravasti," for example, he suddenly manifested himself as a thousand different Buddhas spread across the sky in order to dazzle and disarm some especially aggressive critics and persecutors. As he explained at the time, he resorted to this last-ditch strategy "only to help instill faith in the faithless," who in fact were on the verge of causing him and his disciples bodily harm. In other words, Buddha used supernatural skillful means to neutralize a dangerous foe although he generally considered such capabilities mere special effects rather than the main powers of enlightenment.

Buddhist scriptures after the Buddha's death are filled with stories of human Bodhisattvas who possess extraordinary powers. One that I always enjoy telling is about a Bodhisattva who lived more than two thousand years ago. This Bodhisattva was a teacher known not only for his wisdom and selfless compassion but also for his visionary insights into the unknown. In the same territory lived a Vedic teacher who regarded the Buddhist doctrine of rebirth as "unbelievable" (in the negative, ultra-rational sense of the word!). "If you can prove that rebirth exists," he challenged the Bodhisattva, "I and all my students will convert to Buddhism."

The Bodhisattva simply replied, "I will die, and I will intentionally be reborn in a manner that demonstrates that rebirth is possible, and I will take the king of this land as my witness." Soon the Buddhist teacher did die, immediately after he had put a pearl in his mouth and a dark orange mark on his forehead in the presence of the king. Afterward, the king had the body sealed in a copper coffin. A few days later, a boy was born to a learned person in that region. Much to his family's surprise, the infant had a red mark on his forehead and a pearl in his mouth. When word reached the king, he ordered the copper coffin to be opened. The red mark had disappeared from the corpse's forehead, and the pearl was no longer in the mouth. The astounded non-Buddhist teacher and his followers quickly set forth along the Buddha way.

Who among us has attained this Bodhisattva's level of mastery, this kind of mind-over-matter power? I feel safe in claiming that most, if not all, of us would have to declare, "Not me!" Yet I feel equally confident in claiming that most, if not all, of us are aware at some level that we exist in a universal energy field of mind and spirit that is capable of generating amazing wonders. We all experience and hear about remarkable incidents that defy rational explanation, and occasionally have firsthand experience of them, yet we can't help but suspect that these incidents are mere intimations of a vast ocean of possibility, just waiting for the right creative impetus, the right kind of powerful spiritual mastery. One of my favorite poets, W. H. Auden, said: "We are lived by Powers we pretend to understand."

Not long ago I heard a true contemporary story that reminded me of the ancient legend I just recounted about the Buddhist teacher, the pearl, and the newborn child. My friend Sara has neighbors, Sam and Maggie, who recently celebrated their thirtieth wedding anniversary. They are a devoted couple, but they have fallen out of the habit of giving each other presents. On the morning of their anniversary, Maggie teased Sam by saying, "The traditional gift for a thirtieth anniversary is pearls, so maybe we should get ourselves one?" "Right!" said Sam, laughing dismissively.

That night Maggie and Sam went out to dinner with their pastor, who loved oysters. Sam decided that in honor of the anniversary he was going to do something he had never done before: he was going to try oysters. When the oysters arrived at the table, he ate one, and, much to his surprise, he loved it. The second one was as delicious as the first. Then he put the third one in his mouth and grimaced. "There's something hard in here!" he sputtered. Assuming it was a piece of grit, he spit it out into his napkin. There, to everyone's astonishment, was a large, beautiful pearl!

Now Maggie and Sam are not by any means magicians, at least in any intentional sense. Nor are they highly evolved spiritual practitioners who have trained themselves to create material change in the universe by mere acts of will and imagination. So it would be easy to say that the pearl showing up in Sam's oyster on his "pearl" anniversary was sheer coincidence; but was it? Or is it possible, in some way we can't completely explain with our intellect, that Maggie and Sam were connected with the universe on that particular night in an especially clear, genuine, and powerful way? I definitely believe that somehow, some way, they were in the right place at the right time with the right spirit and their pearl arrived accordingly. In any case, with or without whatever explanation we might like to come up with, the pearl did appear in just the way I have described.

As for "higher accomplishments" and extraordinary powers within a spiritual practice, many of my own lamas possessed documented powers that would commonly be considered superhuman. I have known masters who could read minds, predict the future, heal illnesses and injuries, change people's hearts and minds, and reveal others' past lives.

One of these masters was the Sixteenth Gyalwa Karmapa, Rangjung Rigpai Dorje (1924–1981), my root guru. He was the head of the Kagyu order of Tibetan Buddhism, a grand lama and a *tulku* (a reincarnated lama) in a line of successive reincarnations stretching back to Karmapa Dusum Khyenpa in the twelfth century. Throughout the centuries the

Karmapa lama has been particularly renowned for having prodigious psychic powers. The Sixteenth Karmapa was responsible for recognizing, through his unimpeded clairvoyance, hundreds of the reincarnations of lamas during his lifetime. Among many stories about his unusual capacities, or "higher accomplishments," is one told to me in Nepal by my friend Chokyi Nyima Rinpoche, who was also a student of both the Karmapa and Dilgo Khyentse Rinpoche, the main subject in the story.

Dilgo Khyentse Rinpoche had two brothers: Nyenpa Rinpoche, who was a great lama, and another brother I'll call "the third brother." The latter was not an advanced practitioner, but he had the good fortune to have met the Karmapa a few times. The two men liked each other a lot and often joked together. One day, while all three brothers were traveling toward central Tibet, where the Karmapa lived, the third brother died shortly after falling and breaking off a front tooth. When the other two brothers finally reached their destination, they met the Karmapa, who told them, "I already saw your brother. He came by some time ago. He had broken his tooth but seemed to be doing quite well."

There was no way that the Karmapa could have heard in Old Tibet that Khyentse Rinpoche's brother had died, much less that the brother's tooth had broken off beforehand. Quite astonished, Khyentse Rinpoche said, "How can you know these things?"

The Karmapa replied, "There is not much point in talking about it. I am a Karmapa [*Karmapa* means "Man of Buddha Activity"]. There are certain qualities that happen due to past aspirations and past practice. But there is just one thing that always seems to happen regarding anyone I have met in this lifetime who then dies: whether we have a good or bad connection, the person comes and visits me before continuing on [dying and heading toward rebirth]. Some I can help, but not everybody needs it. Your brother doesn't seem to have any problem."

This is just one of literally hundreds of such amazing personal stories these well-known lamas and others have told over the years, both publicly and privately, as part of their teachings—on top of those found in the sutra scriptures and the biographies of Buddhist saints and sages down through the centuries. Buddhism is truly a miraculous tradition—thank God for it.

An outstanding example of an American of astounding higher accomplishments is Edgar Cayce (1877–1945), one of the best-documented, most versatile, and most credible psychics of modern times. Over a period of forty-three years in the early twentieth century, he delivered twenty thousand psychic readings, many of which helped cure people of profound physical and mental afflictions. He also left a wonderful legacy, the Cayce Foundation in Virginia Beach, Virginia, along with two dozen satellite institutes around the world. These organizations conduct and promote work in the beneficial use of psychic powers and other forms of holistic and spiritual healing. In 2005, on the fourth anniversary of the 9/11 terrorist attacks on the World Trade Center, I was invited to the main Virginia Beach center to lecture on Buddhist meditation practice. While there, I had the chance to visit Cayce's great library, where I could still feel his presence. The books there revealed his tremendous interest in a broad range of areas, including spiritual education, holistic healing, diet, exercise, mental and physical health, the healing power of prayer, meditation, and the power of the mind.

A humble person of great humanity, Cayce was raised on a farm in the Midwest and grew up to become a husband, father, gardener, photographer, Sunday school teacher, and—last but not least—mystic. Referring to all these endeavors, he often said that his main purpose was to "help people walk more closely with God." As a young man, he originally wanted to be a doctor and preacher, but he lost his voice to a serious and lasting case of laryngitis. Physicians told him he would never speak again, but a psychic vision appeared to him in a dream that led directly to a cure. Afterward, others who heard about this miracle prevailed on him to read for them regarding their ailments. He had to struggle to overcome his initial reluctance to do so, not only because of his modesty but also because of his concern about lacking any medical or psychic training.

Cayce's first reported healing was saving a five-year-old girl named Aime Dietrich, who had stopped developing physically and mentally after a bout of severe influenza at age two. She suffered from convulsions, and her doctors had finally dismissed her as "hopelessly impaired." Cayce went into a sleeplike trance and gave a diagnosis and healing regimen, including some osteopathic adjustments. Within three months her mind was able to catch up from where it had left off, and she ultimately blossomed into a normal, healthy five-year-old.

Word of Cayce's healing vision in Aime Dietrich's case made news throughout the country. It was soon discovered that Cayce needed only the name and location of a suffering individual to be able to give a successful reading. This incredible ability puzzled him deeply. Often, when he was awakened from one of his psychic trances and told by a transcriber what he had said, he himself didn't understand it, frequently because it was detailed medical jargon he'd never mastered in his waking life. Nevertheless, he vowed to continue exercising his unusual gift as long as it proved helpful to people. In 1911 his own beloved wife, Gertrude, was diagnosed with terminal tuberculosis. Utilizing information he received in various sleep trances, he cured her by 1912.

Many medical professionals scoffed at his psychic abilities, including Dr. Hugo Munsterberg of Harvard University. Munsterberg wound up investigating Cayce firsthand and became convinced of the legitimacy and effectiveness of Cayce's readings. Similar conversions happened to other skeptics on subsequent occasions, many of which are recorded in two of the most comprehensive books about Cayce, Thomas Sugrue's *There Is a River* and Jess Stern's *The Sleeping Prophet*.

Throughout his life, Cayce refused to claim any personal credit as a miracle-doer and always attributed his good works to the grace of God. His readings never came with a set of beliefs that the recipient had to embrace but, instead, carried the message that each person should test his or her own life for the right principles and practices to live by. Although he was a Christian himself and read the Bible from cover to cover every year of his life, he had sympathy toward and understanding of other major world religions. Accordingly, he championed the importance of comparative study among all the world's belief systems, as does the Cayce Institute today. A major underlying theme in Cayce's readings was the oneness of all beings and the need for people to practice tolerance toward each other, and the first motto of his institute was "That We May Make Manifest Our Love for God and Man."

So what should we make of these examples of higher accomplishments or supernatural deeds? They are certainly noteworthy as feats that confound our reason—or to put it more colloquially, that blow our minds—but to leave it at that is to miss the point. In this chapter, we're concerned with a kind of transcendental magic—siddhis—as *spiritual* power. Psychologists might call it the power of the higher self, a phrase that relates more closely in terminology to my translation of *siddhi* as "higher accomplishments."

As we grow spiritually, we tap into this superior energy latent in all of us. Sometimes it may manifest itself in the form of an obvious miracle; other times it may work more subtly and intangibly. In either case, the result is wondrous evidence of a cosmically wise and compassionate heart-mind. It reveals a person who has broken through the normal boundaries of human existence (remember, *paramita* means "gone beyond") to come more clearly into tune with the universe as a whole. It is why my old friend Ram Dass, in awe of this kind of glorious metamorphosis, once proclaimed, "I don't underestimate the power of the human heart. When I look at the human heart, that link, that doorway to transcendence, I see an institution that makes the Pentagon look like kids' toys."

As Bodhisattvas-in-progress, we don't necessarily follow a particular training regimen to achieve a particular special power. Rather, we open ourselves up to release the powers that are already there within us, inherent in the higher power of our Buddha nature, to express themselves as they will when needed. An essential element in this opening up is accepting these two truths: first, we *can* accomplish things that are extraordinary and beyond our ability to explain in a linear-sequential way, and second, we may sometimes *need* to do so in order to evolve spiritually. As the philosopher Claude Bernard said, "Man can learn nothing except by going from the known to the unknown." I can personally attest to this verity. Although I find it hard to believe in many of these miraculous occurrences, I must admit that I have experienced some and know them to be true.

THE TEN SIDDHIS OF A BODHISATTVA

Who makes much of a miracle?
As to me, I know of nothing else but miracles....
To me, every hour of the light and dark is a miracle,
Every cubic inch of space is a miracle,
Every square yard of the surface of the earth is spread
with the same;
Every spear of grass—the frames, limbs, organs of men
and women and all that concerns them,
All these to me are unspeakably perfect miracles.

—WALT WHITMAN

Most enlightened masters I've known have been quite discreet about demonstrating or even revealing their powers in any way. Time and again, the Buddha warned against paying too much attention to, and putting too much emphasis on, flashy, spectacular exhibitions of power. Humility, discretion, and even anonymity are considered great virtues among highly accomplished yogis and meditation masters.

One of the most remarkable women I have ever known was my late Tibetan mother, whom we always called simply Amala, or Respected Matriarch. Originally a Buddhist nun from Nyemo, in central Tibet, she became the wife of the late great Dzogchen master Kangyur Rinpoche of Riwoche Monastery, who left this world in Darjeeling in 1975. An impeccable individual and an impartially loving presence in my life for decades, she was the mother of our sangha in Darjeeling and southern France. Amala Kunzang Chokyi was the humblest of great meditators and saintly beings. She gave birth to six remarkable children, including my mentor, the contemporary master Tulku Pema Wangyal. When Amala came to her last days, in her eighties, she began foretelling the weather and other things, revealing psychic powers and superknowledge that until then she had been extremely discreet about and had demonstrated only infrequently even to her own grown children. Everyone was amazed at the veracity of her clairvoyance and vision and spoke with awe after her passing of her great, hidden, sublime qualities and humble, impeccable character. Never a day goes by that I don't feel her with me, guiding and protecting me.

Recently, my neighbors' son and I were reading aloud from one of J. K. Rowling's enormously popular books about Harry Potter, the wizard-in-training, when suddenly it struck me how much children today are reinventing the nature of the higher consciousness quest through their enthusiasm for magical questers like Harry Potter. What is the spiritual heart of the Harry Potter phenomenon anyway? Isn't it a desire to find out who we are and can be, what we are capable of, and where we fit into this immense universe? Mythical heroes such as Harry Potter, Hermione Granger, Luke Skywalker, Superman, Wonder Woman, Batman, Spider-man, and even Dorothy of both Kansas and Oz loom large in our culture because they point to a way that transcends material concerns and logical constraints and open up for the little Buddha in all of us the marvelous realm of spiritual possibilities. All of their magical powers serve a much higher and more mystical purpose: achieving the greatest good not only for themselves but also for others, in true Bodhisattva fashion.

The Ten Powers, or higher accomplishments, of the Buddha or Bodhisattva are codified in the classic sutras of Buddhist history. Examining this list can help us move from a worldly, mundane view of siddhis as special effects toward the awakened spiritual warrior's view of higher accomplishments as revelations of the Bodhisattva's wisdom nature, or transcendental ways of knowing. The Ten Powers of the Bodhisattva are

1. Knowing what is positive and negative, good and evil, helpful and harmful, or knowing right and wrong within the path.

2. Knowing the result of every single action of body, mind, and mind, or knowing and transforming the karma of self, others, the community, the environment, the collective whole.

3. Knowing the karmic and ultimate potential of each and every sentient being, or knowing, embodying, and manifesting profound meditation and contemplation.

4. Knowing the five elements—earth, water, air, fire, and space—or knowing the capabilities of self, others, and the whole.

5. Knowing the capacity, aspirations, and motivations of each sentient being; knowing the aspirations, moral direction, and understanding of self, others, and all.

6. Knowing the path of enlightenment completely, or knowing the nature and actions of self, other, and the whole.

7. Knowing the various karmas that lead to profound peace and meditative equipoise (samadhi); knowing the direction and consequences of causes and effects.

8. Knowing previous lives; knowing the results of the past karmas of one and all.

9. Having the power to transfer consciousness at death to higher birth and beyond; knowing, embodying, and manifesting profound insight.

10. Realizing the exhaustion of all phenomena in nirvana; knowing and manifesting the destruction of illusion of any kind.

THE NATURE OF POWERS VERSUS *POWER*

We can experience higher accomplishments and inner illuminations such as the ten I have just described once we learn to make room for deeper realities by seeing through our illusory ego-selves and getting out of our own way. Unlike the aggressive concepts that many worldly thinkers commonly associate with power, the concept of making room for power is gentle, gracious, and peaceful. Sociologists, for example, often define power as the ability to impose one's will on others, even if they resist. Such imposition may not always involve overt coercion or active control that's easy to pinpoint. Instead, it may be manifested in a more diffuse, multifaceted kind of power that resembles what we normally call "influence." In Alvin Toffler's book on the subject, *Powershift,* he considers three main kinds of worldly power: violence, wealth, and knowledge. All other kinds of power, in his formulation, are variations of these three, including personal power, collective power, physical power, emotional power, sexual power, economic power, military power, inherited power, legal power, psychic power, and spiritual power. However, in this chapter about siddhi paramita, we are not examining any complex of power in this sense. What concerns us here is not more might or force, but inner strength and the more inclusive and transpersonal powers that we do not and cannot own but that exist for us to realize and actualize. These powers are the higher accomplishments that live *through* us for the benefit of others.

Each of us has an amazing amount of mental power that can be invested in myriad wondrous ways to make the world a better place for ourselves and everyone else at the same time, as Dorothy discovers in L. Frank Baum's beloved classic *The Wizard of Oz.* In her longing to return home to Kansas, Dorothy seeks out the renowned Wizard as a savior she hopes holds the power to take her there. However, after Dorothy unmasks the Wizard, she realizes that he doesn't have the power she needs to complete her heroic journey of return, a classic metaphor for returning to our true home and source. The Witch of the North then guides her to find it within, saying, "You don't need to be helped any longer. You've always had the power." The point is that pure-hearted Dorothy has had the inner power all along, although she has had to learn that for herself and learn how to use it. She learns that she just has to click together the heels of her shoes to get where she wishes to go.

We too tend to be ignorant of our own powers. Think of how much time, energy, and resources we waste on petty, ego-oriented, short-term, materialistic agendas, not to mention meaningless distractions! Imagine if we could raise our consciousness above these agendas and see how pedestrian they are compared to living the life of the spiritual warrior, the Awakener, the Bodhisattva! Recognizing that can unleash as much power and energy as splitting the atom.

We are all connected with what people call a higher power, or universal energy. However, we must be strong, capable, and conscientious to wield the lightninglike dynamic of power without being fried or even electrocuted by it. Like pure energy, power in and of itself is neutral. How and why it is used, and to what effect, are the real issues.

Most spiritually aware people I know seem especially sensitive to power and its dangers and, as a result, are inclined to be wary of exercising or cultivating power. This hesitancy may be due in part to their unfamiliarity with their own power. It may also arise from their reaction to the many excessive misuses and corruptions of power over the ages by forceful individuals, corporate and political entities, and even churches and other religious institutions. With reflection, however, they find that if and when they feel truly in touch with a higher power—something greater than themselves yet immanent within them—then the worldly power they're worried about pales by comparison and ceases to daunt them. They no longer think of themselves as being powerful in the reckless, dangerous, worldly sense of the term, and they are less likely to be ensnared by egocentric delusions of being separate from and even better than others. James Autry and Stephen Mitchell, in their book *Real Power*, write: "Where does real power begin? On the inside, with self-awareness and self-acceptance. It is a transition from the external to the internal. . . . This is the pathway to leadership and fulfillment." The psychologist James Hillman says, "If we simply and naively dismiss power as old-style white patriarchal thinking, we will be throwing out the baby with the bathwater."

In recent years, my own aging, experience, and attainment of some inner maturity have combined with my efforts to guide and empower my students and others to give birth to my present conviction that the appropriate and conscious exercise of power is the duty of anyone trying to accomplish anything genuine in this world. "How much is enough?" is always a living and breathing question. Bodhisattvas let the Middle Way—not too much, not too little—and the selfless, compassionate, and wise motivation of Bodhicitta be their intelligent guide, witness, and higher conscience.

Bodhisattvas need a certain degree of enhanced abilities to be able to fulfill their vow to be of the greatest service for the greatest number. They also need to be masters of themselves and their own personal world in order to be free from unconscious fears, negative emotions, and psychological shadow, all of which are inevitably acted out semiconsciously in unskillful and even harmful ways. The Venerable Penor Rinpoche, a contemporary Nyingmapa leader who is the head of a large Tibetan Buddhist monastery and refugee camp in Mysore, India, once said to me, "I have a lot of power and know how to use it. Do not let power or the desire for power run your life, but see to it that any powers, assets, talents, accomplishments, or advantages that accrue to you and your work are dedicated and devoted solely to the Bodhisattva's mission to benefit others." In this way, we can learn to offer all we have and are to a greater cause beyond egotistic aims and thus boost our Bodhisattvic progress toward the goal of universal liberation. By offering up ourselves to a higher, deeper, truer cause, the base metal of egotistical desires and ambitions is transmuted into the spiritual gold of Bodhicitta—the gift that keeps on giving, a blessing for one and all. This is the true spiritual alchemy, transmuting human nature into Buddha nature.

The realm of higher accomplishments is a realm of vast perspective that inspires unconditional love, intimate wisdom, connection, and selflessness. Whether or not we eventually wind up like the mythical Superman, with the ability to stop a speeding bullet or leap tall buildings in a single bound, and whether or not we become clairvoyant, develop healing touch, or possess any other mundane siddhi, we can finally bring ourselves to experience the true miracle inherent in even the simplest activities of life and the humblest aspects of creation when they are unpoisoned by selfish greed, anger, and ignorance. We can truly sink roots into the present moment and extract its ambrosial essences, wherever we are, through our own daily life and work and relations. Each of us can be a light-bringer, a veritable beacon, and a miraculous force for good in this benighted world as we transform our karma into Dharma.

Layman P'ang (740–808 CE), Ch'an Buddhism's most highly regarded layperson and master, touched on this way of interpreting "higher accomplishments" when he said, "The most mystical power and wondrous function is carrying water and lugging firewood." Even more significant, once we attain this state of inner empowerment, we can then more convincingly motivate others to strive toward the same magical state of being.

SIDDHIS: OUTER, INNER, AND SECRET

If we as baby Bodhisattvas or even advanced Awakeners wish to effect a spiritual revolution and awaken the world, we need to develop the power and wisdom energy to be able to do so. And moreover, we need to learn how to use that power skillfully to the greatest effect. The fourth-century Confucian philosopher Mencius says, "A mature superior person transforms where he passes, and works wonders where he abides. He is in the same stream as Heaven above and Earth below."

According to the original Pali sutras of Buddhism, purportedly Buddha's earliest teachings, there are Five Powers (*balas*) we need to develop. These are faith, which overcomes false beliefs; energetic effort, which overcomes laziness; mindfulness, which overcomes heedlessness and forgetfulness; concentration, which overcomes distractedness; and wisdom, which overcomes ignorance and confusion.

Through outer, inner, and secret, or mystic, siddhis, the Bodhisattva exhibits a positive and helpful influence in countless ways throughout the world—both seen and unseen. Outer siddhis include skills in leadership, communication, strategic planning, peacemaking, conflict resolution, and timing. Externally, Bodhisattvas often display charismatic attractiveness, which has the effect of magnetizing energy and gathering resources for the common good. With all these attributes, they are able to open and illumine the way of awakening to others.

Inner siddhis manifest themselves as mundane and supermundane powers, such as the power of inner purity, or psychic abilities, a healing touch, magical gifts, a spiritual "green thumb" that can help anyone grow and be empowered, or mystical vision and perspective. Bodhisattvas who are in touch with the true source of ultimate power, creativity, imagination, and meaning have access to the innermost, or secret, siddhis, which give us the power *to* rather than a power *over*. These siddhis enable us as Bodhisattvas to be masters of ourselves and to embody and transmit continuously the edifying and authentically transforming, panacean power of pure Being itself.

To put it more simply, outer-level siddhis give us beneficial power in relationship to others, the environment, and all phenomena; inner-level siddhis allow us to have mastery over ourselves; and the innermost, secret, siddhis imply total illumination, freedom, oneness, and the dynamic life of awakened enlightenment.

THE THREE LEVELS OF SIDDHIS

Once when the Buddha was living at Nalanda in the Pavarika Grove, a man named Kevaddha approached him reverently and said, "Lord, Nalanda is a successful city. The people here are prosperous. It would be greatly beneficial if you appointed a monk to work a dazzling miracle of supernormal power, so that the people of Nalanda might become all the more confident in you and your teaching."

The Buddha replied, "Kevaddha, I do not teach the noble Dharma in that way!"

The Buddha gave the same answer when Kevaddha pressed the issue. Finally, after a third round of entreaty, the Buddha said, "There are three levels of supernormal powers. The first is the power to appear as many persons, to pass through walls, to fly through the air, and other amazing physical feats that ordinary people can't perform. The second is the power to read another person's mind. The third is the power to guide people according to their own mental development toward their own good, using just the right methods.

"The first two levels of power, if displayed for their own sake merely in order to impress people, are no different from the pleasure-feeding performance of magicians. A spiritual person who practices such worldly miracles for show is a source of shame, humiliation, and disgust. Such actions may win converts, but they do not bring enlightenment to help them put an end to suffering.

"The third level of power, however, which can truly be called miraculous, helps people to get rid of suffering and confusion. This is the only supernatural power that is fit to be practiced. The only miracles worth performing are these: When you see someone full of passion, craving, and greed and you teach this person how to free himself or herself from passion, craving, and greed. When you see that a person is a slave to hatred and anger and you use your powers to help this person control that hatred and anger. And when you come across a person who is ignorant and cannot see the true, impermanent, and sorrowful nature of the world and you use your powers to help this person overcome ignorance. These are worthy miracles you can perform!"

The Buddha didn't deny that a practitioner of the Dharma can acquire supernatural powers, in the mundane sense of the phrase, but he insisted that they are simply what we'd call beneficial side effects, not the main thing. I believe that the many stories of magical wonders that occur in saintly literature throughout the world are meant to be taken, at least in part, symbolically. I have always been a bit skeptical about miracles and the countless tales one hears along the spiritual path. Not only Buddhism, Hinduism, and Taoism but all the other ancient religious traditions have tales of human beings flying, levitating, walking on water, traveling or manifesting with great speed over long distances, emanating in order to appear in several places at once, swallowing poison to no effect, reading minds, holding their breath for great lengths of time, living an incredible number of years, returning from the dead, resurrecting the deceased, making accurate predictions, and so forth. Tibetan Buddhist teachers often illustrate their oral teachings with stories and anecdotes about such *siddhas* (accomplished masters with supernormal powers) and their astounding deeds to accentuate the efficacy and power of spiritual practice.

Milarepa, the greatest of Tibetan yogis, is widely believed to have developed the power of flight through his mastery over subtle energy and cosmic forces as well as over his own body, mind, and spirit. There is even a classic tale of his competing with an important Indian yogi to see who could fly faster and higher up a Himalayan peak! This is a story every Tibetan I have ever known has heard and believes. Even the Dalai Lama himself, a modern rationalist with a scientific bent, has said that when Kalu Rinpoche taught him Milarepa's six special yogas, he himself saw Kalu Rinpoche fly. Whether he meant that he saw him soar, levitate, become higher, or something else, I can only speculate. In any case, I am sure these saintly lamas became exceedingly elevated, one way or another, through these profound, esoteric, diamond-path energy yogas.

Traditional and oral Buddhist literature is chock-full of similar stories. Tibetan masters consider the Rainbow Light Body of perfect enlightenment (that is, the physical body turning into a rainbow) the ultimate achievement, signifying utter transcendence, power over life and death, and even omniscience. My own teacher Kalu Rinpoche told us that his root guru in Tibet, Lama Norbu Dondrub, attained the rainbow body and that when he died his body shrank to the size of a thermos and then dissolved into rainbow light as a sign of his awesome spiritual realization. The late great Dzogchen master Dudjom Rinpoche, who passed away near our retreat center in southern France in 1988, was said to have done likewise. I myself saw rainbows all around his shrunken remains when his corpse, in a sitting posture, was interred in a stupa monument built expressly for this purpose at his monastery in Bodhanath, Nepal, where it remains enshrined to this day. Almost everyone present at the time saw many rainbows around the holy mummy, on the windows of the building, and hovering in the air. My friend Pema Yeshe, an American graduate of Radcliffe College who was quite devoted yet also a skeptic, uncharacteristically admitted that she too saw the rainbows. It was a totally remarkable and moving sight, echoing many of the siddha tales told by lamas.

Yogis may well be able to fly, as Tibetan Buddhists believe. My own mentor, the late great yogi Nyoshul Khenpo Rinpoche, told stories about the flying yogis and rainbow-body masters at his former monastery, Katok Gonpa, in eastern Tibet. Even more important than whether or not these stories are literally true, however, is the deeper meaning they convey—wouldn't it be a truly marvelous higher accomplishment to step through our limitations, open the wings of the heart, and soar above worldliness into the space of freedom, uplifting others in the process along with ourselves?

DEVELOPING POWERS

We can intentionally develop some of these powers in various ways. But before going too far in this direction, we need to check our motivations for doing so. There are many stories of the famous eighty-four siddhas (master yoga adepts) in India who initially set out to acquire supernatural powers for their own benefit yet in the process overcame their ego-based desires and used their powers for the benefit of others. The mind is the most powerful tool and force in the world, as far as I can tell. My Tibetan friend Tulku Thondup Rinpoche, an erudite and accomplished teacher and author living in Massachusetts, agrees: "Our minds possess the power of healing pain and creating joy. If we use that power along with proper living, a positive attitude, and meditation, we can heal not only our mental and emotional afflictions, but even physical problems. . . . Learned people realize that all happiness and suffering depend upon the mind, and do not seek happiness from other sources." The late German-born scholar Lama Anagarika Govinda wrote in his book *Way of the White Clouds* that the healing power of saints is not only a Tibetan belief but a general human experience:

> Christ, according to the Evangelists, was first and foremost a healer, who convinced people not by arguments and sermons, but mainly by the power of his saintly personality, which aroused faith in those who came in contact with him. . . . Faith is the capacity to receive the power of the spirit, the capacity to communicate, to pour out and give from the accumulated fruits of inner experience that have matured in the stillness of a composed and devoted mind.

We too can help and heal both ourselves and others, with prayer and awareness practices that purify and clarify our internal being. The potential for almost unimaginable powers of the awakened heart and mind rests within each of us. Today we can go to workshops to develop psychic powers and intuition, if that's our wish. We can also explore the ancient, timeless, tried-and-true contemplative yogic methods for refining the subtle, powerful energies (*prana*) latent within us by using samadhi (concentrated absorption in deep meditation), visualization, chanted mantras, *chakras,* and internal energy channels. This work can bring us to experience superboosted states of consciousness, such as those traditionally called "infinite light," "infinite space," "weightlessness," "deathless bliss," and so on. As I mentioned in discussing the dhyana paramita (chapter 5), recent scientific research has demonstrated that meditation and intention can favorably alter our brain waves and refine our awareness by triggering the release of serotonin and other mood-enhancing chemicals.

One of the best ways I know to develop supernormal powers and abilities intentionally is through the use of samadhi, or the totally one-pointed concentration that leads to total absorption and the union of oneness and noneness. By simultaneously expanding and dissolving ourselves, we reach this inexpressible state of mystic union, nonduality, transparency, and transcendence. Ordinary meditation can sharpen the mind so that it's like a keen knife that cuts deeply into the nature of things. Samadhi is a state of hypersharpened acuity, brightness, and quickness. It's like the scientific process of focusing light into laser beams, which can then be put to all kinds of powerful uses, such as microscopic surgery, superprecise steel-cutting, and instantaneous telecommunications. Similarly, the best-honed states of consciousness can be put to extraordinary tasks, as has been done throughout the ages by the most proficient of yogic adepts who have mastered the various states, degrees, and depths of samadhi concentration.

We may also develop our capacity for higher accomplishments through visualizing and meditating on or praying to Bodhisattva archetypes or grand Bodhisattva figures, whom I'm about to describe in more detail. Each of these grand Bodhisattvas personifies and models for us the ultimate powers of beneficence that we ourselves can realize. We could think of these grand Bodhisattvas as legendary ancient superheroes seeking to be reborn in and through the modern-day spiritual warrior.

BODHISATTVAS AS SUPERHEROES

Fully purifying my body, speech, and mind,
And completely purifying good activity and all worlds,
Like the dedication of wise Bodhisattva Samantabhadra
May I too dedicate my efforts in communion with him.

—FLOWER GARLAND SUTRA

Mahayana Buddhist cosmology features a number of archetypal Bodhisattva figures who function symbolically in both Buddhist literature and the flesh-and-blood lives of Buddhist practitioners. In addition to being archetypal, they are called celestial, mythical, cosmic, or grand Bodhisattvas. Today, in our comic-book culture, we might label these exalted beings "superheroes."

Science speaks about force fields or quantum fields that extend over vast areas of space. In many respects, an archetypal Bodhisattva might be called a virtue field that permeates the universe, serving as a blessed "frequency channel" that we can tune in to and tap for help, guidance, support, and inspiration. Buddhism depicts this Bodhisattva virtue field as a timeless being in idealized, transcendently human form so that our limited human intellect can imagine it and draw on its boundless, transcendental energy more easily. But it is our heart—or, in Buddhist terms, our heart-mind—that instinctively downloads and translates this energy into spiritual power or higher accomplishments here in this world.

Each of the archetypal Bodhisattvas represents a certain cluster of sublime Bodhisattva qualities, both universal and deeply personal. My friend Joan Halifax Roshi, a teacher in the Zen Peacemaker Order as well as an anthropologist, expresses the concept this way: "Though grand Bodhisattvas are mythic figures, they also are functions within the psyche." Buddhists say that if we look carefully enough we can recognize our own face in the different icons of enlightenment.

Because of their overall super-excellence, it is tempting to think of archetypal Bodhisattvas as gods or archangels, in the Western sense of the word, but they are not deities external to ourselves. Buddhism acknowledges a god (deva) realm as one of the six realms of conditioned existence; not entirely unlike our own evanescent world, it is also subject to the universal laws of impermanence, mortality, and decay. Archetypal Bodhisattvas, in contrast, exist for the most part beyond the cycle of birth and rebirth that traditionally includes the godly realm. Buddhist literature is filled with references to different gods, such as Indra or Brahma, that Buddhism inherited from the Hindu culture in which it arose, but again, these gods are not to be confused with archetypal Bodhisattvas—or, for that matter, with Buddhas. Nor are they synonymous with the one God of the monotheistic faiths. (I think that we probably use a king-size word like *God* so as to have an abstract mental placeholder for something ideal and transcendent rather than to refer to something that can be precisely described in worldly terms.)

Archetypal grand Bodhisattvas are potent images of the ideal. They don't by any means rule over life as supreme creators, destroyers, governors, or judges. Rather, they serve universally as focal points of meditation and devotion and as energy sources that play out in the everyday lives

of people living in the world of samsara (or relativity). For our own betterment, these images of enlightened activity mirror in the highest sense
what we are all fundamentally capable of displaying in our lives. I think a
good way to think of these grand Bodhisattvas is as the Buddha assuming
the guise of each of them for specific reasons and purposes in the multitude of different situations throughout all the various realms of existence.

In Tibetan Buddhism, the best-known and most widely revered grand
Bodhisattva is Avalokiteshvara ("he who hears the cries of the world"),
who is closely identified with the Dalai Lama and is considered by many
to be the central or sovereign Bodhisattva deity. Avalokiteshvara assumes
many different forms among various Buddhist cultures and schools but
always symbolizes all-encompassing compassion. The Tibetan name
Chenrezig signifies "he or she who watches over us," like a parent or angelic guardian caring for beloved children. It is from Avalokita's mouth
that the Heart Sutra of Perfect Wisdom issues forth.

In Tibet, Chenrezig's female grand Bodhisattva counterpart is named
Tara (Guiding Star) or Drolma (the Liberatrice), the Protectress of the
high ground. My late friend, the Buddhist scholar and author John
Blofeld, believed that Chenrezig and Tara combined in Chinese history into the wondrously popular form of Kuan-yin. Over the centuries,
Kuan-yin has emerged as the most popular object of reverence in all of
East Asia. Sometimes called the Goddess of Mercy, her image is found
everywhere. In Japan, Avalokita is envisioned as either a male or a female
named either Kannon or Kanzeon. All of these angelic forms are images
or faces of the same principle of divine compassion, forgiveness, tender-
ness, and unconditional love. All Tibetans without exception pray to Tara
and Avalokita and chant their mantra, aspiring to be more like them.

In artistic representations, Avalokita often appears as a radiant, Buddha-
like icon possessing numerous arms, each ending in a hand that holds its
own helpful tool, such as a mirror, medicine vial, wish-fulfilling jewel,
string of prayer beads (mala), or syllable of speech (mantra). In Tibetan
iconography, Chenrezig usually has four hands to symbolize the Four
Boundless Attitudes, also known as Brahmaviharas, or what I call divine "heartitudes": lovingkindness, which wishes others well; compassion, which feels others' pain and is moved to help; joy, which celebrates
the good fortune and virtue of others; and equanimity, which exercises
tolerance, impartiality, objective detachment, and acceptance.

By envisioning Avalokiteshvara or chanting his mantras and prayers, Buddhists invoke the marvelous virtue of heartfelt compassion in their own lives. When they exhibit this compassion, it is believed that Avalokiteshvara is manifesting through them. I'm certain, for instance, that on that wintry Woodstock day in 1977 that I described in the introduction, as I was dangerously pumping gas into the tank of my running car, Avalokita appeared to me in the rough and ready, denimed form of Exxon Ken, who stopped me from almost blowing myself up and then mercifully fixed my car gratis. Within the vast religious world of Mahayana Buddhism, certain revered teachers are officially deemed lifelong incarnations of Avalokiteshvara. Among them are Bodhidharma (c. 470–543 CE), who established Ch'an in China in the sixth century (later known as Zen in Japan), and each successive holder of the title Dalai Lama up to the current, fourteenth, one. The Karmapa lamas and the Gyalwang Drukpas are also considered prime incarnations of this glorious grand Bodhisattva.

In addition to Avalokiteshvara, who embodies active compassion, Tibetan Buddhism recognizes seven other grand Bodhisattvas, each embodying potent images of the ideal:

1. Manjushri embodies transcendental knowledge-wisdom (prajna paramita). He cuts asunder the veils of ignorance and illusion and illumines the darkness of samsara with his flaming, upraised wisdom-sword in his right hand. His radiance dispenses knowledge-wisdom and suffuses the world with the light of discrimination and discernment. He is imagined or visualized as a prince who is always youthful, just as timeless wisdom is always fresh and up-to-date and doesn't age, tarnish, or degenerate.

2. Maitreya embodies lovingkindness and well-wishing beneficence (in Sanskrit, *maitri;* in Pail, *metta*). He personifies the Buddha of the future (that is, the next Buddha to come into history after Sakyamuni Buddha), whom we try to usher in and bring forth by emulating his lovingkindness and selfless, helpful ways. Meditation on lovingkindness and beneficial well-wishing is one of the most popular and effective forms of Buddhist meditation practiced worldwide today. Maitreya is often depicted seated on a chair holding a lotus with a stupa

emerging from it. Sometimes he holds a vase containing nectar, symbolizing the elixir-like Buddhadharma as pure, present, and available.

3. Vajrapani embodies power, energy, dynamism, fierceness, and even appropriately skillful and necessary wrath on behalf of righteousness. He is said to correspond to the five dhyani Buddhas, protectors of the five directions in the Theravadin, the most ancient tradition of Buddhism. Legend tells of him constantly accompanying and guarding the Buddha at his birth, his enlightenment under the Bodhi Tree, his public teachings, and his death at age eighty. Vajrapani is often invoked to dispel hindrances and to remove diseases, natural disasters, and other hardships and calamities. He holds the thunderbolt (*vajra*) of the god Indra and stands in a posture of active, dynamic readiness and is known as "Thunderbolt Wielder." He is surrounded and enhaloed by wisdom flames, which consume ignorance and illumine the darkness of confusion and delusion.

4. Samantabhadra embodies the perfection of all sublime virtues, especially generosity, along with the spiritual qualities of morality, purity, humility, devotion, equanimity, and inclusiveness. He is known as the All-Good Bodhisattva, Worthy Awakener, and Protector of the Dharma; much can be learned about him from the Lotus Sutra, one of Mahayana Buddhism's most important scriptures. In statues and paintings, he holds a wish-fulfilling jewel in his left hand and lotus flowers in his right hand and often rides on a grand white elephant with six ivory tusks, symbolizing—guess what?—the first six paramitas.

5. Kshitigarbha embodies the qualities of a savior and comforter. He concerns himself with beings fallen into the infernal lower realms of existence—hungry ghosts, helpless animals and insects—and vowed eons ago that, "Only after the hells are empty will I become a Buddha." He is one of the most popular Bodhisattvas in Japan, especially among women, because he is regarded as being particularly watchful over

lost and ill children and aborted or miscarried fetuses. Japanese Buddhists also consider him to be the special protector of euthanized pets, homeless individuals, and travelers. His name means "Earth Storehouse"; they know him as Jizo and pay their respects to him at thousands of roadside shrines, a practice that has spread to temples, gardens, and home altars around the world. Kshitigarbha is imagined or visualized in almost every Buddhist culture as a jolly old monk who carries a walking staff with six jiggling metal rings atop it, so that children can hear him coming and run up to him to be blessed and nurtured—making him not unlike an ice cream truck in today's world! I like to think of him as the Buddhist Pied Piper, a totally good version of the more problematic Pied Piper in German folklore, who is beloved of children and animals. Aspiring to be like him, I try to keep my ears open to hear and follow the clarion call of the Bodhisattva Guardian of Children, the Marginalized, and the Underdog.

6. Akashagarbha embodies the infinite: the skylike nature of Bodhicitta and the womblike matrix of sunyata (emptiness), which is the mother of all the enlightened ones and their disciples. Akashagarbha's infinite abundance and vast embrace fulfill the positive needs, wants, prayers, and aspirations of all beings. Chinese masters say that whoever wants to attain happiness, peace, and wisdom should devote himself or herself to this great Bodhisattva. Akashagarbha is golden and may hold a lotus with a sword that radiates light.

7. Dribpa Namsel embodies purification and the removal of barriers. He is the grand Bodhisattva who clarifies the five *kleshas* (obscuring emotions) and clears the way to liberation. He is sometimes associated with the Medicine Buddha. He is royal blue with a moon on his lotus. In the sutras, he is with Avalokiteshvara, praising him after their fortuitous meeting.

There are traditionally said to be three ranks of Bodhisattvas, in ascending order. First are the royal, or kinglike, Bodhisattvas, like Manjushri, who benevolently look after the welfare of all beings as they do with their own people while remaining slightly above and beyond them. Second is the Ship Captain–like Bodhisattvas, like Maitreya, who travel with and remain in the same boat as their passengers on the way to the other shore, nirvana. Third and greatest is the humblest, Good Shepherd–like Bodhisattva, like Avalokita, who is the last to retire at night to the safety of the fold after the entire flock has been brought safely home.

Buddhist lore is filled with stories about the "magical" power and blessings, protection, teachings, and encouragement that individual grand Bodhisattvas somehow transfer, not unlike the saints and archangels of other religions, to faithful individuals who invoke them in one way or another—individuals including masters and neophytes, from trained priestesses and scholarly yogis to illiterate nomads, doddering invalids, and children.

We too can solicit help, strength, and inspiration from the grand Bodhisattvas, and experience great comfort and solace as well as mystic visions, numinous visitations, meaningful dreams, omens, and a variety of extraordinary experiences. We too can turn to them for wisdom and guidance. As we strive to learn from and emulate a particular grand Bodhisattva and to inculcate in ourselves his or her sublime qualities, we can pray in this way: "May I become just like you, a beacon in this benighted world, a true Bodhisattva, a vehicle of your compassionate, wise, and selfless Buddha-activity—an Awakener of all beings!"

Individual grand Bodhisattvas can also be invoked using traditional prayers or rituals, such as the Flower Garland Sutra's prayer invoking Samantabhadra. Alternatively, we can create prayers and rituals ourselves based on our own research into their attributes and images. To inspire myself to be more like Avalokiteshvara, I practice the Tibetan Compassionate Buddha (or Avalokiteshvara) Meditation, which is done on a daily basis by most Tibetan Buddhists. It involves visualizing myself as this grand Bodhisattva, chanting his mantra—"Om mani padme hung"—and radiating compassionate thoughts, wishes, and intentions from my radiant, blossoming, lotuslike heart-mind. In this manner, I cover and transform all aspects of my worldly expression—body, mind, and speech. Liturgically speaking, this kind of practice is called "modeling off an accomplished one." The Compassionate Buddha Meditation was the first practice taught to me long ago by my root lama, Kalu Rinpoche, and it was his lifelong main practice. They say he recited the great compassion mantra well over 300 million times, irradiating all six realms of existence with the six colorful syllables of the mantra, one syllable for each of the six paramitas.

In a less technical sense, I try to bring the ascendant archetypal Bodhisattvas into my life literally by inviting and integrating them into my daily existence, which means taking odd moments during the day to exhort and invoke their help, pray to them, recall their virtues, look at pictures of them, or imagine a symbolic detail of their iconic appearance, such as a lotus or wish-fulfilling jewel. We can also apply this kind of power-stoking, consciousness-stirring practice to the historical Buddha himself or to another historical master in one of the teaching lineages. As we go about turning ourselves into the particular transcendent helper we are invoking—through the combined power of sacred chant, mantra, visualization, samadhi concentration, faithful devotion, lineage blessings, and the like—their powerful blessing begins to emanate within us and through us, as well as to and from us. Thinking about my ongoing communion with Avalokiteshvara and the grace I gain from it, I'm reminded of the celebrated closing lines in the popular Lotus Sutra: "Eyes of true compassion, gazing at sentient beings, bring to focus an immeasurable ocean of blessings."

LET US BE SUPERHEROES!

> As a blind man feels when he finds a pearl in a dustbin, so am I amazed
> by the miracles of awakening arising in my consciousness.
>
> —SHANTIDEVA

I have been mulling especially hard over the relative importance of siddhis—call them higher accomplishments, special talents, magical powers, or what you will—and the shortcomings of becoming overly fascinated with them since I began writing this book about the Bodhisattva ideal and the universal Way of the Wisdom Warrior. Many people are afraid of power and its corrupting, damaging, even violent aspects and implications. Power of various kinds—physical, political, military, personal— has burned many of its possessors throughout the ages, as we already know. We have all heard the historian Lord Acton's famous utterance that "power corrupts, and absolute power corrupts absolutely."

Tibetan Buddhism, renowned as the mystic Vajrayana (the Diamond Path, or tantric path), is a profound and powerful way of dynamic energy coupled with the view that everything is sacred and all are equally sacred. In this sacred outlook, power is always related to compassion and altruistic action, always connected to the sense of unity and interconnectedness with others. "Power to the peaceful," I like to say, echoing our popular 1960s slogan "power to the people." There is no room for megalomania, cultic brainwashing, forceful domination, oppression, hypocrisy, or enslavement here. Yet the tantric Vajrayana does make skillful use of energy, passion, power, and powers in the quest for enlightenment.

Extraordinary fearlessness and audacity are crucial elements in the Bodhisattva career; we must transform ourselves into dedicated spiritual warriors or even knightlike superheroes. Stop for a moment and think about what an outrageous ambition it is to strive through many lifetimes, worlds, and dimensions of existence to end the sufferings of all sentient beings by delivering them to the deathless other shore of freedom, bliss, and enlightenment! How long is *that* going to take? Is there really an end in sight? This infinite journey is certain to require every bit of paramita power we can muster, don't you think? So let's not timidly shy away from the source of true power, in the name of simplistic, limited notions of purity, selflessness, nonviolence, and love.

Fortunately, the timeless wisdom and insight into reality pervading all the paramitas is the gift that keeps on giving, and it can help each and every one of us do what might otherwise seem impossible. It is universally true and applicable, far beyond mere local beliefs, religious politics, doctrine-based power struggles, religious isms and schisms, or even apparent success or failure. We can't possibly bring about the highly positive global results we long for if we, as Bodhisattvas on the path of universal awakening, don't have sufficient discriminating wisdom combined with each of the other precious qualities that are encoded within the ten transformative practices of the stainless Bodhisattva Code.

Altogether, these qualities truly do equip us to perform miracles. And how much our world needs them! We must work with all the capabilities we possess to bring about a more benevolent world, one that is less selfish, greedy, hardheaded, hardhearted, violent, materialistic, and anxiety stricken. Mahatma Gandhi exhorted us to "be gentle, truthful, and fearless." Just look at how much he accomplished, a principled advocate of nonviolence. As Bodhisattvas, we must strive, like Gandhi, to keep ourselves committed to making a positive difference in every way we can.

We must elevate our sights, raise our dreams, and summon our higher powers—for all higher powers are welcome!

To do this, we first need to cultivate a mentality of sunrise, with all its intimations of boundless energy, light, dawn, and possibility, as opposed to a sinking mentality of sunset, which suggests weakness, blindness, degeneration, and despair. We must never lose sight of the fact that life is an inconceivably wondrous mystery, a splendid combination of energy, reality, time, and luminous spirit. We must not squander it! To waste and kill time only deadens ourselves. Transforming ourselves and, in common cause, healing our differences, we *can* save all sentient beings. Magically enough, awakening oneself does help awaken the world, just as one small morsel of yeast can leaven the entire loaf of bread.

I revere the wisdom of the ancient lineage of Buddhist masters, who have mined the treasure trove of wisdom over time and preserved and transmitted it to us for our unending benefit. It is my great hope to pass on to the next generations an offering of whatever wisdom I have been fortunate enough to gather and make my own and, in so doing, to pay back my own gracious teachers and benefactors. Timeless wisdom is the ultimate form of power, wealth, and blessedness, far beyond mere worldly power, riches, and success. With wisdom comes boundless peace of mind, compassion, unselfishness, generosity, and kindness. "Blessed is the man who finds wisdom, who gains understanding, for he is more profitable than silver and yields better returns than gold" (Proverbs 3:13). From this inner power all good things become possible.

As for higher accomplishments, I try to empower each and every one of my students to surpass their teacher in becoming all they're capable of becoming. Pure water, even if it issues from a dirty pipe, can help plants grow and flourish. We are all somewhat "dirty," flawed, imperfect, and dispensable as mere human beings, but our innermost nature is perfect, pristine, and deathless. It is essential for everyone's benefit that we cultivate, embody, and dynamically transmit this elixir-like inner essence for the boundless benefit of one and all.

Mindful of the Buddha nature that resides within each of us, I see the individuals who come before me as being like stars. I try to help them gather and focus their light so that it can shine forth not only for themselves but for the world, which sorely needs to wake up from delusion's darkness. I truly believe that if we treat each student in our schools as a star, as a kind of revered tulku (a reincarnated lama and Bodhisattva)—in other words, as a genuine prodigy—our society will be vastly transformed for the better. I think the same truth applies in regard to each individual in our lives who in any way looks to us for anything worth having.

I believe that it is in our power to cause such a miraculous, widespread change, and that it is incumbent on us to try. That is why I am calling for a spiritual revolution—a revolution of our hearts as well as of our consciousness. Heeding this call means assuming universal responsibility and laboring diligently together for the good of all with open hands, open arms, open hearts, and open minds.

The Buddha himself advocates just such a revolution through his Bodhisattva teachings. Like other great sages, saints, and heroes throughout human history and even today, he pleads for us not to withdraw into our narrow circle of self, family, friends, and acquaintances. Instead, he bids us to engage ourselves more fully in the life of the universe and to achieve a higher, more potent level of existence by serving all sentient beings. This is how the caterpillar-like light-seekers can shed their cocoons, spread their wings, and fly.

During the yearlong writing of this book, perhaps the most inspiring historical story I found concerns the superhuman faith, perseverance, and selfless giving of Father Damien de Veuster (1840–1889), the saint of the lepers. He said, "My greatest pleasure is to serve the Lord in his poor sick children rejected by other people." As a young and idealistic Belgian priest, he went to the remote Hawaiian Islands during the American Civil War and devoted himself to alleviating suffering and saving souls in the leper colony on Molokai, the most out-of-the-way island. At the time it was described by one observer as "a living graveyard, a land of lepers without law, doctors, nurses, infirmary or administration." His Jesus-like labors there eventually cost him his life, although his efforts saved the lives and relieved the misery, loneliness, and fears of so many abandoned souls. The *London Times* called him "one of the noblest Christian heroes ... who has well earned his beatification and divine rest."

When I visited the castaway colony of Kalaupapa on a rugged, windswept spit of land extruding from Molokai Island out into the Pacific Ocean, I could not believe that people survived there before the age of airplanes, electronic communications, and even lighthouses. In fact, the famous Molokai lighthouse on the tip of the Kalaupapa peninsula, erected early in the twentieth century, was until recently the most powerful beacon in the Pacific, owing to the extremely dangerous and unpredictable nature of the straits between Molokai and the neighboring islands.

The Scotsman Robert Louis Stevenson, one of the most popular writers of the nineteenth century, said his heart was all but broken by the plight of the abandoned outcasts of Molokai. He also suffered from a terrible wasting disease—in his case, tuberculosis—which would claim his life at an early age. After visiting the notorious leper colony in 1889, shortly after Damien's death, he said: "They were strangers to each other, collected by common calamity, disfigured, mortally sick, banished without sin from home and friends."

One of the last admonitions of Father Damien's bishop before he left Honolulu for Molokai was not to touch anyone or eat anything he had not prepared with his own hands. Father Damien, however, could not in good faith live like that, distancing himself from the poor sufferers he had come to identify so closely with and to see as God's smallest children. He gave himself unstintingly for sixteen years to the outcasts, and the worldwide attention he brought to their plight garnered humanitarian aid that was previously unseen in the Pacific. Before succumbing to leprosy himself at the age of forty-nine, he said, "Suppose the disease does get my body. God will give me another one on Resurrection Day. The main thing is to save one's soul, isn't it?"

Father Damien was beatified in 1995. Mother Marianne, the mother superior who eventually brought her nuns to help a year before he died, wound up staying thirty-five years more and also ending her life there. She was beatified in 2002. Like Father Damien, she saw her own salvation in the service and salvation of others less fortunate than herself. In the lives of both Father Damien and Mother Marianne, we see the sweet, secret wisdom of the Bodhisattva's commitment to selfless dedication. They knew that liberating others liberates oneself, healing others heals oneself, and transforming others transforms oneself.

Nascent Bodhisattvas, I exhort you to find where you are needed and can provide help, where you can truly make a positive difference and unselfishly give yourself to doing so. Anyplace could be your Molokai, your mission of mercy. When you learn to give yourself, it may claim all of your energy, body and soul, but you will receive in return God's heart, Buddha's mind. By getting out of your own way, superpowers beyond belief and blessings too shall be yours. Losing yourself, you'll be rewarded by finding your higher self, your best self, your divine Bodhisattva self—thus creating a paradise wherever you are.

We cannot afford to wait. We must prepare ourselves to be the guides we have so far only waited for, the promised messiahs who will help usher in the kingdom of heaven for everyone. We must bring into our daily lives this servant leader dwelling within ourselves, no matter when, where, how, and whatever it takes. We can do it through teaching, parenting, mentoring, inspiring, motivating, volunteering, healing, and helping in whatever ways present themselves to us. We can do it because underneath our mild-mannered exteriors we are indeed superheroes who create our lives and the world around us every single moment of every single day.

> *Ultimately the power is within us,*
> *and is greater than ourselves.*
> *Don't unconsciously give it away,*
> *disempowering yourself and others.*
> *Power should be used for good, to help and to accomplish,*
> *not used over others.*
> *Never underestimate the power of mind and heart,*
> *the power of intention,*
> *the power of vision and of leadership,*
> *the power of prayer and meditation,*
> *the power of creative imagination,*
> *the power of community and of connection,*
> *of silence and simplicity,*
> *of patience,*
> *of impeccable action,*
> *of love,*
> *of acceptance,*
> *of fearlessness,*
> *of humility,*
> *of reverence,*
> *and of authenticity.*
> *Power to the peaceful!*

TEN

THE PERFECTION OF AWAKENED AWARENESS

May I realize the supreme virtue of primordial awareness,
which intuitively recognizes the innate purity
and perfection of all that is.

One particular Zen teaching tale always makes me smile. In a clear, concise way, it reminds me that enlightenment, the ultimate aspiration of every Buddhist, comes about primarily through nonattachment, wise awareness, and clear vision. The tale also conveys that things are not always as they appear to be and, miracle of miracles, that enlightenment can be a lot closer than we think.

Long ago, in a Chinese monastery, there lived an aged monk who had been seeking enlightenment for many years. No matter how long and hard he meditated, however, that great goal still eluded him. Finally, he decided that he might do better if he left the monastery and found an isolated mountain cave where he could meditate alone and undistracted. He put all of his possessions—including his robes, his begging bowl, and his umbrella—into a bundle, tossed it over his shoulder, and headed off into the wilderness to begin his climb up the highest mountain in the region.

On the way, the monk ran into an elderly man who was also carrying a huge bundle over his shoulder. Unbeknownst to the monk, this man was really Manjushri, the supreme Bodhisattva of wisdom. Of course, the monk had studied Buddhism long and hard, and he certainly knew that Manjushri occasionally appeared to seekers in order to help them complete their journey to enlightenment, but it never occurred to him that he himself could have this kind of extraordinary visitation.

Manjushri-in-disguise asked the monk, "Where are you going?"

"I am going high up the mountain to find a cave," answered the monk, bowing to the Buddha nature in the person before him, because that's what monks do. "I plan to stay there until I die or attain enlightenment."

Manjushri suddenly shifted his weight and dropped the heavy bundle he was carrying to the ground with a huge *thud!* Instantly, the monk was enlightened. He too had simultaneously lost a large, weighty burden. When Manjushri dropped his bundle, the monk was genuinely inspired for the first time to drop his whole separate and defensive self, his own personal story and sense of identity, the weight he had been carrying around throughout his life.

Amazed, the monk asked, "Now what?"

The wise Manjushri simply smiled. He reached down, picked up his bundle again, and continued peacefully down the path.

One of the only things we can say for sure about enlightenment is that it's not what we think it is. Neither is the tenth transformative practice, the final step on the Bodhisattva path and the immediate precursor to enlightenment. Awakened awareness (in Sanskrit, *jnana*) is not about striving to be a Bodhisattva anymore or gradually growing the seed of Bodhicitta into a fully flowering, fruit-bearing, and shade-providing tree of enlightenment. It is not *about* anything, really.

Michael Lee, my Chinese friend in Hong Kong, an aged puppet-maker and longtime Zen man, once told me his favorite old Taoist story, and it is relevant here. One day some disciples found the Taoist philosopher Chuang Tzu in front of his house, sitting peacefully on the ground in the sun with his fresh-washed long hair cascading down around him. The students gathered around him and waited patiently for him to say something. "What are you doing, master?" they finally asked.

"Drying my hair in the sun," the old sage replied.

"Can we help you?" they wanted to know.

"How can you help me?" he said. "What is there that I need? The hair is being dried by the sun, and I am resting at the origin of all things."

Jnana paramita is simply authenticity in *being*, in all its incandescent immediacy—alive, wakeful, and free. Whenever I try to describe this ineffable, self-existent, unconditional state of heavenly grace, I think of something amusing that Rumi, the most popular poet of the Islamic Sufi mystical tradition, once advised: "Try to be like a duck, with its joyful body paddling along in the loving water of the river. Just enjoy that." Being *is* it, totally. Sometimes Buddhists call it "is-ness." In the Tibetan meditative tradition, we might term it ordinariness or natural-ness or nowness—Trungpa called it ordinary mind—free from concepts, fabrication, and striving. This implies the authenticity and scintillating brilliance of pristine, innate awareness. Awareness itself is self-arisen and timeless, all-pervasive, immutable, and yet not a solid thing or entity in and of itself. It is more like grace than something we plant, grow, and develop, yet it can be cultivated and polished, and its potential skills and radiant qualities can be further stabilized and unfolded.

The tenth paramita reflects what it means to be like that joyful, un-self-conscious duck: splendid in our natural simplicity regardless of what is going on around us, what has occurred in the past, or what might happen in the future. For want of an exact explanation, since it's essentially indefinable, we can jokingly call it being "ducky." In Rumi's sense of the word, ducky means taking everything with lightness and grace, like water off a duck's back, floating along, always doing wholeheartedly what we are doing and being wholeheartedly who we are being, whether we're engaged in what the world labels "serious" matters or "trivial" ones. This level of spiritual achievement shows that we have finally let go of our attachment to ego concerns, strategies, self-improvement plans, stories, and agendas. We are finally beyond delusion. We have finally stepped out of our own dualistic way, and the true path is clear. The brilliant wisdom of awareness is an eye-opener. The unaware life is hardly worth living.

As I indicated earlier, this kind of awakened awareness represents the penultimate stage in the Buddhist way, the tenth panacean practice, the tenth bhumi level of the exalted Bodhisattva. This state is as evolved as it gets before we cross over to the next level of full and complete Buddha-hood. Most of us will have only rare glimpses of what it means to reach this level of expansive, uncorrupted, pristine awareness, although it is possible for all of us. In Buddhist iconography, awakened awareness is often portrayed as a full moon, and as the song goes, the moon belongs to everyone just as the moonlight spontaneously and impartially illuminates everything. Sometimes Buddhist artists and writers imagine awakened awareness as a radiant, lustrous, unsullied pearl, an image closely related to that of a full moon. Often this kind of pearl appears on the roof of a temple or in statues or paintings of a dragon; grasping the pearl in its mouth or paw, the dragon symbolizes a magnificent enlightened being. In China awakened awareness is called the Pearl of Wisdom; Jesus called it "the pearl beyond price." Better than gold and jewels, it is the most valuable thing there is. In spiritual life, we practice polishing this pearl so that its inherent radiance may shine ever more splendidly.

In addition to awakened awareness, jnana can be translated as primordial awareness, pristine awareness, innate wisdom, or innate wakefulness. It's what might be called clear, inner-core light, as opposed to the bright, external light that's picked up by the eyes or the keen metaphorical light and illuminating power that's shed by brilliant intelligence. Jnana is the sheer luminosity of being itself. It's the source and the groundless ground of all. Tibetans call it *yeshe,* which means "immaculately wakeful since the beginningless beginning." Thus, it is termed self-arising, self-existent, unborn and undying, primordial and unconditioned, clear light.

Because jnana, by its very nature, is so difficult to define, it's often confused with prajna, or wisdom, the sixth transformative practice. How do they differ? Prajna is everything, includes everything, suffuses everything, manifests as everything; jnana is realizing this. Prajna is to be grown and developed through progressive steps, including learning, reflection, meditation, and experience. Jnana is to be recognized by the Awakener, always innately present and inherently complete, deeply within us. Jnana can be considered an aspect of prajna, but prajna wisdom is like gradually growing up and becoming a mensch, while jnana awareness is more like waking up to the fact of being a mensch. Jnana is like the mythical celestial hawk of Indian cosmology, which emerges from its shell fully hatched. I recall the wisdom deity Manjushri saying in a tantric text, "One moment of total awareness is one moment of perfect freedom and enlightenment." This trenchant observation explains jnana in a nutshell.

The traditional explanation of prajna wisdom, as you'll recall, is that it includes two kinds of knowing: knowing how things appear and function, ranging from individual phenomena in the real world to the principles that govern the universe, such as the law of karma; and knowing how things truly are—their illusory and transitory nature, the pervasive emptiness of things (sunyata). Prajna implies knowledge-wisdom, sagacity, clear vision, discernment, and discrimination. In Western philosophy, we use the Greek word *gnosis* (supreme understanding or sagacity) to describe this kind of wisdom.

Jnana, on the other hand, is our innate wakefulness that precedes *conceptual* knowledge of specific things and even general principles. It's not something, like prajna, that we learn or develop, but rather the penetrating higher consciousness and innate cognizance already perfect and complete that is hidden within us. It can sometimes shine through spontaneously even in the middle of our most deluded moments, like a flash of lightning in the dark sky. When we break through illusions altogether and stop clinging to things—like the notion of a separate self and concrete reality—the innate wakefulness of awakened awareness (jnana) steadily illuminates our entire existence. Prajna is like a sharp sword; jnana is like lightning.

In Dzogchen lingo, jnana is closer than prajna to what Tibetans call *rigpa* (pure presence) and what I call Buddha-mind, BuddhaVision, or total Presence. My late guru Dilgo Khyentse Rinpoche used to introduce rigpa—the intrinsic nature of our mind, what we're calling "awakened awareness"—by holding up a radiant crystal, pointing to it with one finger, and abruptly shouting, *"What is mind?"* This kind of direct, mind-to-mind, mouth-to-ear teaching of the Dzogchen tradition's "pointing out" instructions—in which a master puts a short, shocking, mind-shattering question to a disciple—often provokes a spiritual breakthrough for the disciple, startling him or her into a fresh new way of seeing and being. In this way, the student can intuitively realize the utter unity and inseparability of his or her own Buddha-mind and the guru's Buddha-mind, far beyond joining and parting. For Buddha, guru, and oneself are ultimately one.

To answer this particular question—"What is mind?"—Khyentse Rinpoche would go on to say that the radiant, sparkling, transparent yet lucid nature of the crystal represents the magic mirror of the mind with its limitless potential. It is empty of feature or hue, yet capable of taking on the color of whatever is held to it. In other words, the crystal is clear yet luminously "aware." This lesson is known in Dzogchen as "the direct introduction to the nature of mind—one's true [Buddha] nature" or "the recognition of our primordial nature." It is the first vital point of Dzogchen and Mahamudra, the nondual direct-access teachings of advanced Tibetan Buddhism.

Another one of my masters used to pound on a table or clap his hands loudly and shout, *"Who is hearing and experiencing?"* The first time I heard him do this, I realized that his mind and my mind were not two but rather inseparably one with each other and with Buddha-mind, or ultimate reality. It actually felt as if he and his words were coming out of me and not just to me. Using the same shouting technique, my first Dzogchen teacher Kangyur Rinpoche would ask his students to look directly into their heart-mind to determine its color, shape, and size in the immediate moment and where it could be found. This inquiry often brought his students to a direct, nonconceptual realization of the nature of primordial identity, of selflessness, of sunyata-jnana: the empty yet cognizant lucidity and brilliance of innate awareness.

Buddhist masters of almost every school say that we are all Buddhas by nature; we only need to realize that fact, in an authentically integrated, whole-mind-and-body way. This is the core meaning of pristine awakened awareness. It is so close to being possible for us that we tend to overlook it. It is so clear and ever-present for us that we're inclined to see right through it. It is not outside of ourselves, so we can't grasp or obtain it as much as we continue trying to do so. It seems too good to be true, so we don't let ourselves believe it. Awareness of the true nature of our heart-mind answers the questions "Who am I?" "What is real?" "What is the meaning of life?" and all of the many other inquiries we might have about God, the soul, the afterlife, the material world and our place in it, or our purpose in life. However, it doesn't necessarily answer these big questions in any way we would have imagined it might.

Once, during a conference on brain science and Buddhism, the Dalai Lama was asked, "Do you think there is something—I am not sure what to call it—a kind of awareness that can exist independent of the brain? For example, something that survives death?"

The Dalai Lama's reply is worth quoting at length:

Generally speaking, awareness, in the sense of our familiar, day-to-day mental processes, does not exist apart from or independent of the brain, according to the Buddhist view. But Buddhism holds that the cause of this awareness is to be found in a preceding continuum of awareness, and that is why one speaks of a stream of awareness from one life to another. Whence does this awareness arise initially? It must arise fundamentally not from a physical base but from a preceding continuum of awareness.

The continuum of awareness that conjoins the fetus does not depend upon the brain. There are some documented cases of advanced practitioners whose bodies, after death, escape what happens to everyone else and do not decompose for some time—for two or three weeks or even longer. The awareness that finally leaves their body is a primordial awareness that is not dependent upon the body. There have been many accounts in the past of advanced practitioners remaining in meditation in this subtle state of consciousness when they died, and decomposition of the body was postponed although the body remained at room temperature.

In other contexts, the Dalai Lama calls what continues beyond the demise of our mortal body "the subtle clear light of consciousness."

Too often we think of ourselves as existing in the narrow confines of a particular body and lifetime in a particular world, but awakened awareness is primordial, deathless, unborn, and undying—to use Buddhist jargon. When we experience it, we realize our primordial and transpersonal "being-ness."

THE POWER AND JOY OF INCLUSIVENESS

I want you to bring Kuan-yin down to your own cushions,
your own desk, your own sink, your own response. The jnana
paramita is the perfection of this process. Like Kuan-yin herself,
it disappears in the dance with your friends.

—ROBERT AITKEN ROSHI

Awakened awareness may seem to some people like a state of consciousness that is completely above and beyond the world of everyday life, yet nothing could be further from the truth. Jnana does represent our communion with the universal mind, the Big Mind that transcends space and time, but once we wake up to that awakened mind, jnana transforms every aspect of our existence, including everyday life. In fact, it gives us the capacity to live our everyday life more fully, productively, dynamically, intentionally, gracefully, and meaningfully.

How exactly does the tenth panacean paramita, awakened awareness, function in this way? In a word, it helps us *connect* more vitally with everyone we encounter and everything we experience. We don't necessarily lead a whole new life once we tap into jnana. Instead, we proceed from where we are to live the life we already have with greater wisdom, compassion, clarity, and power. Why? Because we are so much more consciously aware of and attuned to reality as it is, around us and within us, in the very present, the eternal moment, the holy now—unmediated by conceptual fabrications. That's part of the message contained in the teaching tales concerning Manjushri and Chuang Tzu I recounted at the beginning of this chapter.

Bodhisattvas are experts at connecting. This is one way in which they fulfill their vow to help deliver all beings together to the far shore of nirvana, or enlightenment. They do it through the magic of what Thich Nhat Hanh describes as "interbeing": remaining fully aware of, and functioning in perfect accordance with, their interdependent unity and interwovenness with all of creation. Those who live with this spirit practice inclusiveness. They intuitively perceive and embrace all in each one, and the oneness in all, without making much ado about it.

Today we are increasingly witnessing the distress and damage caused by dogmatic, exclusionary thinking: extreme religious views about what's right and what's wrong, social intolerance of people whose lifestyles are different, and rigid political-economic lines drawn between the world of the haves and the world of the have-nots. We can help reverse this trend by working more conscientiously to practice inclusiveness in our own lives, to demonstrate open-minded tolerance and patient acceptance, starting right now and continuing on a day-by-day basis. We simply need to notice each of the times and ways in which we exclude people and things from the circle of our embrace. We can then begin to seriously reconsider why it is in our best interest, as well as the best interest of the world, to do otherwise. Finally, we can make the effort to change, to widen our circle until it opens up into infinity. As the Sufi Hafiz wrote in his poem "I Saw Two Birds":

Keep thinking about God
Keep thinking about the Beloved

And soon our nest will be the
Whole firmament.

As this widening and deepening process escalates, we'll find ourselves gradually enlarging our perspective and awakening our minds, thus connecting with all that is—from the higher power, however we may conceive of it, to the smallest of God's creatures and the entire environment that we are so much a part of and that we ignore and deny at our peril. Never underestimate the deleterious power of denial! Never overlook the panacean power of relatedness!

Bodhisattvas do not generally focus on differences between themselves and others, though they may be well aware of such differences; instead, they strive to see others in themselves and themselves in others. When we grow into this inclusive vision of interbeing, how can we harm, use, abuse, or exploit anyone else? Here lies the transcendent logic behind Christianity's Golden Rule: "Do unto others as you would have them do unto you." Putting this sacred outlook into action is the very means to recondition our selfish, separatist behavior. It is practicing what we preach.

Tolerance and acceptance is also a central and original theme of every major world religion. I write a regular "Ask the Lama" column for Beliefnet.com, an Internet clearinghouse for matters relating to all the various religious and spiritual paths. In a recent Beliefnet interview, the popular actress Susan Sarandon contributed the following spiritual insight that relates directly to the subjects of inclusiveness and primordial awareness: "When you start to develop your powers of empathy and imagination, the whole world opens up to you. As my little guy said when he first learned about the origins of man ... 'So, Mom, I guess there really isn't such a thing as a stranger, is there?' It's a spirituality that's empowering and inclusive and gives you a world that's so large and full of possibilities and so full of rewards. That's joyful."

Who can say that the love and wholehearted attention of a devoted mother watching over her infant all day is less holy and Bodhisattva-like than the ministrations of Mother Teresa's angelic nuns reaching out to the poorest and most helpless street people of Calcutta, or the austere spiritual strivings of any priest, yogi, monk, or nun meditating and praying alone in a solitary cell, cave, forest hermitage, or chapel? Doesn't holiness depend on how and why someone is doing what he or she is doing, rather than on the external form of that person's worshipful adoration and one-pointed concentration? The famous Trappist monk Thomas Merton, who wrote eloquently about the strong connections between his own Roman Catholic faith and Zen Buddhism, believed that what makes a saint saintly has nothing to do with being a perfectly sinless paragon of virtue. The more important measure of sanctity, he said, is one's ability to see what's good and beautiful in other people. The truly godly person, in his words, "retires from the struggle of judging others."

I believe that parenting is a sacred trust. Similarly, I think teaching, coaching, mentoring, healing, and engaging in charitable endeavors are sacred Bodhisattva professions. In fact, any true vocation plays a vital part of our spiritual evolution. All of life can be integrated and assimilated into the great highway of awakening. Shall we perceive the innate incandescence and splendid radiance of all beings and of Being itself, or are we totally restricted to seeing things in more self-oriented, worldly ways, as a result of our past conditioning, sensing only what can be weighed and measured and thus easily named? Do we habitually look on others either as objects for our own profit or pleasure or else as threats, enemies, or nonentities? Why can't we open up our awareness of others as freely, innocently, and automatically as children do before they are socialized otherwise? Then we'd at least have some chance not only of genuinely experiencing others but also of experiencing ourselves in the ever-present moment, so that we'd be capable of thinking, speaking, and acting more wisely, compassionately, and appropriately. Why don't we bring an unguarded open-mindedness to every moment of noticing, approaching, engaging and communicating with, and then leaving and sustaining contact with another person, regardless of the specifics involved? Why don't we converge and "inter-be" with this person before immediately evaluating, analyzing, judging, and reacting? These are all parts of what I call Steps to Conscious Connection, through which we and the people we influence learn to open up to each other and dance together to life's music. The process has to start with someone: can't it begin with us?

Life is about relatedness, as Jewish mystic Martin Buber said. Nothing exists in isolation. Even the Dalai Lama, who as a celibate lifelong monk might be expected to think more solitarily, has said that we need others in order to become enlightened, because compassion is necessary for genuine enlightenment and we need others to help us develop it.

I myself notice that when someone comes up to me, I sometimes slip into a reactive mode, the most common modus operandi among us. How much better I feel, and how much better the encounter unfolds, when I don't turn away and hide behind the supposedly safe barrier of self, but instead turn my heart and mind, body and soul, *toward* the person. Each time we meet another person is a special opportunity to reexperience our connection with the universe and to gain important insights into living that are unobtainable any other way. Why blow this opportunity by being defensive, halfhearted, or half-asleep, as if sleepwalking through life? No wonder we so often feel something is missing—for it is. *We* are missing.

THE FIVE WISDOMS OF AWAKENED AWARENESS

> Unify your attention. Do not listen with your ears but with your mind;
> do not listen with your mind but with your essence.
>
> —CONFUCIUS

Awakened awareness brings with it new and more powerful, more inclusive ways of directly "sensing" the world around us; the source of that awareness is a cosmic consciousness far greater than our merely personal one. One of my favorite poets, Amherst native Emily Dickinson, captured this truth in a poem:

> I heard, as if I had no Ear
> Until a Vital Word
> Came all the way from Life to me
> And then I knew I heard.
> I saw, as if my Eye were on
> Another, til a Thing
> And now I know 'twas Light, because
> It fitted them, came in.
> I dwelt, as if Myself were out,
> My body but within
> Until a Might detected me
> And set my kernel in.
> And Spirit turned unto the dust
> "Old Friend, thou knowest me,"

And time went out to tell the news
And met Eternity.

The fresh new way we sense things when we experience awakened awareness is not handicapped by dichotomies and dualisms such as self and other, good and bad, inside and outside, wise and foolish. Nor are the immediate perceptions and physical sensations themselves separate entities that our mind obsesses over, needs to suppress or indulge in, or tags and exploits for its own purposes. In other words, these sensations are experienced freely, naked and unadorned by conceptual imputations and interpretations, beyond the scope of greed, anger, ignorance, expectation, confusion, or negativity. Seamlessly interconnected with all of our thoughts, words, and actions in an all-knowing, all-loving, expansive state of being, everything is grist for the mill of empty, open, lucid, and penetrating awareness—jnana.

This implies a sort of mutuality and reciprocity between us and the world, between human being and God, between transcendent God above and the immanent Godhead within, between the small, egoistic, limited self and the supreme Self or Buddha nature. It brings to mind the Buddhist notion that Bodhicitta—awakened heart-mind—is both the goal and the seed within us aspiring toward the goal, bridging the supposed gap between getting there and being there. Here's how medieval mystic Meister Eckhart expressed this heightened form of perception in terms of Christian theology:

> Some people want to see God with their eyes as they see a cow and to love him as they love their cow—they love their cow for the milk and cheese and profit it makes them. This is how it is for people who love God for the sake of outward wealth or inward comfort. They do not rightly love God when they love him for their own advantage. Indeed, I tell you the truth, any object you have on your mind, however good, will be a barrier between you and the inmost truth. . . . I pray to God to be free of God.

This is universal wisdom, beyond the divisions of religious isms and schisms. It was also Eckhart who said: "The eye through which I see God is the eye with which he sees me." This wisdom eye is none other than the pristine innate awareness called jnana. Until we awaken to that innate awareness—until we ourselves experience that heavenly nirvana within ourselves—we are like sightless men blundering around in the dark, arguing about who has rights to the miraculous sunlight.

With awakened awareness comes an unspeakably vast, cosmic joy in living, the ducky quality I mentioned earlier. In using the word *joy* to describe this oceanic feeling, I don't refer to the giddy, ephemeral happiness associated with sensual pleasure. Instead, I mean the blissful feelings of profound fulfillment and certainty concomitant with an openhearted recognition and acknowledgment that the eternal, ever-buoyant life force is always operating naturally in our world and that it works in infinitely wondrous and mysterious ways. It isn't a joy that denies pain and difficulty, but rather one that understands and transcends them. Just as our physical bodies are intrinsically geared toward staying healthy, and health, not illness, is the original state, so our spiritual being is fundamentally drawn toward the affirmative, whatever circumstances may present themselves.

Jeff Barge, a publicist in New York City, once described to me an incident that, insignificant as it may appear at first, nevertheless reflects what I mean by a joyful affirmation of life. He was walking down Broadway on a very windy day, and he noticed that the street cleaners were out, pushing their huge, heavy garbage containers on wheels. Suddenly, a great gust of wind blew one of these unattended containers directly into the path of a lady walking toward him from the other end of the street. And she instantly broke into a big, hearty laugh.

What a great way to live life—to be able to laugh even when life is hurling a giant garbage container in your direction! It brings to mind the words of the fourteenth-century Dzogchen master Longchenpa: "Since everything is but an apparition, perfect in being what it is, having nothing to do with good or bad, acceptance or rejection, one may well burst out in laughter." Emaho! as we say in Tibetan. Wondrous, marvelous, amazing.

Of course, the woman in the story was also quick to jump away from the garbage container. The joy she was exhibiting was by no means scatterbrained or mindless. Fully aware of the situation, she embraced the absurdity of garbage-laden existence even as she took a practical step to handle it, to roll with the punches, as Exxon Ken said. This incident reminds me of the appreciation shown by enlightened masters I have known for all the sides of life, even those usually considered negative, without undue attraction or aversion. The pure appreciation inherent in awakened awareness can see and value things just as they are, regardless of whether they are pleasant or painful, helpful or harmful, beautiful, ugly, or disgusting. In Dzogchen lingo, we call this virtue or perspective One Taste. It represents a great deal of inner freedom, equanimity, and detachment combined with profound amusement at the absurdity and amazing nature of existence as it continuously presents itself—"the entire great catastrophe," as Zorba the Greek affectionately called it.

Recently I've seen the same kind of cosmic joy exhibited in a different way by some of my young friends responding to the needs of the people suffering in the aftermath of Hurricane Katrina. These volunteers didn't waste time bemoaning the disaster, assigning blame for it, or arguing about disastrous climate changes due to global warming. Instead, they immediately let go of their grief, fear, anger, and feelings of being overwhelmed by the enormity of it all. With nothing but love and hope in their hearts and on their faces, they loaded up their cars with food and clothing and drove down to Louisiana. Once there, they brought as much joy as they could to every hurricane victim they met, volunteering in any and every capacity. Doesn't this kind of fearless, selfless, spontaneous altruism embody all the Bodhisattva virtues, the powerful and profound paramitas, all at once? For Buddha is as Buddha does.

The woman in the path of the runaway garbage container and my friends working courageously for weeks in the wake of Hurricane Katrina revealed the same instinctively positive, upbeat universal mind—a sincere and heroic, one-people–one-family Bodhicitta response to troubling events. How can we characterize this inconceivable state of genuine awakened awareness in mere words? In Buddhism (and in Asia in general, for that matter), the mind is regarded as a sensory organ, just like the eyes, ears, nose, tongue, and skin. As the eyes see, for example, so the mind thinks. So how does thinking differ for someone who has awakened in the way we're considering in this chapter? What would the world look like through the unitary eye of such BuddhaVision?

With all the other transformative practices, we have discussed their manifestation on the outer, inner, and secret levels of our being. Jnana is more all-of-a-piece: ineffable and all-pervasive, infinite, encompassing and subsuming everything. It is not a particular entity or thing but a luminous, peaceful, potent, coherent oneness of being.

To better understand its full ramifications, however, jnana is traditionally broken out into the five jnanas (in Tibetan, *yeshes*), also known as
the Five Pristine Wisdoms. In Tibetan Buddhism, ancient commentators
arrived at the doctrine of the Five Wisdoms to describe the various facets
of the all-embracing nature of awakened awareness. The doctrine of the
Five Wisdoms is as close as we can get to a diagram of what constitutes
awakened awareness. These five forms of well-developed pristine awareness, or wisdoms, are symbolically represented as the Five Dhyana Buddhas
or Meditational Icons/Archetypes adorning the Bodhisattva's shining five-
leafed crown. This symbolic headdress, often worn by the grand Bodhisattvas like Avalokiteshvara, Tara, and Manjushri, represents their full
endowment with these enlightened awareness-wisdoms:

1. *Mirrorlike wisdom* clearly reflects whatever is, without distortion.
   The essence of mind is emptiness, or formlessness, represented
   in mirrorlike wisdom as unimpeded clarity and veridical reflection.

2. *Discriminating wisdom* can make fine distinctions and discern-
   ments that are true and undefiled by desire or fear. It understands karma and all interconnecting causes and origins and
   can be most directly associated with prajna wisdom (although
   prajna permeates all forms of wisdom). As the empty essence of
   mind manifests the individuality and variety of phenomena, it
   displays discriminating wisdom.

3. *Equalizing wisdom* sees the oneness or equality of everything
   and recognizes that the essence of all is emptiness. It registers
   the One Taste, or the essential oneness, interwovenness, and
   homogeneity of the myriad things and their coherence within
   the holographic mandala principle.

4. *All-accomplishing wisdom* is resourceful and can do anything
   that needs to be done. We could say this is wisdom-in-action,
   the wisdom that results in skillful means, because it equally
   and instantaneously understands all details, origins, consequences and implications, needs, methods and benefits.

5. *Spacious, all-encompassing wisdom* includes everything and excludes nothing. It is analogous to what theologians might call "divine vision" but Buddhists call BuddhaVision, or *Dharmadhatu* (the domain of ultimate truth). It is displayed when one realizes the true nature of mind—when one connects fully with the source of awakened awareness, the universal mind.

In itself, the doctrine of the Five Wisdoms is a skillful means to assist us in our individual quests for the awakening of jnana. It is by honing and refining our practice of the five forms of wisdom that we can attain universal wisdom and total awareness. In other words, it is by striving toward realizing and perfecting these higher or more cosmic levels of consciousness that we finally and truly awaken and ascend the Bodhisattva's ten-step stairway to enlightenment.

IDEAL HUMAN BEINGS

Every individual human being, one may say, carries within him, potentially and prescriptively, an ideal man, the archetype of a human being, and it is his life's task to be, through all his changing manifestations, in harmony with the unchanging unity of this ideal.

—FRIEDRICH VON SCHILLER, GERMAN POET

Just for a few moments, please stop reading and answer this question for yourself: When do I most feel I am being my true and authentic, ideal self?

It's not an easy question to answer, is it? Unfortunately, given the culture in which we live, we don't get much training in authentically "ideal" states of being, or even in reflecting on our lives, so we may not recognize an ideal state when we're caught up in it. Instead, society—in its own interest, of course, and for its own reasons—imposes on us highly questionable, one-size-fits-all, collective ideals that relate more to consumerism, conformity, social roles, and politics than to authenticity and the true meaning of our lives—not to mention our spiritual awakening and liberation. Generally, we are socialized to believe only that we need to go-go-go, pay attention to the media, buy the best products, hold the correct opinions, dress for success, and join the right groups so that ultimately we can think smart, behave flawlessly, get ahead, look like movie stars, feel like winners, and wow our neighbors. And if we're really lucky, we might even win a huge lottery payoff, or even live forever!

But we might very well wonder, who are we truly meant to be? How are we really supposed to live? What is our true purpose here in this fleeting, ephemeral world, this Spaceship Earth? How are we ever going to realize our full potential to help ourselves and others unless we know the answers to life's big questions? How are we going to find the answers unless we learn to reflect and pay attention to the deepest, most original and fundamental part of ourselves?

I know that I am never more myself than when I am in nature or writing and teaching. I have no good explanation for this, except that I feel as if I am the right person in the right place at the right time, doing the right thing unequivocally, regardless of outcome, feedback, or strategic considerations of any kind. It's as if I'm simply flowing and experiencing oneness, as if the notion of the dancer and the music being separate has fallen away and there is just the dance itself going on through me—I am the dance. There's no sense of anyone looking on, not even some detached part of myself. The French artist Paul Cézanne knew this truth through his own art: "If I think while I am painting, if I intervene with the process, everything falls apart, all is lost." We could just as well say that about meditation or any practice that, in its highest expression, can become like an art form.

Romantics might say it's like making love as if the world has ended and is just about to begin again. There's a timeless and authentic quality about being in this sacred zone that resonates throughout our consciousness and verifies it as an ideal experience. Inexplicably, all meaning and purpose is included in the experience itself. This kind of sensation has a lot to do with just being, which, at its most intense, turns into incandescent Being. It's a matter of discovering our true self—the Buddha-like, transpersonal self that is already there and has always been there, hidden amid the chaos and cacophony of everyday life. In the idiom of self-help, it's finding our voice, our true vocation, higher calling, or reason for being. It is finding ourselves, and a beautiful thing it is.

Awakened awareness enables us not only to recognize this state of being but also to live, work, and play in it. What's more, others see this state in us and, consciously or not, can't resist gravitating to it and benefiting from it. I am thankful to have encountered it in a significant number of my Dharma teachers over the decades. For example, my late mentor and Dzogchen master Nyoshul Khenpo Rinpoche was well known for being able to transmit the essence of Dzogchen without using words or rituals, although he was a greatly learned and accomplished meditation master steeped in all the Tibetan traditional arts and inner sciences. This was certainly true for me as his student. He touched something deep within me simply because of his authentic presence and dignity, his self-command, his radiant, peaceful buoyancy—all manifestations of innate wakefulness. Just to be in his presence was enough. His awakened state of being naturally and spontaneously present communicated with us on a level beyond the verbal or physical.

Khenpo told us that he often saw strangers at a distance whom he wanted to awaken, and could probably have done so, but that he didn't, because the conditions weren't right and intruding upon strangers like some kind of missionary didn't seem appropriate. One time when we were in Paris together in the late 1980s, he told me he felt this potential for awakening while riding the Metro subway and observing some of his fellow passengers. In my little mental amusement theater, I imagined that perhaps these passengers were ripe enough anyway and, unbeknownst to my teacher, he had provoked some great awakenings in the Metro without even overtly trying to do so.

Garab Dorje, another teacher of the Dharma who was renowned for his spontaneous awakened awareness, lived less than a century after the lifetime of the Buddha. Appropriately enough, this master's name means the Laughing Vajra or the Joyful Diamond. Upon instantaneously receiving direct transmission of the intrinsic nature of Buddha-mind from its primordial source in the form of the Buddha Samantabhadra, he awoke into peals of laughter. This response is said to have resulted from his sudden understanding of the cosmic emptiness and absurdity of it all. That insight has come down to us in the form of a famous Dzogchen teaching: the Twelve Vajra Laughs of the Primordial Buddha. As the masters say, if you have to ask what they are (as most of us do), you just haven't gotten it yet!

With lightning directness, Garab Dorje pointed out to his main disciple, Manjushri Mitra, the Buddha nature and ultimate reality within his own mind. Manjushri Mitra did the same service for his main disciple, Sri Singha, the Lion-Face Master of Crazy Wisdom. The latter, in turn, introduced his main disciple to the inseparability of his Buddha-mind from the wisdom mind of his guru and the Buddha himself simply by suddenly pointing upward at the sky in a startling, powerful gesture. Thus, the teaching of innate wakefulness and primordial awareness was passed down through the Dzogchen lineage, beyond words and concepts. This teaching speaks of our innate radiance, which combines primordial purity with spontaneous creative manifestations. This inner incandescence—from which emerges our highest identity as a Bodhisattva warrior, the ultimate spiritual activist, heroic awakener, and enlightened leader—is jnana paramita.

Among well-known contemporary figures, the person who I feel most clearly exhibits this inner incandescence is the Dalai Lama. Residing in political exile in Dharamsala, northern India, ever since the Communist Chinese Army drove him from his native Tibet in 1959, he has inspired the world with his inexhaustible compassion, courage, goodwill, patience, wise words, and nonsectarian messages of peace. Over the past few decades I have come to know him well in my many different relationships with him: as his visitor, auditor, student, attendant, bodyguard, adviser. From these multiple perspectives, I have seen him ceaselessly exemplify the Bodhisattva way, including all ten of the transformative practices outlined in this book, while simultaneously functioning with great practicality as a major spiritual leader, wisdom elder, world teacher, and nonviolent moral conscience on the international stage.

Despite the Dalai Lama's celebrity and far-reaching influence, he always tells people that he is no different from them—except, possibly, for that fact that he has been "trying to develop spiritually for a little while." In exercising this humility, he echoes the Buddha's teaching: anyone can follow the path he follows and evolve in the same way.

The Dalai Lama maintains time and again that the secret to spiritual evolution is to think of others before oneself. He likes to call it "intelligent selfishness," because helping others toward fulfillment is the best way to achieve it ourselves. He also emphasizes the virtue of cultivating joy in even the most taxing circumstances, just as he strove to remain cheerful despite being forced to leave his country and people. "A sad human being cannot influence reality," he writes in *The Buddha Nature*. "If *you* are sad or depressed, *you* cannot influence reality. When you face a so-called enemy, that enemy only exists on a relative level. Then, if you harbor hatred or ill feelings toward that person, the feeling itself does not hurt the enemy. It only hurts your own peace of mind and eventually your own health." This is the secret of peacemaking.

The Dalai Lama is a well-recognized and highly regarded figure around the world, but that level of recognition doesn't necessarily go hand in hand with having awakened awareness. Many ordinary folk, unknown outside their own network of family, friends, and acquaintances, also exhibit jnana awareness and wisdom. One such person is my American teacher, who lives in the mountains of New England. He prefers to remain anonymous, so I'll merely call him "H" here.

H is several years older than I am. During the early 1970s, H and I were among the Western students of a blanket-wrapped wandering guru in India named Neem Karoli Baba, who, as Maharaj-ji, was made famous in the West by Ram Dass's stories about him in his many books, including *Be Here Now.* H found what he was looking for there, returned to the United States with his wife, and moved into a small mountain house deep in a woods near a stream. He and his wife have lived at that sylvan New England location ever since. To just a handful of sincere students, and in a discreet way, H teaches "Self Inquiry," a form of enlightened nondualism and introspection influenced by Zen, Advaita Vedanta, and the Socratic method. Otherwise, he remains below the radar of the spiritual education scene, living simply and in harmony with all things. He never lectures, publishes, advertises, proselytizes, or charges for the thrice-weekly private group teaching he provides, nor does he accept gifts or donations. Moreover, he does not seek followers; more than once he has told me not to advertise him among my students and friends.

H is clear and transparent like a glass window, yet he also reflects undistortingly, like a bright mirror. He is sharp as a diamond, luminous as crystal, graciously accommodating, and as spacious as space. He is wise and caring but brooks no nonsense. He is also extremely practical, with a lightning-quick intelligence. For example, he lives entirely off his investments, which he manages himself. Because H is totally present in each moment, keenly sensing whatever is going on, he always seems to know exactly the right thing to do in any situation. I remember that one time his roof needed fixing, so he called professional roofers, for despite his expertise and research abilities in a number of fields, he was by no means an expert in household repairs. Three days later, while the roofers were still working, his well started failing, so he called in the well guy. By the time these two repair jobs were finished, both the roofers and the well guy had asked H if he would work with them, so successfully had he learned difficult aspects of their respective businesses and demonstrated helpful insight into their labors. They had no idea that he was a spiritual teacher, rather than a retired musician, professor, or engineer, because he appeared so ordinary and straightforward to them—just another friendly down-jacketed denizen of the Green Mountains.

Talking with H is not like talking with anyone else I know. Whether in person or by phone, it is a fascinating, instructive, and challenging spiritual practice in itself, not unlike the Zen image of two arrows meeting head-on in flight. If H is like anything, the image that comes readily to mind might be my alarm clock, which rings loudly but awakens me only when I'm ready to take the pillow off my head, open my ears, and stop hitting the snooze button.

I find that I can discuss anything at all with H, and he always seems right on the beam, whether we're talking about health problems, cars, or yoga and meditation practice, with never a word more than is needed. That is not to say we don't occasionally converse for an hour or two together, because we do—and laughter is plentiful! I can't really compare him in manner to my Eastern gurus, although I do think he embodies awakened awareness and pure presence in their sense of that paramita. All I can say is that somehow when I'm around him he helps me gain direct access to the immanent reality of the glorious, radiant, undeniable here and now, in which nothing is lacking and nothing is extraneous. I feel as if I'm in a state of pure, authentic being, aliveness, and truthful simplicity. As our friendship has endured over three decades, I have increasingly felt that he lives within me, sort of like an inner guru or conscience reminding me of my own authentic nature, assisting me in staying on the ball and living in the point where arrows meet in flight, the timeless time of nowness, of total immediacy. Once when I thanked him for this gift, and for talking long and strong to me, he replied, characteristically and not without humor, "Thanks, but you're just talking to your Self."

YOU ARE A BODHISATTVA

The important point of spiritual practice is not to try to escape
your life, but to face it—exactly and completely.

—DAININ KATAGIRI ROSHI

The tenth transformative practice, awakened awareness, or jnana, is a thoroughly manifestational one, representing not only the culmination of the Bodhisattva Code but also the penultimate stage before full enlightenment. It's the stage in our spiritual evolution when we realize ourselves as full-fledged universal Bodhisattvas and evince it in our lives.

When we look at this stage from the outside, it can easily appear to be an incredibly exalted, inconceivably difficult state to attain. But to look at it from the outside is to take a dualistic perspective, and that is exactly the wrong conceptual perspective to take. The essential beginning point in pursuing the Bodhisattva way is to accept the fact that we are Bodhisattvas already, in our heart of hearts. We are meant by nature to be wholehearted, generous, sincere, patient, heroic, caring, loving, and wise, with the full capacity to exercise skillful means, accomplish higher things, fulfill our spiritual aspirations, and live in wakeful awareness. Only our acquired greed, anger, and ignorant conditioning prevent us from recognizing this truth and living it.

When we finally see through these three principal forms of illusion and uproot them, we can start soaring on the buoyant updraft of bliss that is the freedom of natural being, transcending mere temporal pleasures. We can also connect more profoundly and beneficially with everyone around us, so that our own spiritual awakening helps catalyze a worldwide revolution of the heart. In the words of Mindroling Khandro Rinpoche, an energetic young female lama from India who has recently established a meditation center in Virginia called Lotus Garden:

You are a Bodhisattva. You are the future Buddha. In your hands and in your realization lies the liberation of all sentient beings. You cannot make a mistake because you will not make a mistake. One must have courage and know existence for what it is. In this existence, imperfection is a quality that is there. Yet even within the discursive thoughts and delusions, wisdom is there. Through that imperfection, there is no imperfection.

"Through that imperfection, there is no imperfection." We can apply this statement directly to ourselves as individuals. Yes, in our day-to-day existence we are not always ideal human beings in all of our specific thoughts, words, and deeds. How can we be, living in a world that is less than ideal? Beyond that personal imperfection, however, is a basic core of no-imperfection, our immaculate Buddha nature, the force that gives us life in the first place. The more we identify with this fundamental, eternal, nirvanic level of our being, and not with our self-oriented ego that craves and suffers in samsara, the more we actualize our Bodhisattvic potential and live up to our boundless potential.

My Buddhist teachers have graciously taught me many powerful methods for tapping into my Buddha nature and bringing more lov-ingkindness and wakefulness into the world. As an aid in your own endeavors, let me give you one of my favorite awakened awareness ac-tivities to start doing right now. As you encounter each person during the day, imagine your heart center opening like a rose or a lotus to wish this person well. (Remember, the root of the Sanskrit words *Buddha* and *Bodhisattva* is also the root of the English word *bud*—indicating a blossoming or awakening.) Make a concerted effort to undertake this activity, however briefly, for every person who crosses your path, be-ing careful to include those you don't like or don't even know, as well as those you do. This heart-opening practice will transform all your relationships as you gradually decondition and recondition your own egotism and learn to relate genuinely and totally to the Buddha light within each sentient being you encounter, unhindered by preconcep-tions, illusions, and negative habits.

This simple awakened awareness activity could be called an everyday way of reconditioning your heart-mind. Another, more generalized awak-ened awareness activity I recommend involves making an effort to open up each and every one of your other senses. For example, develop the habit of regularly taking a solitary walk—or an intentionally silent walk with a friend or loved one—through a nearby natural environment: a woods, meadow, park, cemetery, riverside, quiet neighborhood, or coun-try road. Pay special attention not only to the sights along the way but also to the smells and sounds. Touch things you encounter that have in-teresting textures, like tree trunks, flowers, leaves, or stones, and as much as is practical and safe, get a taste of whatever you can, such as the air, a blade of grass, a drop of sap, a colorful berry, or the dew that has collected on a patch of moss. I myself love the sounds, smells, and tastes of the salty seaside. Enjoying them feels like a natural meditation experience in itself. Some people can naturally settle into meditative calm and mental quiescence just sitting or standing near a body of water.

This kind of wonderfully revitalizing sense awareness practice brings to mind the words of Irini Rockwell in her recent book, *The Five Wisdom Energies* (a title that refers to the Five Wisdoms I defined earlier in this chapter):

> When we are fully present, we are receptive to the phenomenal world around us. Opening to sense perceptions, we become a sensate being, embodied. Being fully present, when we look, we actually see; when we listen, we hear; when we smell and taste, we smell and taste, we savor it; when we touch, we truly feel. Connecting to the phenomenal world in this way is the key to contacting reality directly, beyond concept. We are able to experience the play of energies that is life itself.

I wish you many glorious, refreshing, and inspiring moments in life as you progress along the Bodhisattva path, which I'm sure will present you with many challenges that will require all your courage, faith, and steadfast discipline. I'm equally certain, however, that you'll be rewarded beyond your imagination. You will be able to fly, spiritually speaking, if and when you can step out of and drop away from your outdated, self-protective cocoon.

Above all, please bear in mind that the Bodhisattva Code is a matter not of overidealistic perfectionism or of taking on more burdens in your life but of letting burdens and hangups go. A few years back, I heard a delightful awakening story from Spanish television. A man was knocking on his son's door one morning, trying to wake him up and calling to him again and again, but his son just didn't seem to want to wake up. "You have to go to school today. Wake up!" the man shouted.

"But I don't want to go to school," said the sleepy voice inside.

"Why not?" his father retorted.

"For three reasons," replied the son. "First, because it's dull. Second, the kids tease me. And third, I hate school."

His father responded, "I have three reasons you must go. First, because it is your duty. Second, because you are forty years old. And third, because you're the headmaster!"

How much longer can we afford to stay like children and remain somnolent, as if sleepwalking through our lives? Isn't it our duty, as well as our ultimate purpose and desire, to awaken, to learn to love life in all its outrageousness, and to truly live—for ourselves, for the world, and for the generations to come? Let us join hands, heads, and hearts as Bodhi-sattvas in this joyous pursuit, this great awakening.

As a parting gift to help guide you and keep you, here for your study and practice is a beautifully wise and appropriately mysterious poem from Tibet's master yogi-saint, Milarepa.

THE TEN TRANSCENDENTAL VIRTUES OF THE BODHISATTVA

Perfectly give up belief in any true existence,
There is no other generosity than this.
Perfectly give up guile and deceit,
There is no other discipline.
Perfectly transcend all fear of the true meaning of emptiness,
There is no other patience.
Perfectly remain inseparable from the practice,
There is no other diligence.
Perfectly stay in the natural flow,
There is no other concentration.
Perfectly realize the natural state,
There is no other wisdom.
Perfectly praise Dharma in everything you do,
There are no other skillful means.
Perfectly conquer the four demons (death and illness, defiling
*   obscurations, prideful ignorance, and sensuality),*
There is no other strength.
Perfectly accomplish the twofold goal (liberation of both self and others),
There is no further aspiration.
Recognize the very source of negative emotions,
There is no other primal wisdom.

SPIRITUAL REVOLUTION, ENLIGHTENED LEADERSHIP

Prayer of Accomplishing the Paramita Virtues

With one eye on this world and one on the next,
And a third focused on the timeless dimension,
Throughout this life and all possible lifetimes
Until enlightenment be achieved,
May I inexhaustibly endeavor in the Bodhisattva way
And follow the path of unconditional compassion
And selfless altruism,
So that all beings everywhere may be delivered
And freed from the ravages of suffering and confusion
And reach the other shore, great peace, deathless nirvana.

May I perfect the sublime virtue of generosity,
which brings contentment through liberating
craving, grasping, and attachment.
May I develop and accomplish
the pure virtue of ethical self-discipline,
which dries up the boiling river of greed,
hatred, and delusion and is a kindness to all.
May I perfect the noble virtue of patience,
which can face naked reality, forgive,
accept adversity, bear hardship,
and turn it into an ally.
May I perfect the noble virtue of enthusiastic effort
and fearless perseverance, which heroically strives
for the ultimate benefit of all.

*May I perfect the subtle virtue of concentration
and alert mindfulness, which clarifies the heart
and mind and allows awareness
to dawn within.
May I perfect the profound virtue of transcendental
knowledge-wisdom, which knows
how things actually are as well as how they arise and operate.
May I perfect the multifaceted virtue of skillful means,
and resourcefulness, which makes all things possible
and swiftly accomplishes all that is wanted and needed.
May I perfect the adamantine virtue of unshakable resolve,
determination, and inspired aspiration,
which has universal vision and scope.
May I perfect the radiant virtue of spiritual empowerment
and positive influence, which accomplishes unselfish service
and active love far beyond the limits of mortal beings.
May I realize the supreme virtue of awakened awareness,
which recognizes the innate purity
and primordial perfection of all that is.*

*May all that has been prayed for and here affirmed
be realized and accomplished by one and all!*

ACKNOWLEDGMENTS

I want to thank Jack Maguire, Leslie McClain, Gideon Weil, and Lisa Zuniga for their editorial help, patience, and skill; Paul Crafts, John Makransky, Willa Baker, Denise Montana, Linda McCarley, Susan Burgraff, Roz Stark, Christopher and Daniella Coriat, Lewis Richmond, and Susan Lee Cohen for transcriptions, conversations, and other helpful assistance without which this book would not have come into being; my Tibetan lama teachers, who exemplify and illumine the Bodhisattva's altruistic way of awakening; and as always, my wife, Kathy Peterson, for her good heart and loving support.

May longevity, health, joy, and well-being be theirs!

ABOUT
DZOGCHEN CENTER

Lama Surya Das founded Dzogchen Center in 1991 to further the transmission of Buddhist contemplative practices and ethical values to Western audiences and the transformation of these teachings into forms that help to alleviate suffering and create a civilization based on wisdom and compassion.

The Dzogchen Center Web site, www.dzogchen.org, is a regularly updated resource for Dzogchen Center information, teaching and retreat schedules, local meditation groups, and online registration.

 DZOGCHEN CENTER

P.O. Box 340459
Austin, Texas 78734
Phone: (617) 628-1702
E-mail: info@dzogchen.org